GORILLA TACTICS

HOW TO SAVE A SPECIES

GREG CUMMINGS

CHICAGO
REVIEW
PRESS

Published by Chicago Review Press Incorporated
814 North Franklin Street
Chicago, Illinois 60610
ISBN 978-0-89733-031-2

The author's piece "A Day in the Life of a High-Tech Gorilla Tracker" previously appeared in *A Day in the Life of Cyberspace*, MIT Media Lab, October 1995.

Library of Congress Control Number: 2023945936

Typesetting: Jonathan Hahn

Printed in the United States of America
5 4 3 2 1

CONTENTS

ACKNOWLEDGMENTS

I WISH TO start by thanking my amazing wife, Roberta, for taking care of my mother, Monica, at Sampaquita, which allowed me to write seven hours a day, six days a week, for two months straight, while her own elderly parents in Sicily missed her terribly, and she them. Sadly, Mum passed away before my book was published, but I couldn't have written it without her generosity. I'd like to thank all those who helped me recall the details of some of the more obscure events described in this memoir: Vince Smith, Geoff Carr, Kevin D'Souza, Richard Harris, Dan Richter, Liz Gebhardt, Sophie Astin Dolley, Michael Backes, and Jason Drangel, your memory's clearer than mine. Thanks also to James Fry and Lindsay Taylor for proofreading and providing valuable feedback, and to Prof. Richard Dawkins and Dr. Nathan Myhrvold for granting me permission to use their words. And thanks to William Finnegan, who encouraged me to write this book, saying, "Now that's a memoir I would read: the sad reflections of a burned-out fundraiser." Finally, a heartfelt thanks and a big gorilla hug to all those who have done their bit to protect mountain gorillas and their habitats. This book is dedicated to the rangers who loyally protect them. Facing impossible conditions, low pay, and sometimes no pay at all, gorilla park rangers are among the bravest conservationists in the world, staying at their posts no matter what challenges are hurled at them and proudly maintaining their vigil through the darkest days. More than two hundred park rangers have died in the line of duty, brave environmental warriors who have made the ultimate sacrifice for the endangered mountain gorillas. Glory to you!

1

APRIL 11, 1994

IN A BALLETIC display of science and rocket engineering, the space shuttle *Endeavour* rolled onto its belly and deployed a large radar in its payload bay. Flying upside down and backward, at a speed of eight kilometers per second and an altitude of 138 nautical miles, with its payload bay doors wide open, the spacecraft appeared to be embracing Mother Earth. In a way it was. *Endeavour*'s payload, the shuttle-based SIR-C/X-SAR large-array radar, was scanning the ground on three different frequencies, capturing detailed data sets of the vegetation, agronomy, and topography below. It could even search for underground water. Earth would thank it for it.

For STS-59, *Endeavour*'s sixth mission, NASA had turned its attention to the home planet. Mission to Planet Earth aimed to develop a scientific understanding of the Earth system and its response to natural and human-induced changes to enable improved prediction of climate, weather, and natural hazards for present and future generations. In just nine days, the most complex flying machine ever built would make a complete and detailed map of the planet's environmental hot spots, ostensibly checking for ecology's vital signs. A second shuttle mission in four months' time would gauge the rate at which environmental degradation was occurring.

Day three of STS-59 and, on its fifty-eighth orbit of Earth, *Endeavour* was about to aim its radar at the Virunga volcano chain— the habitat of the mountain gorillas. But as the orbiter approached its target, and the great expanse of Lake Victoria came into view, the astronaut crew on board would have noticed something peculiar. Between the volcanoes and the lake, scores of blue smoke tendrils betokening death and destruction rose up from the hilly terrain and ascended into the atmosphere to converge into one drifting cloud. Rwanda was on fire.

Effie had no way of knowing a radar was probing her habitat. Its emissions were imperceptible on the ground. As the space shuttle flew overhead, she and two dozen other gorillas were blithely foraging in the subalpine zone of Mount Karisimbi, surrounded by meters-high sting-ing nettles. Mist as dense as wool enveloped them and hung between a grove of Hagenia trees whose short trunks were all but invisible. At 4,507 meters, Karisimbi, the tallest of six dormant volcanoes in the mountain gorilla habitat, was continually mantled in mist. If the temperature dropped to freezing at night, the next morning its summit would be capped in a frost. Still, at least once a day, the equatorial sun broke through the cloud cover and warmed its fertile slopes for a spell. That is when gorillas frolicked. For now, though, they were swathed in a dense, chilly fog. Their thick, furry black coats provided some insulation from the cold. When it rained, they sat still and let the raindrops roll off their fur. But in a light drizzle, as was falling then, they continued foraging.

Carefully grasping the giant nettles with her black rubbery fingers, Effie removed and folded the stinging leaves, which made them easier to eat. She would have eaten anything to alleviate the ache in her chest, yet stinging nettles were part of a mountain gorilla's diet. Her mate, the dominant silverback Ziz, had died the year before. At 220 kilos he was probably the largest gorilla ever documented. Veterinarians said the cause of death was respiratory failure, but the constraints of time made it difficult to be sure.

Lately the din of war had died down, and the report of AK-47 and mortar fire could no longer be heard echoing in the valley. The gorillas had grown accustomed to gunfire and rarely reacted when they heard it, unless it was a bomb. If they heard the screech of an incoming projectile, they knew to run. Now the forest was strangely quiet and absent of soldiers. And the researchers who used to follow them every day were no longer around. The gorillas saw only ragged people, hundreds of them, frightened, running, desperately seeking refuge in their habitat.

Dazed and confused, I sat at the bar in the Engineer drinking straight bourbons on ice. I didn't usually drink during working hours, but I was gutted. I felt like a prizefighter who'd just lost a bout he was meant to win. A week had passed since surface-to-air missiles brought down the jet carrying the presidents of Rwanda and Burundi. At first, we thought the fallout from the assassinations, however severe, would quickly blow over, like so many other "security incidents" in Rwanda's three-year-long, on-again, off-again war, which began the year before I was appointed director of the Dian Fossey Gorilla Fund UK. Gorillas lived in a densely populated, highly volatile part of the world. There had been insecurity in the region for decades. I took the unrest for granted. But no one, except those behind the killings, could have imagined the wanton bloodshed we were now seeing on the nightly news. And there was no stopping the mayhem. The machete was proving to be a more effective weapon of mass destruction than a nuclear bomb.

All our foreign staff had been evacuated to Nairobi. However, we still had not located Louis Nzeyimana and his family in Kigali. I called Lars Rasmusson at the Red Cross to ask if he had seen them at the Hôtel des Mille Collines. He had not. "I'll try to locate him at his home," he said. "Only the Red Cross are permitted to move around the city."

"We need to evacuate the Nzeyimanas as soon as possible," I told him.

"As far as I know, no Rwandans have been evacuated," he said.

"Are you serious? Aren't there any flights out of Kigali?"

"The Rwandan Army controls the airport. But the RPF [Rwandan Patriotic Front] are just on the outskirts of town. Evacuation is risky. However, I don't object to trying to get them out by road."

Louis, our education officer, was six feet tall with long limbs. He could easily pass for what people perceived to be a typical Tutsi, the tribe being massacred, when in fact he was a Hutu, the tribe behind the massacres. And his petite wife, Agatha, was a type-defying Tutsi. Fortunately, Louis had bribed an authority to register her as Hutu on her ID card the year before. That they had to be classified in this way was a vile legacy of colonial rule. Every minute that passed without hearing news of them and their eight-month-old baby, my hope crumbled. I shuddered to think what could have happened. That I was not there was only a matter of timing. But being powerless to do anything for the Nzeyimanas made me feel sick to my stomach.

At the outset, Jillian Miller, my wife and codirector, and I had made a conscious decision to always include a positive slant. We avoided guilt and shock in our emotive appeals. In the last few issues of *Digit News*, our in-house newsletter, we had prematurely declared that war was over in Rwanda. What naive fools we were, tenderfoots in the right place at the wrong time.

Meanwhile a goddamn space shuttle was orbiting above the killing fields of Rwanda, scanning the gorilla habitat to make a detailed map of its ecology. We had been gearing up for this momentous mission for months. Arthur C. Clarke, an early proponent of spaceflight, had doorstepped NASA to get us included in the mission. Gorillas from Space was meant to be our crowning moment, a public relations coup, and a shoo-in for major gifts—and after just thirty months on the job. For the first couple of days of the mission, we remained enlivened by it all, read every online post by the *Endeavour* crew on the space shuttle newsgroup. But as the reports from Rwanda grew increasingly grim, our bold endeavor for the gorillas became eclipsed by the unfolding human calamity. It was out of our hands now.

How quickly things had changed. A week ago, no one could even point to Rwanda on a map. Few people had even heard of this tiny, landlocked country in the heart of Africa. In my fundraising spiel, I usually had to explain where mountain gorillas lived. No longer. We had not seen this coming. I hadn't seen it coming. I never expected to face such a harrowing moral dilemma within my little niche-cause fundraising job. I was thirty-two years old, for Chrissake. What would become of my livelihood now? Would they even need me after this? Surely gorillas would be massacred too. Such horrifying thoughts I could not shake as I drowned my sorrows in bourbon.

It was spring. Primrose Hill hadn't dazzled like this in months. The neighborhood's enameled Georgian facades were awash with bright sunshine. But to me, the days were just as bleak as in deepest winter. Waiting in the office for the phone to ring had been unbearable. I couldn't get any work done, so I shifted to the pub. Jillian was working from home. Rosemary, our office administrator, was manning the phones and was under strict instructions to come and get me if and when Louis called. I was only fifty meters up the road, close enough to run back and speak to him.

"C'mon, Louis," I whispered, "I know you're still out there. If you can just get to a phone and let us know you're all right. Please, *rafiki*." I ordered another Maker's Mark to calm my nerves. The bartender raised an eyebrow but served me anyway. I was listening to Pink Floyd's new album, *The Division Bell*, on my Discman headphones. Its mournful, psychedelic guitar riffs and theme of communication breakdown went some way to soothing my anxiety. I was disgusted with myself. My friend and his family were trapped behind a wall of death and all I could do was drink whiskey and listen to the Floyd. If I kept going like this, I'd soon be too drunk to talk sense to anybody. Goddamn it!

Within minutes of the president's plane getting shot down, the killers set up roadblocks in Kigali and then later on all roads leading in and out of town. The Interahamwe, as they called themselves, or "Those Who Attack Together," willingly slaughtered Tutsi men, women, and children as well as anyone suspected of being one or sympathizing with them. Nightly patrols were mandatory in Kigali. Every resident had to participate. Anyone found not participating was assumed to be either a Tutsi or a sympathizer, and was killed. Most who were not able to escape the capital had already been killed. A few may still have been in hideaways, but they would eventually be found.

Meanwhile, there were shortages of everything, food supplies mostly. Everyone in the city, those who were still alive, were hungry. The killing spree had slowed the movement of food into town, and the Interahamwe had looted whatever was left. Mass murder was a hungry business.

The radio announcements grew more alarmist, claiming a Tutsi revolt was gaining ground, amassing by the day. "The cockroaches are rising up to reclaim their kingdom," they said. They blamed the Tutsi army for the massacres, said that after shooting down the president's plane they had unleashed an evil-minded plot to kill every Hutu in Rwanda. Of course, Hutus fought back. They swallowed the official narrative, even when they were the ones going out there every day and participating in the massacres. Who among them had actually seen a Tutsi with a weapon in his hand? No one had seen a living one in days. Some people, especially those with an education, doubted the propaganda they were hearing on the radio, though they dared not express those doubts out loud. Every rational being alive feared for their life. Now Hutus were turning on each other. Bodies were strewn everywhere, and the streets ran red with blood. At night, untold apocalyptic fires burned on Kigali's thousand hills that were visible from space.

Rain fell heavily on the slopes of the Virunga volcanoes, washing over the slippery undergrowth. Streams burst their banks, and new waterfalls emerged as an airborne river plunged into the mountains. Rather than sit out the deluge under a tree, as they usually did, Group 5 gorillas made a beeline up the slopes of Mount Bisoke. The old matriarch Effie was exhausted. She was finding it hard to keep up. She would have preferred to climb down to the edge of the forest and gnaw on the bark of a eucalyptus tree in the buffer zone. Although an exotic species, eucalyptus had proven to be a good medicine for respiratory illness among mountain gorillas, and they had added it to their apothecary of natural remedies. But Effie had no way of letting the other gorillas know of her need and she could not go there by herself.

As the rainclouds descended to lower altitudes, the rain eased off and a mist returned. Effie's deep brown eyes darted nervously up the slope. She could no longer see the gorillas in her group. Soaked through to her skin, cold, and feverish, she found herself alone in the Afromontane forest. She coughed repeatedly, hard hacks from the depth of her lungs, and her eyes were heavy with mucus. In an attempt to get warmer, she feebly pulled together a few twigs to make a day nest, then curled up inside it. She remembered how Ziz would position himself so that his broad silver back shielded her from the cold. And as the hours passed, her life began to ebb away.

Somehow she knew her time was up. No matter—she had lived a long, fruitful life. At forty-two, she was the oldest gorilla in the Virungas. Few lived beyond forty. And no other female had been as nurturing a mother. Among Group 5's number, more than a dozen were healthy, well-adjusted gorillas that Effie had raised. And she extended her mothering skills to other females in her group too, not only her daughters, making sure they brought up their own infants well. It was a meaningful legacy. Now, as the mist lifted, and she felt the sun on her back, she leaned forward, put her face in her hands, and died.

During 100 days of killing in Rwanda, Effie was the only gorilla we lost. She died of natural causes, with dignity, in the place where she was born.

It was too much for my ingenuous mind to process at the time. My whole world was coming apart. Four years after leaving my bartending job to become a charity fundraiser, I was suddenly faced with an epic humanitarian crisis. It would be my bloody baptism. Growing up in Africa, I had witnessed some bad scenes before—in Biafra in 1969 and Ethiopia in 1985—but nothing like this. Would Rwanda ever recover? Would our "all-singing, all-dancing, gorilla-loving nation" be forever mired in the killings, like Bosnia, Cambodia, Germany, and Turkey? Would my character ever recover from the emotional battering I took in those dark days? I never made the time to reflect on it, to disentangle myself from the mayhem. My wife and I simply forged on, working side by side, never realizing that we too, despite our physical distance from the Rwandan genocide, were experiencing post-traumatic stress disorder. We were in too deep.

2

A NEW CAREER

In April 1967 my family moved from Canada to Kenya. I was four, too young to grasp the magnitude of the move. I had no idea of the distance, let alone the vast cultural and economic divide, between Montreal and Nairobi. All I knew was that it was hot and sunny and smelly. And I was unhappy to miss Canada's centenary and Expo 67. But Africa aroused childish delight in me. My curiosity and imagination ran wild.

We lived in Muthaiga, a Nairobi suburb on the edge of Karura Forest. Built in the 1920s, our house was made of blue granite. One half was occupied by the owner, an elderly White Kenyan widow, and we occupied the other half. Its dark, hardwood-paneled rooms smelled of lingering woodsmoke and stale linseed oil. A sloping garden led down to a creek. While I innocently played in the African light, my transition began. It was gradual at first, subtle and subliminal. It happened when I ate fresh honey from a beehive at the bottom of our garden, when at a trade fair marking the fifth anniversary of Kenya's independence I saw a live cow with its stomach cut open, and when I heard hyenas howling in the wilderness at night.

I met my first lion at Nairobi National Park, a short drive from our house. I recall the warmth of the rising sun against my small face as Dad drove us into the park escorted by a park ranger. The

ranger pointed to a patch of savanna beside the road ahead and said,
"Simba!"—meaning "lion." Dad inched the car closer and turned off
the engine. A lioness was hunched over her kill: a young wildebeest.
Steam rose from both predator and prey. I did not know if I should
feel sorry for the wildebeest or happy for the lioness. Mum said her
cubs would get fed. Dad said there were plenty more wildebeest on
the savanna. I was not entirely satisfied with either explanation. The
lioness's eyes glowed as she panted. Her snout was bloody and scarred.
Seeing her awoke something in me—a spark, what would become a
lifelong passion for wildlife. It was my wild baptism, a rite of passage.
A safari guide was born.

The Rift Valley is the landscape of my soul. The first time I saw
it, we had driven, *en famille*, some fifty kilometers north of Nairobi
in our Peugeot 303, to arrive at the Great Rift Valley View Point.
The official roadside viewing deck offered a panoramic view of the
landscape: a vast grassland dotted with acacia trees, hills, and lakes
that rolled on to the horizon. Seeing it stirred something in me.

Back when fire walking was more a necessity than a rite of passage,
our ancestors lived in the Rift Valley. The oldest fossil evidence of
hominids come from there. Some of the hottest temperatures on Earth
have been recorded in the Rift, both above and below ground. It is
where tectonic plates come to play. The temperature was particularly
high around two hundred thousand years ago when seismic and volcanic activity discharged some 2.5 billion liters of lava per year into
the Rift Valley. This cataclysmic rain of fire eventually abated, and
by one hundred thousand years ago, the lava flow had reduced to
about a fifth of what it had been. That is when anatomically modern
humans emerged.

In 1969 we relocated to Ibadan, Nigeria. The country was in
the midst of a civil war at the time. Not sure what my parents were
thinking when they accepted that posting. Seems damn irresponsible
to take three young kids into a war zone. I had a front row seat to

the Biafra War. It was a lot to take in for a seven-year-old. Dad owned a copy of a book by war photographer Peter Obe that he left lying around the house. As I pored over every black-and-white image of charred and dismembered bodies in the rubble and destruction, I became desensitized to images of war dead. During prime time on a Friday night, a local TV station broadcast, live from Apapa Beach in Lagos, the execution of political prisoners by firing squad. I knew then my life was abnormal.

Nigerian culture was rich and deep and diverse. Drama, sculpture, literature, and art thrived. Writers of the era met at a rooftop restaurant in Ibadan that we frequented. I would watch them engage in heated debates—playwright Wole Soyinka arguing with novelist Chinua Achebe between forkfuls of the local specialty, fried pig's brain. I followed Mum on her many forays into the slums where the humid air was filled with the bittersweet odors of sewage, rotting vegetables, squashed oranges, kerosene, and boiling beans. Mum was braver than Dad, who, when visiting an African slum, always wore the armor of a development man. Clearly his intentions were good. Mum simply used her charm to go as far as she needed to go to search out a renowned master carver, tailor, or ghost painter.

Brief summer home-leaves back to Montreal painted a rosy picture of my home and native land. In my childish mind I formed a dreamscape of rolling green lawns shaded by maple trees where kids rode skateboards and jounced yo-yos, grown-ups tended sizzling barbecues—all in slow motion—and aunts, uncles, and cousins vied for my attention with jokes, money, and inane questions about Africa. "Do you swing to school on a rope, like Tarzan?" "Do you live in a grass hut?" "Must be scary living with lions and tigers."

My cousins grew up in one culture, their own. And as they advanced through early development, they lived in one place. Their world was constant and consistent. They had a solid place to test the rules. Grandparents, uncles, aunts, neighbors, and teachers looked on, nurtured them, encouraged their psychological and emotional growth. It all happened naturally like learning to walk and talk.

Not me. I never knew where I was going next. "Pack up your belongings, say your goodbyes," was something I got told again and again growing up. And I had to juggle a multitude of rules and customs. Cross-cultural mobility added to the normal stresses of childhood, which stunted my development. We moved so often that my cultural anchors were in constant flux. My head was a carnival fun house filled with every shape and size of ethnic mirror: French Canadian, English Canadian, Swahili, Kikuyu, Maasai, Yoruba, Hausa, Ibo, and the legacy of British colonialism. African communities played a big part in my upbringing.

In 1972, when I was ten, we moved from Ibadan to Dar es Salaam—from an up-country city to a coastal port. Mercifully, we chose to remain in Tanzania for five years. The pause in our unrelenting uprooting helped me get my head right. The Indian Ocean was teaming with tropical fish, shells, and spiny sea urchins. Dad loved it for the sailing. I was out on the reef almost every day searching for cowries at low tide, or exploring caves, or snorkeling at high tide.

I once made a spreadsheet of all the dates and places stamped in my passports. By the age of twenty-one, I'd lived in seven countries on three continents and traveled more than one hundred thousand miles, circling the globe three times. On average, my family uprooted every three and a half years. I still grieve for the places, people, and pets they left behind. Then, at the age of twenty-three, on my own volition, I moved to London, England, where I began working as a bartender in the West End.

"Yo, Danny," I said to my cobartender, "do you mind if I take a smoke break?"

"Go right ahead, mate," said Danny, a long-haired cheery cockney with a toothy grin. Two Yuppies with a mobile phone the size of a Wellington boot plunked down between them sat at the end of the bar. Danny served them. "What can I get you gentlemen?"

"Tossers," I said to myself as I sat down for my smoke break. The bar was long and wooden and riddled with crescent-shaped dents from shot glasses getting slammed against its surface, back when that was a thing. It had a smooth rounded edge and a tubular brass footrest, and the stools were just the right height. Easier for punters to prop up the bar for longer. The American owners had modeled the place on a Mexican cantina circa 1940s. From the ceiling hung industrial light shades and a maze of water pipes and ventilator shafts. The walls were yellow brick and decorated with beer brand neons, photos of sunny taquerias, and dark, seductive señoritas from a bygone age. The glamour was more implied than stated, like a south-of-the-border joint where movie stars and writers came to hide from the paparazzi. No other bar in London had a wider selection of tequila. Dozens of brands were lined up in tall teak shelves behind the bar, lighted yellow and red. Premium brands were arranged in a pyramid in front of a big mirror encircled by fairy lights, as though a shrine to the Madonna. And above the display hung a wooden plaque with the names of the half dozen patrons who'd paid as much as seventy-five pounds for a shot of the best tequila. "Tossers." I looked around. Most of the current staff had worked there for years. Cafe Pacifico had hardly any turnover. Everyone loved working in the cantina.

A minicab driver—I'll call him Mark—pulled up a barstool next to mine. His arrival could only mean one thing: someone was scoring cocaine.

"How's tricks?" he asked.

"Not bad," I said, as I lit a Marlboro cigarette. "But I've been mulling over a career change. Turn of the decade, turn over a new page. Know what I mean?"

"Bartending is bloody hard work, mate," he said.

"Tell me about it. You work vampire hours. In winter, you never see the sun. Tequila oozes from my skin. I've no idea what it's like to wake up *without* a hangover. Don't get me wrong, Pacifico is a cool place to work and the pay is stellar, but I need something with a bit more respectability, you know. This job is taking me nowhere. I'm getting married this summer."

"Congratulations, mate," smiled Mark. "May I buy you a drink?"

"Van Gogh," I quipped, raising a half pint of lager. "I've got one 'ere. Get it, got one 'ere, as in got one ear, like Van Gogh. It's something we bartenders say to sound clever."

"Right. Have you thought about raising money for a good cause?"

"You mean shaking a bucket on the high street?" I laughed. "Not likely, mate."

"No, I mean like getting on the phone and soliciting donations," he said. "There's a children's charity in East London that I drive errands for, delivering balloons and whatnot. They're always looking for fundraisers. Pays commission only, but I reckon you'd be good at it."

"What, you mean like a sales job, except for charity?" I asked. "Well, I've done sales before   door to door. And bartending trains you in how to relate to all sorts of people."

"If you're interested, I'll give you the number of the bloke you need to call."

"Sure, I'll give it a go. Any port in a storm, mate. I need a proper job."

————————

Howard Saddler was working as a server that night. Howard was an aspiring actor. We had become close friends over the past year. We would do back-to-back shifts together (night shifts followed by day shifts followed by night shifts) and I'd drop acid in between our working hours. It was a hurdy-gurdy existence. Howard was Black, strikingly handsome, had perfected an erudite style, and taught himself society's mores, just to rattle the prejudices of the people he met.

"Looks like your missus has arrived," said Howard. I looked across the room to see my fiancée striding across the restaurant. She moved with the confidence of a fashionista, her dark gray Strenesse jacket swishing from side to side. She had friends in the rag trade who kept her in chic threads. She was tall, blonde, and appealing—both physically and intellectually. Born and raised in Salford, in the north of England, she'd taught herself to speak with a southern accent. "I got tired of people saying, 'There there, dear. What part of the north are you from?'" I'd asked her to marry me. She was the closest thing I had to stability in my life. She owned her own graphic design company in Covent Garden. She was smart, powerful, and wounded. And I admired her deeply.

I met Jillian in February 1987 while I was working lunchtime shifts at Palookaville, a basement jazz bistro in Covent Garden. Ted Porter, a fellow Canadian and a regular at the bar, introduced us. She was his ex-partner. I needed little persuasion to chat up a leggy blonde in a business skirt, but the demands of my lunchtime punters kept me from having a meaningful chat. As she watched me pop open bottles of champagne and fill rows of flutes, she asked, "What do you think of the assumption that a woman who dresses suggestively is simply asking for it?"

I rang open the bar till, which was stacked with red and blue bills, and said, "Just because that cash is there, within my reach, doesn't make it mine to grab." She liked my answer. Indeed she liked me, which became more apparent over the next couple of months. But I was not as enamored with her as she was with me, and I had doubts about a relationship. I found her audacious, Salfordian attitude a little unsettling. And she was nine years my senior.

I quit my job at Palookaville and tried to revisit my ambition of publishing a novel. My flat, on the tenth floor of a council tower block in Child's Hill, was west-facing and on a clear day I could see airplanes taking off from Heathrow Airport, some twenty kilometers away. Watching their fuselages shimmer in the pale winter light, I longed to return to where I was raised: Africa. The Bright Continent, as I liked to call it, held so much promise for me, and I knew I'd find inspiration there. But I could not afford an air ticket. My net income from bartending got spent on drugs and alcohol, and I had no savings.

On the dole, I began to write feverishly. But I soon came to the conclusion that a catalog of exotic episodes is no basis for a book. I had neither a compelling narrative, believable characters, nor convincing plot. So, after three months of false starts, I gave up my literary ambitions and returned to slinging drinks in the West End.

It didn't take long before Jillian found me and began wooing me again. I was more inclined to build a professional relationship with her, rather than become romantically involved. But faced with a powerful woman, I lacked the balls to say what I really wanted. We began seeing each other. We had only been dating for a month when an opportunity to work together came up. "You should've been there," I told her after I returned from a world music festival in St. Austell, Cornwall. "Bright costumes and colorful banners fluttering in the wind. It was like an army of African drummers had taken that Cornish beachhead. And no one was bloody filming it!"

"Well then, let's make the movie!" said Jillian. "You and me."

"OK, I'm in. But I have no idea how to make a movie."

As we struggled to bring our vision to the screen, saddling all our film project's expenses on the back of Jillian's business, we traveled to Paris and met West African artists and talked to music producers. A Dutch production company took an interest, pitched our treatment to Island Records, Channel 4, and Working Title. But before we could secure any financing, Jillian ran out of cash. We had driven her business into the ground. Her bank foreclosed. The movie never got made. The BBC ended up making something similar to what we had imagined. I was glad somebody made it. In retrospect, our failure to raise money was partly what tweaked my interest in becoming a fundraiser: I wanted to know how to raise money for something I truly loved.

Like me, Jillian enjoyed partying. All-night liquor licenses had come into effect in the West End, making it easier to unwind after a busy shift at the bar. Los Locos stayed open until 4:00 AM. It was our Summer of Love, and the acid-house scene was emerging in London at the time. Our favorite haunt on a Wednesday night was Shoom, an acid-house club that regularly changed locations: Soho one week, Kensington the next. Danny Rampling was the DJ, spinning Balearic and Chicago House grooves all night long, and always knowing exactly when his ravers were peaking on their psychedelics. Jamie Principle's "Your Love" was our song. And as the dry ice poured onto the dance floor, and the quadraphonic sound system took hold of my nervous system, we both moved seductively through the mist. The ecstasy had taken effect.

Known as the "love drug" for its prosocial effects—a truth serum for genuine affection—ecstasy revealed the faker in me. When I was on E, even with oxytocin levels sufficiently boosted in my brain, I did not feel amorous toward Jillian. The neurons in my overworked hypothalamus were trying to tell me that I was not in love with this woman. So what? For all I knew, I had a dodgy hypothalamus. It would be a marriage of convenience.

In July 1990 Jillian and I were married in a registry office in Diss, Norfolk. Howard was my best man. My brother David and my best friend Doug were witnesses. (The same two would witness my second marriage twenty-seven years later.) Doug led the wedding party—most of the newlywed's family members and a handful of friends—in a procession across town, while playing his kora, a twenty-one-string lute harp from West Africa, to a champagne reception at Ted's cottage. What could go wrong celebrating our union at my new bride's ex-partner's home? Nothing—we were cool like that. I did, however, get stung by a bee. Nature's nudge.

The wedding reception was held at Strenneth Farmhouse—a pig of a seventeenth-century building. Holding it outdoors in the gardens was a brave choice for the middle of the English summer. But the weather held up, and we couldn't have asked for a finer day. We fed our guests rabbit. Howard stood up and gave a drunken best man's speech. Jillian and I sang Monty Python's "Philosopher's Drinking Song." My dad never got the chance to give his speech. We didn't realize he'd prepared one.

Dad was first to take to the dance floor. Crazy Legs Ian, they called him. He was clearly relieved that I'd married a serious woman with marketable skills. "But I cannot for the life of me understand why in the hell the two of you want to work in the voluntary sector. You haven't a pot to piss in," he said, handing me a small ceramic toilet, "which is why I got you one as a wedding present." Later that day, my dad had an epileptic fit.

———

The eastbound Thameslink train tilted as it rounded Primrose Hill, an affluent suburb in North London. I was on my commute to my new job, trying to wrap my brain around my new profession. Since moving to England four years before, I'd attended a couple of garden parties and chatted up a few socialites in their Georgian townhouses. I saw how glad-handing was done. And I was gregarious by nature—sycophantic if I needed to be. Growing up in a multitude of cultures, I learned how to make friends fast. But in order to raise serious money, I needed to ask the rich, and I did not know any wealthy people. Still, Britons were less concerned about net worth than they were about class. Upper, middle, working—the classes stuck to their own. They were more likely to donate to one of their own too. Having said that, Canadians got a hall pass on class. Besides, I was a culture chameleon: I could blend in well with cultures far different from my own, which gained me stealthy access to otherwise closed social circles.

"Alight here for Canning Town," came the announcement on the platform Tannoy. My workplace was twenty minutes walking distance from the station. I wasn't sure what to expect. The East End was new territory. The sun was shining. The day was warm. But a gloom hung over the neighborhood, which had a distinct Victorian character, as though it hadn't had a lick of paint in over a century. The roads were empty, pubs and houses boarded up. I passed a brick warehouse stained black with coal and damp. Seemed an unlikely place to raise money. Still, as ever, I was optimistic. The future looked bright.

The Wheelchair Trust operated out of a converted classroom in an abandoned school. The room was humming when I arrived. Two dozen fundraisers were on the phones cold-calling companies that they had looked up in a business directory. I listened in. "We're raising money to buy electronic wheelchairs for handicapped kids. Would you like to buy a balloon for a hundred pounds? We'll later release your balloon at an event, and it will have your name on it. It's good advertising for your company." I thought their sales pitch could do with a boost.

I got straight to it. It wasn't rocket science. Plus, I had the gift of gab, could talk the stripes off a zebra. In my first month, I earned a tidy commission. And I quickly made friends with coworkers, most of whom were poor, single mothers. The hours of work—4:00 PM to 9:00 PM—suited their mothering duties.

Soon I was leading the team. Using my culture chameleon skills, I won them over with cockney kidology. "Nothing wrong with your phone banter, love," I'd say. "It's your call list that's all Pete Tong. Joe Blogs of Canning Town can't afford to spend a ton on a balloon."

I found them directories to the fashion, music, and publishing industries, wrote them a new script that focused on the importance of the
cause, and motivated them with a pep talk at the start of each day.
Sometimes I stood on a table to express my passion for the cause, or
to announce a big donation. "George Harrison just gave us £5,000!"
They responded well to my coaching. I turned a motley crew of ne'er-
do-wells into a dynamic team of telemarketers.

Come December, we had raised enough money to buy a wheelchair
and had more than five hundred balloons to release. Jillian organized
an event for the charity, an outdoor concert in Battersea Park. She
got the stage, rig, and lights donated and booked a stellar lineup of
chart-topping acts to perform live for free. On the day of the event,
however, freezing temperatures kept people away. Nevertheless, most
of the acts showed up and performed despite the weather, including
Doctor and the Medics, who played "Spirit in the Sky," albeit to an
audience of no more than twelve. It was surreal—all dressed up and
nowhere to go.

Battersea was a salutary lesson for Jillian and me. The most important thing about staging an event, no matter who agrees to perform for
free, is getting bums on seats, filling the venue with paying patrons.
Afterward we learned the Wheelchair Trust was simply a cover for
East End gangsters who were siphoning off funds from the donations
to pay off their debts, and we both resigned. I told my story to the
Daily Mail.

We each got short-term jobs. Jillian organized a fundraising event
for Inter-Action, an education charity. Aboard the HMS *President,* a
ship moored on the banks of the Thames, she staged a glittering soirée
attended by Tom Stoppard and Diana Rigg that raised £40,000. I
worked from home applying for grants from foundations on behalf of
Farm Africa, a development charity. At the Directory of Social Change,
a bookshop in Hampstead specializing in charity guides, I bought
A Guide to Company Giving and *A Guide to the Major Trusts*—all I

could afford. I'd go down to the Spanish Café in Soho and, while drinking dreadful cappuccinos, pore over every detail: the backgrounds and giving preferences of corporations and trusts, and how to tailor a grant application to each of their finicky requirements.

I understood that to make a living at it, a fundraiser had to be able to at least raise his or her own salary. But Farm Africa couldn't afford to pay me, and foundations were unwilling to fund a fund-raiser's salary. Plus, it turns out commission-based fundraising, as I'd been doing in my previous job, was a no-no. The public was wary of this type of remuneration. Rightly so. What are you going to do if you bring in £1 million, pocket a six-figure commission? Not ethical. Better to bring in enough funds so that the beneficiary charity can afford to pay you a salary. A bit of a chicken-and-egg dilemma in the early stages of a charity's life, though. The best way around this conundrum is to avoid being straitjacketed by restricted grants, and to raise unrestricted funding, from appeals and events.

I was hired by the Core Trust, a holistic drug and alcohol rehabilita-tion center located in a Georgian mews off Lisson Grove, Marylebone. In the midst of a recession, I took over a hand-to-mouth fundraising operation that was barely keeping the charity out of bankruptcy. When I started, a fully funded upgrade was underway at the rehab center. It was being renovated to include six places for residential patients. First off, maximizing the upgrade's potential, I negotiated a contract with Westminster Council to house three of their recovering addicts at our center. In a matter of months, we had signed the contract. I sent off letters to trusts and foundations appealing for grants to close the gaps in our expenditure. And I set up a membership scheme. Carol Wolf and Jackie Leven, the charity's founders who were former heroin addicts, had backgrounds in the music business and were well connected. We signed up fewer than fifty members that summer, but they included MPs, lords and ladies, captains of industry, and celebrities such as Hayley Mills, Pete Townshend, Phil Collins, Ringo

Starr, and Gary Lineker. Most of our members had either personally experienced addiction or knew someone who had.

The Core Trust used alternative medicine to rehabilitate addicts. Detox involved a team of volunteer therapists using treatments such as moxibustion, acupuncture, and Chinese herbal medicine, and took about two weeks. Under Core's system, patients claimed to have endured none of the psychological distress associated with withdrawal. Detox was followed by a three-month rehabilitation period during which therapists helped heal the underlying suffering of addiction. Alongside the more traditional methods of counseling and group therapy, patients were given a cornucopia of alternative treatments like Shiatsu massage, reflexology, and gong therapy. Core considered this to be the most important part of its program. The patient was encouraged to find an identity and lifestyle without drugs, one that was more rewarding and satisfying and imbued with more self-esteem. We had an 80 percent success rate.

That summer, to benefit the charity, Princess Diana agreed to be guest of honor at a gala lunch at the Savoy. Jillian helped organize the event, which involved soliciting 350 guests to pay £250 each for a ticket. The princess had incredible pulling power, and the organizers had little trouble filling the Savoy restaurant. Kensington Palace told us there was just one person on our guest list that Diana wished to avoid: "Black Jack" Dellal. "He is stalking her," they said. But the sixty-seven-year-old banker was willing to pay £10,000 to sit at her table. Recognizing the value of this, the palace suggested we seat them opposite each other and place a large flower display in the middle so she could avoid eye contact. Every one of our flower displays was thus enlarged.

Back from vacationing in Brazil, the Princess of Wales had acquired an alluring suntan and a new bob hairdo, and she out-fashioned every-one in her strawberries-and-cream Chanel outfit. As she advanced along the protocol line, holding a bouquet in one hand and shaking each person's hand with the other, Jillian and I giggled and pinched each other. Barely a year into our new careers and we were already rubbing shoulders with royalty. I was introduced as the fundraiser. The princess stopped, struck a schoolgirl pose with her head tilted to one side, and stared into my eyes. "Are you using me?" she asked. Her choice of words made me blush. But I understood what she meant. Charities are obliged to use star power to get noticed. Lending her name to our cause helped grow public awareness of our work and attract funding. And as a patron of our charity, she gained some added kudos for herself as well. More important, she did not want me to squander the prestige of having a royal patron; she wanted me to use her.

"Yes, I am," I replied. "You're not just a name on our charity's letterhead."

"Your patronage has brought all these paying guests to this benefit lunch," said Jillian. Diana nodded graciously and moved on. After the benefit lunch, the charity hired Jillian to produce a brochure. Her beautiful gatefold pamphlet was designed with a color scheme of saffron, ocher, and orange, reflecting the Eastern influence in Core's therapy, and blended snapshots of the various treatments with photographs of the center taken by rock paparazzo Adrian Boot. The tone conveyed was one of a Buddhist temple.

It wasn't the addicts who made me want to quit my job, but rather the fights between Carol and her husband, Murray Douglas, the therapy coordinator. They were always at each other's throats. There were other conflicts too. Core's code of practice was unconventional and didn't meet current standards for the voluntary sector. Take my pay raise, for example. One day Carol, who had quickly taken a shine to me, noticed I looked glum, so she invited me into her office and asked what the trouble was. "I'm not earning enough to pay my bills," I sighed. She stood directly in front of me, held both my hands in hers, closed her eyes, and told me to close mine.

"Now, Greg," she said soothingly, "try and visualize the salary you need."

I closed my eyes, let the moment sink in, played along, then said, "£15,000."

"If that's the salary you need," said Carol, kissing me on each cheek, "then you've got it, my love." She gave me a 25 percent pay hike! Who knew visualizing worked so well?

Soon after our gala lunch, the trustees had a crisis of confidence. They doubted Carol was capable of leading the charity into a much-needed growth phase. She dug her own grave after she recklessly sacked two of Core's counselors for practicing psychotherapy. The way she and Murray talked about them, you'd think they'd been practicing witchcraft. In the ensuing chaos, Carol resigned then quickly reneged on her resignation. The trustees chose to hang on to her resignation letter nonetheless. The rift between them widened as Carol's friends on the board were successively replaced by tougher, less impressionable bureaucrats from government grant offices who began picking apart the organization and micromanaging her. To begin with, they left me well alone to do my job and fundraise for Core, but they soon began sending critical messages my way. They were worried about cash flow. I told them funding was on its way, but they weren't inclined to believe me.

I remember having a conversation with Ted, Jillian's ex-partner, as we rode along the Finchley Road on a number 82 bus. I told him I thought maybe it was time I moved on from Core. "The atmosphere at work is toxic," I said. "They never stop screaming at each other."

"You should spruce up your CV and send it out to other charities," said Ted.

"Yeah, but with my limited experience I'm not likely to get a job with the same pay."

"Take your time, you've already come a long way from bartending. It's a new career."

"I'm not so sure I like it," I frowned. "Bartending was a lot less stressful."

Fundraising is a form of mendacity. Like sales and diplomacy, it's all about little white lies. We do a dance as we pander for money without ever revealing the hideous nub of the problem. You don't need formal training to become a successful fundraiser. Just put on a supplicating smile and follow the advice of Johnny Mercer & the Pied Pipers, in their song "Ac-Cent-Tchu-Ate the Positive."

Uprooting every three years or so as a child, I quickly learned how to accentuate the positive, eliminate the negative, latch on to the affirmative, and never mess with Mr. In-Between. My family took no prisoners as we bounced from one continent to the next. "Don't worry, you'll make new friends," I was told time and again. I became a world-class liar, which got me into a lot of trouble. I could act, too, starred in school plays, staged variety shows for my parents' party guests. As a young man I took on sales jobs, selling encyclopedias door-to-door in Toronto and theater and cable subscriptions by phone in Victoria. I was a damn good salesman.

I understood the importance of a good cause too. I was raised with high-minded values and endowed with an acute sense of injustice. My father, who worked in development, which is why we moved so often, was hell-bent on making the world a better place. He taught me about social change and wanted me to follow in his footsteps and work for the United Nations. But I believed I could make a bigger difference as a writer. Dad and I fought over that choice for years to come. In 1985, after dropping out of university for the third time, I moved to Singapore and tried to make it as a freelance journalist in Southeast Asia. I hitchhiked to the Golden Triangle and sold stories and photos of my adventures along the way to the *Singapore Monitor* and the *Bangkok Post*. Had I remained, I might have found lasting work. But after a catastrophic brush with heroin and a military coup in Bangkok, I opted to bail out—and not a moment too soon.

My parents sent me the airfare to join them in Ethiopia, where an unrelenting drought had driven its people to starvation. I was thrown in at the deep end of a harrowing story of human suffering on an epic scale. Writing about the Ethiopian famine awoke something in me, and I began to see many more grave injustices in the world. Seeking an outlet where I could voice my angst and dread, I moved to London on a working holiday visa with the aim of becoming a full-time news reporter, sending back gritty dispatches from deepest darkest, but instead I wound up bartending in the wild West End of London. The pay was far better, and I lacked the will to apprentice at some filthy tabloid on Fleet Street. Fundraising was my second chance, a new means to social change. As a fundraiser I would simply be selling a good cause. I also had the ability to turn on a ten-pence piece should an opportunity present itself, change careers or countries with very little fuss. Consequently, I was locked and loaded for my new profession.

Core's trustees became increasingly critical of my role, though never to my face. "What does he actually do all day?" "Why are we paying him so much?" and "Where are the grants?" These would be reasonable concerns for any board had its trustees not been in hiding all these months, never offering me any support or asking to meet me to discuss the charity's progress. When they summoned me to Jackie Leven's flat in Lisson Grove, it was the first time I had met any of them. Jackie, who cofounded the charity with Carol but then bowed out, was a Scottish singer who rose to fame in the New Wave band Doll by Doll. His career was cut short after his vocal cords were severely damaged in a mugging. Years of subsequent alcohol, drugs, and smoking had taken its toll. But he still had money. His home was decorated like a rock star's pad with Persian rugs, Indian wall hangings, and Eastern throw cushions. I told them that Core needed a strategic plan, a document that would clearly state where the charity was headed and what kind of resources it would need to get there. "If you don't take this course," I said boldly, "then I will tender my resignation as Core's fundraiser." They took it as an idle threat. So be it.

Soon after that, I was riding on the upper deck of a bus, this time the number 13, browsing the *Guardian*'s charity classifieds when I spotted an ad no larger than a postage stamp: "The Digit Fund, founded by the late Dian Fossey and dedicated to protecting mountain gorillas in Rwanda, seeks an executive director to establish a UK office . . ." The ad spoke to me like a jungle drum. Africa, the continent that raised me, was calling. I could feel its warmth, hear its birdcalls, and see its wide, teeming grasslands. *Could this be my ticket back?* I wondered. Up until then, I'd never aspired to find a career in animal welfare, though growing up as I did exposed me to a heap of nature, so I certainly appreciated the importance of wildlife conservation. As I read on, my heart sank. "Must have at least two years fundraising experience." I circled the ad and when I got home, I threw the paper on the coffee table in front of Jillian.

"My dream job," I sighed, "but I don't have the goddamn experience they're looking for. Why should they hire *me*?"

"They certainly won't if you don't apply, darling," said Jillian as she read the ad.

Deeply skeptical about my chances of getting this job, I nevertheless sent off my CV with a cover letter waxing lyrical about my experiences in Africa and saying that I could speak a few words of Swahili. A week later I received a phone call from a very posh-sounding gentleman with a deep, booming voice. "Hello, this is David Rogers," he said, "chairman of the Digit Fund. We'd like to invite you to an interview at the Royal Thames Yacht Club next Wednesday."

It was a moment brimming with promise and possibility, like a whirlpool of beautiful light that had formed out of nowhere, opening up a portal that led back to the Bright Continent. I was determined not to fuck it up. The night before my interview, I rented *Gorillas in the Mist*, the biopic of Dian Fossey starring Sigourney Weaver. Watching it for the first time, I was enthralled by Fossey's story. The movie was filmed on location, so I was in no doubt about the setting of the cause. I got a taste of the challenges I would face as director of the Digit Fund, protecting wild gorillas in their natural habitat, and I was overwhelmed with nostalgia, even though I'd never visited Rwanda before. A torrent of emotions flowed over me, feelings I'd thereafter associate with Maurice Jarre's haunting score. Sigourney Weaver's performance is powerful, and in the scenes where she's among the gorillas, it is hard to tell whether she is acting, her reactions are so genuine. As the credits came up, I felt like I had already stepped into my dream job.

The next day, in an oak-paneled board room at the Royal Thames Yacht Club, I told my interviewers how valuable I thought the movie would be in leveraging donations. "It means never having to make a cold call," I said. "And if we can somehow manage to solicit a donation from every moviegoer who ever had a lump in their throat after seeing that film, like I did, then the gorillas will be saved."

UK chairman David Rogers liked my account of meeting Princess Diana. US trustee Pat McGrath was happy I spoke some Swahili, and Ruth Keesling, who was on both boards, felt my knowledge of Africa compensated for any lack of experience. I told them about my wife's design skills and talent for organizing events and PR. I impressed them enough to get invited back for a second interview, this time with Jillian. "We rather hoped we could get two for the price of one," said David Rogers. Jillian was not amused. In the end, they hired her as a PR consultant and offered me the position of executive director of the Digit Fund UK.

By the time I handed in my notice at the Core Trust, there was no longer a cash flow crisis. Grants had begun rolling in: £5,000 from the Tudor Trust, £5,000 from the Moorgate Trust, and £20,000 from Smith's Trust. I made it rain grants. The trustees told me I could not leave. Like Yossarian in *Catch-22*, they wanted me to fly another round of missions. Hearing I'd been offered the directorship of the Digit Fund left them slack-jawed, wide-eyed, and scratching their perfumed heads. During a two-week notice period, £30,000 more came in, bringing the total I raised in nine months to £130,000. Only a fundraiser feels schadenfreude when his detractors are overwhelmed with money. Now I was no longer just a fundraiser, I was executive director.

3

MONKEY BUSINESS

IN JANUARY 1992 the Digit Fund UK began operating out of a shoebox-sized office in a business center in Primrose Hill. The address was as prestigious as the rent was extortionate. Still, as a charity we were exempt from the neighborhood tax, which mostly offset the extra cost. The office was close to Chalk Farm tube station, Camden Town Market, and Regent's Park zoo, and within spitting distance of two great pubs, the Engineer and the Pembroke. Our location allowed us to mix with media stars. The district was so popular with film industry types that the British press referred to it as the "Primrose Hill set." Rock stars were frequently spotted in pubs, restaurants, and coffee shops. It was an exciting and thriving part of London to work in.

Jillian worked from home. She was juggling a handful of other clients as well as the Digit Fund. I worked at the office. I had a desk, a filing cabinet, two chairs, and a phone, but no computer. David Rogers thought it imprudent to spend donors' money on such an extravagance. Apart from that, he and I saw eye to eye on most things. David, Jillian, and I met at the Oasis Leisure Centre in Swindon to discuss the immediate way forward for the charity, along with Ian Redmond, a primatologist who had worked with Dian Fossey in Rwanda and had been overseeing the Digit Fund on a volunteer basis up until then. By coincidence the band Oasis was named after the same leisure center, and Creation Records, where Oasis was signed, would soon open near us in Primrose Hill. Thereafter brothers Noel and Liam Gallagher would regularly get into fights at Pembroke Castle.

"First order of business is to send off an appeal letter," said David. "Greg, you have the names and addresses of some twenty-five hundred people who filled out that card outside the cinema after seeing *Gorillas in the Mist.* You should write to introduce myself and to report how our antipoaching efforts in Rwanda are keeping the endangered mountain gorillas safe."

"But what address shall we use for the Digit Fund?" asked Ian.

"The new address," snapped David. "Where else?"

"Well, do we really want to alienate those volunteers who've managed the fund?"

"Our supporters are confused by all the addresses we've used in the past, Ian. The fund is no longer run from shoeboxes in volunteers' homes. We'll put a notice in the newsletter saying we're now operating out of a shoebox-sized office in Primrose Hill, and offer our heartfelt thanks to the very special volunteers whose hard work has brought the Digit Fund to this stage. And we'll thank our members and supporters for their forbearance."

I liked David. Lofty, gray, and balding, he always had a cheery disposition and we got on well. Old school and yet not too priggish, he took great pains to point out that he had chosen a membership to the Royal Thames Yacht Club over the more ostentatious London clubs. He was dynamic. As head of Abercrombie & Kent Europe, a luxury travel company, he had his fingers in various travel industry pies. And he knew Africa. He was a trustee of ActionAid, a development charity with projects across the continent. As a young man, he'd served in the colonial police force in Zambia, where he claimed he went out of his way to be fair to Black people. While studying law at Cambridge, he became smitten with the beautiful Elizabeth Bagaya, princess of the Kingdom of Toro. After she returned to Uganda, in a fit of romance, he drove across Africa in a Land Rover in the hopes of reuniting with her. In time, his unwavering support for me would cement a lasting friendship that helped me de-stress from my career.

In addition to my appeal letter, our first mailing included a large color poster of a silverback gorilla, and the very first issue of *Digit News*, a full-color, four-page newsletter designed by Jillian and edited by Ian Redmond. *Digit News* was packed with upbeat stories about gorillas, their human neighbors, volunteer fundraising activities across Britain, and our donors. My face was on the cover under the headline DIGIT FUND UK APPOINTS DIRECTOR. Above me was a photo of a handsome American couple, Dr. Dieter Steklis and his wife Netzin, who at the same time began running the Karisoke Research Center in Rwanda. Within six months, our mailing had raised over £32,000 (twice my annual salary), an average of £12.80 donated for every letter sent.

I read up on the cause and the charity's origins. In 1977 Dian Fossey's favorite gorilla, Digit, was decapitated by poachers in Rwanda. His death gained worldwide attention after Walter Cronkite announced it on the *CBS Evening News*. The resulting outcry compelled Fossey to found the Digit Fund in his memory. Ten years earlier, with funding from the Leakey Foundation, Fossey had begun one of the longest field studies of primates. Louis Leakey believed she was the "gorilla girl" he'd been looking for. The Rwandese named her "Nyiramachabelli"—"the woman that lives alone in the mountain." She courted controversy. "Get off my mountain," she screamed at interlopers to her forest while brandishing a loaded pistol. Sometimes she'd shoot over their heads.

Dian Fossey's confrontational style gained her a few enemies. On Boxing Day 1985 she was found dead in her cabin at the Karisoke Research Center. She too had been brutally murdered. She was buried near camp, next to Digit's grave. Three years later, *Gorillas in the Mist* was released to worldwide acclaim. And three years after that, in 1991, war broke out in Rwanda.

Africa is home to four subspecies of gorilla: western lowland, eastern lowland, Cross River, and mountain. The world's largest primates
range through forests in Nigeria, Cameroon, Central African Republic,
Equatorial Guinea, Gabon, Angola, Rwanda, Uganda, and Zaire (now
the Democratic Republic of the Congo). With a combined population of 120,000, western and eastern lowland gorillas are far more
numerous than their mountain cousins, though no less endangered,
and range on the eastern and western rims of the Congo basin.

Only a few hundred mountain gorillas remain in the wild. They
are restricted to just two isolated highland areas in the border region
of Uganda, Rwanda, and Congo: Virunga and Bwindi. They were
brought to the brink of extinction by deforestation, poaching, human
disease, and war. Since there are none in captivity, the future of "the
greatest of the great apes," as Fossey described them, depends on their
survival in the wild. I was proud, if a little apprehensive, to be given
the responsibility. In less than two years, I'd gone from West End
bartender to executive director of an international organization. Was
someone having a laugh at my expense?

Peter Elliott was my first visitor. The English actor lived nearby.
"I heard you had moved in up the road," he said as he sat in my one
spare chair. Peter had acted in dozens of ape movies. He played the
lead chimp in *Greystoke: The Legend of Tarzan, Lord of the Apes*, and
Digit, the lead gorilla in *Gorillas in the Mist*. His build—short and
stocky with long arms—made him ideal for ape roles, and he had
studied clowning and movement at a Method acting school.

"You know about the new IMAX movie about mountain gorillas
that's showing in Bradford?" he asked. I nodded. His accent was
Hereford with a hint of Hollywood. "Well, it was meant to be a
documentary," he smiled, "but just in case they needed an actor to
stand in for a gorilla, they had a few sophisticated gorilla suits made.
I'm going to see if I can get one donated to you guys. That way I
could make appearances and scare the hell out of people." I asked

him to give me a demonstration. "Without a suit, it's better I do a chimp than a gorilla," he said. He climbed up onto my desk and began slapping his torso and screeching. He tossed papers about, kicked my phone off the hook, and ripped up my pack of cigarettes. It was a very convincing performance. Good thing my new computer had not yet been delivered.

"Occasionally, at night," he said breathlessly, as he sat back down, "I'll do a pan hoot for the chimps in London Zoo. And they call back to me . . ."

———————

At the southern end of our street was a pathway leading down to the Regent's Canal. The canal's towpath, used in olden times by horse-drawn barges, is flanked by brick embankments and shaded by willow trees. It provided me with a tranquil waterside walk on which to ponder my challenges and get things into perspective. One way led to the Regent's Park zoo and the other Camden Lock. Camden Market, a thriving, youthful bazaar spread across a warren of alcoves, was a focus for the latest street fashion and drug paraphernalia. One day, while exploring the neighborhood, I stumbled on Primates restaurant. What luck finding an ape-themed, up-market bistro within walking distance of the Digit Fund. The restaurant's decor was less jungly than its name implied—a tasteful tribute to the great apes, exemplified by elegant wall hangings and fine illustrations on the menu. The owner, Marie Taylor-Clarke, was a socialite who simply loved gorillas, chimpanzees, and orangutans. And the food was fantastic; her chef wasn't monkeying around with his delectable lamb shanks. It became my go-to gorilla meeting venue.

Ashley Leiman, director of the Orangutan Foundation, lived and worked nearby. She and I regularly met for lunch at Primates along with the director of the Jane Goodall Institute. Our Leakey's Ladies

Lunches, as we named our meetups, were an opportunity to share successes, bolster each other's confidence, and whinge about our respective employers.

"You're lucky," said Ashley. "You've got a Hollywood movie about your cause."

"So do you," I said. "*Every Which Way but Loose?*"

"Oh, please, Clint Eastwood and his orangutan sidekick Clyde who packs a punch is hardly representative of the cause."

"Yes," I smiled, "but your ape is orange. You must be able to do something with that."

I also met Mark Rose, director of the Fauna and Flora Preservation Society, which, together with the African Wildlife Foundation and World Wildlife Fund, operated the International Gorilla Conservation Programme (IGCP). Uniquely, and in keeping with how mountain gorillas ranged, IGCP coordinated cross-border antipoaching patrols and multilateral conservation measures, like censuses and the standards of tourism facilities. Relations between the IGCP and the Digit Fund were frosty at times, especially when vying for dollars from the same public purse. However, as one would expect, in the field we cooperated. Mark and I got along fine from the get-go. We may not have been working for the same charity, but we *were* working for the same cause. And I wanted to show solidarity with my fellow gorilla people. Strength in numbers.

Five months into my new job, I turned thirty. No place better to celebrate than at Cafe Pacifico in Covent Garden. It was a Friday and the place was hopping. Lots of mates, including Howard, had shown up to wish me well, and his girlfriend, Natascha McElhone, who at the time was waitressing at the cantina, though she would go on to be a famous movie star after being cast in *The Truman Show*. A few brought presents. Everyone bought me drinks—beers, margaritas, and shots of tequila.

Jillian was bristling over all the accolades I was receiving because of my new career. She too had accomplished a great deal in a short time. As well as producing *Digit News* and an arsenal of publicity material for the fund, she'd just completed a contract for the Central Middlesex Hospital. They paid her thirty pounds an hour to help them to prepare an application for a "Charter Mark," a mark of excellence awarded to public sector industries, like hospitals and schools, for implementing the new Citizen's Charter, as directed by UK prime minister John Major. From what Jillian had told me about her final package, the hospital had a jolly good chance of winning. But I got all the attention. Even so, she made sure the mood remained buoyant. Tonight was the birthday boy's night. The cantina's co-owner, Jeanie Estes, an attractive blonde Californian in her midforties with decades of experience in the catering business, sidled up to me and said, "I'm proud of you, Greg. Sounds like it was a smart move you quitting your bartending job here to go work as a fundraiser in a wildlife charity."

"Thanks, Jeanie," I said. "But I didn't quit. I was fired."

"Fired?" she laughed. "For what?"

"For smoking a spliff," I smiled.

"Well, then," she said, "you were obviously looking to get fired."

"It was two o'clock in the morning. The place was empty, punters had all gone home."

"Still . . ." She had a hint of admiration for me. "Let me buy you a birthday tequila."

——————

In early May, Ruth and her multimillionaire travel agent husband Tom Keesling flew in from New York on the Concorde and checked into a suite at Claridge's in Mayfair. They had just completed a grueling eight-week high-end tour of Indonesia. "It's been months since I've had anything to do with gorillas," said Ruth as we sped away from Claridge's in a chauffeur-driven Jaguar. We were headed to Chessington World of Adventures to collect a check. The whole way there she tried to win me over to her side and I wasn't even aware of the debate. Ruth was an operator.

Chessington had organized a reception for us. The day was warm and sunny, the hors d'oeuvres were exquisite—cheese and wine. Two councillors from Kingston town hall, the local press, the director, zoo manager, and primate keeper were there. Ruth gave a speech that Tom had written for her on his laptop that morning. We posed for photos outside the gorilla enclosure, holding a giant check for £4,000—all coins and bills stuffed into a collection box by visitors in recent months—bringing the total raised for the fund to £17,000. No one seemed bothered by the captive gorillas behind us. Their stiff postures and grimaces, however, suggested they were bothered by us. It didn't help that a monorail passed overhead every few minutes, broadcasting a recorded message that pointed out their pungent body odor. Poor fellas. Meanwhile Faust here, the brown-nosed salesman, as I saw myself, sweet-talked the dignitaries before riding back to London with Ruth in her Jag. I was starting to get into the swing of things.

The next day, the trustees convened a meeting to evaluate my performance as the Digit Fund UK's new director. Ruth and Tom wanted to hold the meeting at Claridge's. But UK chairman David Rogers was not comfortable with that arrangement, even though we would get the room for free. Saying that Claridge's was where Belgium's King Leopold held court in 1881 to convince a stupid high-society set of his good intentions in the Congo, David insisted we hold the meeting at his club. The RTYC charged a fee, albeit at member rates. The UK trustees in attendance were Ruth, David, Barclay Hastings, and Tony Elischer. I was preoccupied at the start with placing in their correct spots specially prepared folders that contained a copy of the poster and first edition of *Digit News*. But they were only interested in the figures.

Tony Elischer, London Zoo's fundraiser, thought I could have done
better with corporate donations. He rubbed me the wrong way. We
were both young Turks, too close in age and vocation for me to hold
him in esteem. Dr. Barclay Hastings was a handsome Californian. He
was a wildlife veterinarian and had worked at the Volcanoes Veterinary
Centre (VVC) in Rwanda, which was funded by the Morris Animal
Foundation (MAF). Until recently, Ruth Keesling, née Morris, had
been a trustee of her family's foundation. But no longer. MAF's trustees had voted her off the board, which infuriated Ruth. Conspirators
in our organization, too, wanted her out. "She's too much of a maverick to be at the helm," they said. Ruth and Tom were wealthy,
card-carrying Republicans who possessed a few prejudices inherent in
that demographic. Ruth demonstrated her racism by being unbearably
condescending. A New York debutante who was heir to a cat food
empire, she used her wealth and influence to get what she wanted.
She was remarkably energetic for a woman in her sixties and reminded
me of a female Ronald Reagan in both looks and attitude. She joined
the board of the Denver Zoological Foundation and was elected as a
lifetime trustee. She helped to develop and expand its education and
veterinary programs, and she was instrumental in developing the $16
million Primate Panorama exhibit, a modern habitat for zoo gorillas
and orangutans. Her many gorilla hats—two Digit funds, MAF (as a
Morris she still retained some influence), and the VVC—demanded
a Machiavellian MO in her dealings with others.

I didn't know how to play Ruth Keesling at first. Dr. Barclay
Hastings knew her well and seemed to like her. So soon after I started
at the Digit Fund, I invited him for a pint in the Albert and asked
for his guidance on how best to get along with her. He told me that
in 1988, when an outbreak of measles spread through the wild gorilla
population and six gorillas died, he proposed inoculating them all.
The intervention was controversial. No one had ever attempted to
vaccinate an entire subspecies before. Critics feared it would turn a

wild population into a managed one. Ruth, whose family foundation funded the VVC, supported the intervention. She and Barclay felt strongly that because the disease had been introduced to their habitat by humans, we had an obligation to intervene on the gorillas' behalf by whatever means necessary. Ruth's relentless haranguing eventually trounced the naysayers. A team of veterinarians, including Barclay, darted seventy gorillas.

It worked. Coughing disappeared and there were no more deaths. "Just go along with what she says," Barclay laughed. "Don't take issue with her outrages. Stay close to her and you'll do fine. Remember, she's in the driver's seat. And many who have tried to remove her are now gone." His sobering advice would make my job much easier in the coming years.

The trustees seemed happy with my figures. My performance in office pleased the Senate. I was given signing privileges of up to £1,000 and the go-ahead to hire an administrative assistant. Then, under the stone-faced oil portraits of the club's past commodores, David instructed me to fly across the Atlantic and attend the next US board meeting. "Take those glowing reports of your success to Indianapolis and see if you can't stir up a joint strategic plan with the US," he said. This was the first of many surprises that summer.

Sunday morning, a week after the board meeting, the phone rang in our flat. We had not yet had breakfast. It was Ruth calling from Denver, Colorado. "Mrithi is dead," she said. "They killed him. He got caught in a military cross fire in the park."

Believing a slain silverback was reason enough, I called David straightaway to relay the news. He said he was in his dressing gown listening to Verdi's *La Traviata*. I apologized for intruding. "No, no, you did the right thing, Greg," he said. "I suppose I'll have to get used to this sort of invasion of my privacy."

"Mrithi was a gorilla who had it all," Barclay wrote in an obituary in *Digit News*. "Tall, dark, and handsome and in the prime of his life,

Mrithi had achieved the aspirations of every male gorilla when I first encountered him in 1988. Every gorilla has a different personality, and he quickly became my favorite, not only because of his good looks, but also because of his calm gentle nature. When visiting Mrithi, the initial excitement of coming face-to-face with a wild gorilla was soon replaced by a feeling of tranquility. No conflict, no tension. *It is possible for man and wild animals to live in harmony*, I thought.

Barclay had just taken possession of a donated portable anesthetic machine for the VVC. He asked me to organize its shipment to Rwanda. I did not have a clue where to start. Tom Keesling came to my rescue. He had high-level contacts at British Airways, so he pulled a few strings and the airline agreed to ship the machine for free. What I didn't know was that there was already a guy working in cargo at BA who regularly shipped out stuff for us for free. That I had seen fit to go over his head was enough to get me blacklisted. The anesthetic machine went, but nothing else ever again. Major faux pas. Could have been avoided with a bit more research.

In June I flew to the States on my first-ever business trip. Never would I have dreamed, even a year ago, that I'd be on a four-day, all-expenses-paid business trip to the United States for a wildlife conservation organization.

A destination feels different when you go there on business. As my DC-9 from Detroit descended into Indianapolis airport, the Midwest's corn country seemed to roll on forever. I shared a limo into Speed City with a psychotherapist from San Francisco. The fare was four dollars. I made a note and kept the receipt. I gasped when I saw the size of the Hyatt Regency, and was doubly blown away by its cool air-conditioned interior and twenty-story central atrium. Just hearing the sound of clinking cutlery in the eatery, smelling the aromas of cinnamon and coffee, and seeing the two glass elevators swiftly racing up and down the atrium filled me with childish excitement. In time, business-trip trappings would become so commonplace I would wearily drift through them in a numb trance, but for now I was wide-eyed and mystified. Soon I was kicking off my shoes and falling back into a king-sized bed in a spacious room. My name was on channel 88 on the TV, and papers for the three and a half days of meetings of the Digit Fund's US board and Scientific Committee were in a kit on the desk.

The next morning, I dressed in a suit and tie. The tie, burgundy wool embroidered with navy gorillas, was David's idea and an item in our merchandise catalog. When I arrived in the conference room, the day's first meeting—the mission statement debate—was already underway and, to my surprise, delegates were deep in discussion about a strategic plan. The meeting attracted the cream of primate academia.

Listening to their presentations, I began to get a clearer picture of the challenges ahead. Dr. Alexander "Sandy" Harcourt, a former Karisoke researcher, stressed the need for a more holistic approach to gorilla conservation. He said seven hundred people per square kilometer lived in the communities adjacent to the gorilla habitat in Rwanda. "Human encroachment and loss of habitat are growing threats to the mountain gorilla's survival," he warned. "So it makes sense to include the local people in our efforts." This was an eye-opener for me and spoke directly to my sensitivities about Africans. I furiously took notes.

My own report, covering the establishment of the London office and the money that had been raised in the first six months of our operation, was met with enthusiasm and concern. With respect to our funding of Karisoke and the antipoaching patrols, they saw an urgent need for a division of responsibilities between the UK and US offices. Consternation would be the US fund's first reaction to all my achievements in the years to come.

A bold new decision was made at the meetings to change the organization's name in memory of its founder. Both the UK and US boards subsequently agreed to become the Dian Fossey Gorilla Fund (DFGF). Mary Smith, senior editor of *National Geographic* magazine, revealed a new DFGF logo designed by her art department: a woodcut of an adult and infant gorilla in profile surrounded by jungle ferns. She also donated a catalog of Bob Campbell's photographs. Bob's timeless photos and two cover stories in *National Geographic* are credited with turning Dian Fossey into a household name in America and for raising awareness around the world of these shy, gentle giants in the Virunga volcanoes. "They're for both the UK and US fund's use," added Mary.

Ruth introduced me to Betty White, a TV star and a trustee of the Morris Animal Foundation. Betty was bubbly and charming and full of jokes. She congratulated me on my appointment and wished me well. She also asked Ruth when I was going to be allowed to meet gorillas in the wild. "Oh no, dear," laughed Ruth, "it's far too soon for him to go there now. He needs to learn the ropes of the organization and to better understand the challenges."

"Yes, but if I could see what I'm raising money for, connect with the cause emotionally," I said, "I'd understand things a darn sight better and raise more money to save the gorillas."

"Well, you'll just have to hang in there a while longer," said Ruth, pinching my cheeks.

I arrived in the States as director of the Digit Fund UK, and I departed as director of the Dian Fossey Gorilla Fund UK. In short order, the UK board held another meeting in London to confirm the name change. Ruth flew in to join the meeting. I reported on what I had heard from Dr. Harcourt about a more human approach to conservation, one that took into consideration the needs of local people. My board was enthusiastic about the idea, though Ruth attempted to pour cold water on it. This new direction would set us apart from the United States. Beyond paying for antipoaching patrols and continuing

Fossey's gorilla study, the US board wanted little to do with the locals. David clarified our position. "A UK charity is an autonomous entity," he said. "Its trustees cannot delegate their duties. By law, we alone are responsible for overseeing how UK donors' money gets spent. Hence it is unlawful for us to send funds to the States to let them spend it as they wish. We must have a say in the matter. And whether the American trustees are on board with it or not, UK intends to fund community conservation in Rwanda." A schism had been established.

Ruth raised an eyebrow but understood this was the direction we wished to go in. Just before she departed for Denver, she pulled me aside and said, "I've got some good news for you, friend. A few US trustees are booked on a trip to Rwanda in October, to celebrate the twenty-fifth anniversary of Karisoke. I've discussed it with David and he agrees: you can join us. So get packing, kiddo. You're going to meet wild mountain gorillas!"

It had all come true. On that cold and wet November night, when I rode on the number 13 bus up the Finchley Road and happened on an ad that spoke to me, my wish had come true. I was going back to Africa, back to the tree where man was born. I could not believe my good fortune.

The last of the summer surprises came in late August when, straight out of the blue, I received a call from a woman who introduced herself as Maggie Todd from 20th Century Fox. "You requested a meeting with Sigourney Weaver?" she asked. "She'll see you at four o'clock at the Berkeley hotel in Knightsbridge." Months before, I'd written to Sigourney Weaver's company, Goat Cay Productions, asking for a meeting with the charity's honorary chair but had heard nothing back. It was 2:00 PM. I looked at my outfit. I was dressed down for a no-meeting day at the office. I couldn't possibly see her dressed in jeans and a T-shirt. Jillian came to my rescue, drove down to the office with a clean shirt and my olive silk jacket, the one with the

stylish collar that I'd worn on our wedding day. At 3:20 PM I caught
a cab to the Berkeley.

Seated in front of a large poster for *Alien 3,* the Hollywood movie
star was holding court in a hotel suite, fielding questions from the
British film press about her latest movie role. Her hair was no longer
than a pixie cut. In this sequel, they had shaved her head for the part
of Ripley, and her hair had not yet fully grown back. They asked her
if she planned to make a fourth *Alien* movie. She told them calmly
and clearly that she did not.

"Follow me," said a woman with an earpiece who then took me
upstairs to an empty suite. "Sigourney will be with you shortly," she
said. "You're her last appointment before she heads to the airport.
Feel free to use the phone to call to anywhere in the world you like."

Who would I call? Sure, I had mates all over the globe, but did
I really want to be caught midcall with Allan in Australia when the
star walked in? Left alone in the hotel suite, I slumped into a plush
beige chair and leafed through a copy of *Cosmopolitan.* I adjusted the
collar of my suit and brushed off a fleck of lint. *Any minute now,* I
thought, glancing at the door, *a screen idol is going to waltz through
that door thronged by an entourage of entitled movie people.* But when
the door opened, it was just her.

"Hi, Greg," she smiled. "Sorry I kept you. It's been nonstop here
all day." She wore black linen trousers and a bright red top punctuated
with half a dozen fist-sized circular holes. Relaxing into the chair next
to me, she seemed pleased to meet me.

We talked for twenty minutes. She offered the UK fund the roy-
alties from the *Aliens* power loader, a merchandise item. I told her
about our name change. "So, I'll have to work harder now," she said,
"because people identify me closely with Dian Fossey." She told me
that while she was in Rwanda making *Gorillas in the Mist,* she had
fallen in love with a mountain gorilla named Maggie, whom she had
"adopted." She also confirmed that she was not acting in her scenes

with the gorillas. "The gorillas helped me prepare for motherhood," she laughed. "Being jumped on and peed on by baby gorillas was good training for it. Now, you said in your letter you wanted me to help you with an appeal. Do you have a tape recorder with you? We can record it now." I was impressed by her readiness to act, but alas, I had come unprepared. Never come unprepared.

That evening I met my wife for drinks in Soho. She had a beautiful smile that belied an inner turmoil. She needed looking after, more than I could do at times with the demands of my new job. Nevertheless, she continued to work her ass off. She laughed when people asked her as a freelancer what work she had going at the moment. Now that the fund had changed its name, she was hired to embark on a major package of publicity for us, which included a review of our merchandise, a color brochure as well as various other publications. She showed me her design for a full-color sticker in an elongated portrait shape with our logo. It read, THERE ARE ONLY 650 MOUNTAIN GORILLAS LEFT IN THE WORLD. I told her I thought it looked stunning and was a snappy catchphrase.

We ordered more drinks. "So, of the candidates we interviewed this week, who do you think we should hire?" I asked. She had also been helping me recruit an office administrator.

"I liked Janet Wilson best," said Jillian. "She seemed confident about handling the organizational needs and she knew her way around a computer, plus she could copy-type."

"I see your logic, but I have to say Rosemary Godfrey made an impression on me. In her previous job she was assistant to Mark Carwardine, the rock-star zoologist who cowrote *Last Chance to See* with Douglas Adams. And she left with Mark's address book. Don't you see the value of that?" I asked. "When I get back from seeing the gorillas, I'll be gagging to tell the great and the good about my jungle experience, which is when Mark's address book will be invaluable."

"Are you excited?" asked Jillian.

"Are you kidding?" I said, tinkling my iced bourbon. "It'll be the thrill of a lifetime—returning to Africa on a paid, fact-finding mission to go meet the endangered mountain gorillas in their natural habitat. I can't wait!"

"I wish I was going with you," she sighed.

4

INTO AFRICA

NIGHTFALL OVER THE Sahara Desert. Fulani fires beneath me, a billion stars above. Bounding across the desert at thirty-two thousand feet filled me with calm. Cruising altitude was one of my favorite places. Flying to Nairobi in economy on Kenya Airways, I was headed back to the Bright Continent. It's where I felt most at ease in the world, and I hadn't been back since moving to London six years earlier.

Jomo Kenyatta International Airport was throbbing at midnight. A chaotic throng of people pushed and shoved. For every arriving passenger, there were half a dozen Kenyans soliciting taxi rides or game park excursions. It made me smile to see the familiar pandemonium.

I was met by Mwamba Shete, assistant director of the East African Wildlife Society. David Rogers had asked him to look after me during my overnight layover. He drove me into town. Flat-topped acacia trees lined the route, and we passed giraffes grazing in the grassy median strip. Mwamba and I talked about the issue of people versus wildlife and how it might be resolved. It was my introduction to African conservation.

"For centuries, Africans lived side by side with wildlife in a symbiotic arrangement," he said. "The land and wildlife surrounding a village were considered communal property. And because animals provided food and other products vital to the survival of the community, they received special protection. Then along came the Europeans with their conservation policies. Suspicious of our intentions and abilities, they fenced off protected areas, established ranger patrols, and severed our connection to wildlife and ecology."

"How do we get back to that?" I asked.

"It's no longer possible," sighed Mwamba. "Landownership has put an end to it. What we *do* need is professionalism. For years, wildlife conservation has been left to people who lack any training. If you want to work in conservation, it's enough just to be interested. Academic and professional qualifications don't matter. *This* has got to change."

"I am also a dilettante," I smiled. "But at least I'm a fast learner."

"And you have an African perspective, my friend," he said. I straightened up and took a deep breath. As we passed landmarks from my childhood, the smell of eucalyptus woodsmoke in the cool night air stirred a few fond memories. The Bellevue Drive-In cinema where I saw *Cowboy in Africa*, which was released in the United States as *Africa: Texas Style*. The cathedral where my brother had his first Communion. The 680 Hotel where our family once stayed after driving up from Dar es Salaam and where my brother and I, so easily entertained, spent hours riding up and down in the elevators. My wistfulness swiftly gave way to frustration, however, when we hit gridlocked traffic at the edge of town. We were one of a cluster of poorly maintained vehicles that crawled over the rutted and potholed tarmac like an immense crocodile that hadn't eaten in a year. Two-thirds of the time that it took us to get from the airport to my hotel was spent driving the last third of the distance, even after midnight.

The next morning, I explored Nairobi's dusty streets on foot. Monrovia Street, Market Street, and Kenyatta Road put me in a nostalgic stupor. Some of the buildings I remembered from my youth were still there, only smaller. The downtown gas station with the familiar globe in its forecourt surprised me. "I recall the world being so much bigger." I wondered how my father felt when he first arrived in Nairobi twenty-five years earlier. I hailed a taxi. On my way to the airport, I almost wept. I so longed for that time in my life when I believed we would live forever on the teeming, grassy plains of East Africa. *Stop whining*, I told myself. *You're five years younger than Dad was when he got here and already the director of an international NGO.*

As my 737 taxied along the runway and we awaited clearance for takeoff, I spotted two C-130s bearing the Red Cross insignia parked on the apron. That was a familiar sight in Addis Ababa during the famine in 1985. Eighty percent of Africa's elevations over three thousand meters are in Ethiopia. Food drops were the only way to get aid to the more remote parts of the country. Hercules planes (or C-130s) were flown by the RAF, Luftwaffe, and Air America on a number of daily food drops to drought-stricken regions.

In my early twenties when I visited my parents in Ethiopia and wrote about the famine, I was invited on a food drop. The Hercules I flew on traveled at an altitude of twenty-six hundred meters above the plateaus north of Addis Ababa as we headed seventy-five kilometers north into Wollo Province. I was standing in the cockpit. The land below looked like a beggar's faded patchwork cloak. "We're actually going down in altitude from Addis," said RAF Captain Baring, as he piloted the big plane freighting sixteen thousand kilos of food. "We'll come in for the drop at around forty feet to unload four single-ton packets of food to a feeding center there before flying to another drop zone. We must take care when dropping the food. The other day the Luftwaffe hit someone with a two-hundred-mile-an-hour relief bag. Poor chap died."

I looked at him furtively then quipped, "Ironic end when you're starving."

"No, it should never have happened," said Baring.

"Quite. . . . Heartening to see the Iron Cross and the roundel flying side by side in this international war against hunger, sir."

"Quite."

As we approached the drop zone, I moved to the aft of the Hercules's fuselage to observe how the food drop was managed. It was like a warehouse back there. The loading ramp was wide open, revealing the arid landscape below. At four hundred klicks, the ground flew past in a blur, moving closer and closer as we drew nearer to the drop zone. Tethered airmen manually rolled pallets along tracks to the back of the plane and waited for a signal. As we flew over two red markers, the squadron commander yelled, "Ready . . . steady . . . *drop it!*" With brute force, the airmen shoved the load off the loading ramp. It fell to the ground and exploded into a torrent of wood and plastic and food bags. The plane then circled around and returned to examine the drop zone. Every food bag was intact.

The squadron commander turned to me and said, "Our boys drop some sixty-four metric tons of food a day, the Luftwaffe thirty metric tons. No one knows how much Air America drops. But the Yanks use an automated drop," he jeered. "Not like this balmy lot."

As we flew back to Addis, to release stress the airmen went "air-skiing" out the back. Secured only by their tethers, they leaped from the loading ramp and flailed about like marionettes in the airstream. Utter madness! Working as a stringer in the Horn of Africa, I learned a couple of things: how money flows from donor to donee via agencies and nongovernmental organizations, and the vast chasm between First World sentiments and Third World realities. I also learned a maxim that would inform my later career: there's no such thing as donor fatigue, only fundraiser fatigue.

Now, as my Boeing 737 sped up the runway at two hundred kilometers per hour, and a million vibrating rivets bore the stress of its shuddering fuselage, I could feel a new beginning quaking in my bones. Kenya fell away beneath us. We flew over the Ngong Hills where Karen Blixen, author of *Out of Africa*, once had a farm. Clouds were obscuring Kilimanjaro. *Damn!* But that meant the rains would soon come. The land was very dry. Looked like old bark cloth.

I was excited to be going to Rwanda, a place I knew little about, other than it was the land of the Watusi and the mountain gorilla and the focus of my inspiring new job. I had visited a dozen African parks and reserves and completed a wildlife checklist as long as my arm, but I'd never met a wild gorilla. It was not for want of trying. My family made two bold attempts. In 1971 we went looking for Cross River gorillas in Jos Plateau, Nigeria. And in 1967, we drove from Kenya to southern Uganda with the aim of seeing mountain gorillas in the Impenetrable Central Forest Reserve near the Uganda, Rwanda, and Zaire border. In Jos we found only empty night nests. In Uganda, political unrest kept us away, the same unrest that forced Dian Fossey to abandon her study in Zaire and begin again on the Rwandan side of the border, where she set up her research facility in the saddle between two volcanoes, Karisimbi and Bisoke: the Karisoke Research Center. That is where I was now headed. Going where few had previously ventured to go.

Within fifty minutes, we had begun our descent into the land of a thousand hills. The terrain was fertile and emerald and looked like a rug that someone had skidded into. The two-story airport terminal was simple, airy, and characterless. At Kigali airport, the actual officials, I'd been warned, were the ones out of uniform, which made them impossible to identify as I queued to enter their country. Being in the same time zone as London helped me stay focused. I was jet-lagged but not zoned. No worries. Gorillas were my visa. I was waved through immigration.

Tom Keesling greeted me with a hug. Unruffled and beaming, he wore a bolo and a Western dress shirt and looked and sounded like Bob Hope. A Rwanda tourist service driver grabbed my luggage and led me to a courtesy car in the parking lot. As we drove into the city, I breathed in the new air. Every place smells different. In Kigali I could smell the soil. The air was cool and thin. At fifteen hundred meters and two degrees south, altitude and proximity to the equator competed to regulate Kigali's temperature. Depending on cloud cover, it could be hot one minute and chilly the next. Half a dozen yellow-billed kites circled overhead, riding the thermals formed by hundreds of thousands of inhabitants burning charcoal for their supper and to stay warm. Despite its sprawl, I was amazed by how clean and prosperous the city looked. By all accounts, Kigali lacked the corruption and chaos that typified other African cities. Sort of how I imagined Addis must have been before the revolution. Soldiers were omnipresent but I was used to that.

On a leafy hill near the center of town, I checked into a room with a view at the Hôtel des Mille Collines and was unpacking my things when the phone rang. It was Dieter Steklis, the director of Karisoke, inviting me to dinner. He took me to a restaurant in a nice part of town that was strangely empty for a Friday night. We were joined by Charlene Jendry, who was studying gorillas at Karisoke for the better management of captive gorillas at the Columbus Zoo. Charlene was bubbly and funny but tended to dominate the conversation. The meal was superb. I had four seasons pizza, washed down with a large bottle of Primus beer. The other two ate a local fish specialty that I would have to try before I left. The night was cooler from the rains and the air was sweet. Our table overlooked Kigali's hills, strewn with countless flickering lights.

Dieter briefed me on the security situation in the country. "The war is so stop-and-start that no one is sure when the hell it actually began," he said. "But for the time being, it's all quiet on the north-western front." He was tall, good looking, and hunky and had a full head of blue-rinsed gray hair. He had flown in just before me from Paris and was jet-lagged and a bit grumpy, which framed my initial impression of him. But as the night progressed, I discovered a calm and considerate man with a great sense of humor. It was a privilege to dine with him on my first night. He and Charlene made fun of me for not bringing a sleeping bag or Wellington boots. "You're gonna wish you had," he said, recalling how bitterly cold it could get at Karisoke. "Your nose is either frozen or filled with charcoal soot."

At 10:00 PM I was alone in a chair on the balcony of my room, watching the lights in the hills, breathing in the highland air, listening to the night sounds and the tinkling of iced bourbon in my glass, and thinking I'd only be happy when I figured out how to live this way all the time. My hunch had been correct: fundraising for a wildlife cause would ultimately be my ticket back to the Bright Continent. Now I just had to convince Jillian to move to Africa with me. She would need to see it first.

———————

A caterwauling Hadada ibis with a cry like a work-whistle cartoon bird awoke me. Its shrill call was a shock to my system. The Hadada didn't range in the places I'd grown up.

It took me a moment to adjust to my new surroundings. The view from my balcony was of a rolling, leafy, tidy city, scintillating in the morning equatorial sun. In the hotel dining room, I met the Keeslings and Dieter and enjoyed a breakfast of cut fruit, eggs, and assortments of breads and jams. Dieter introduced me to our new education coordinator, Dr. Louis Nzeyimana. "Apart from the men working in antipoaching patrols and domestic duties at camp," said Dieter, "Louis is the first professional African we have employed at the fund." His appointment was reassuring for me, an Afrophile. I told Dr. Nzeyimana I was keen to pick his brain about conservation education.

"Oh no you don't, friend," said Ruth. "You're not snatching him away from us. We've got him lined up to roll out our Denver education scheme." I bit my lip. This was how it was going to be with Ruth. She was a one-woman strategic plan who objected to having to reveal any of her ideas to others. Liz Macfie, director of the VVC, joined us. She lived in Ruhengeri, the town closest to the gorillas, and had driven up to meet her benefactors and me. Although she was American, her husband was Welsh and she had acquired a muted, Anglicized manner, which helped her in her dealings with Ruth.

After a few minutes of idle chitchat, Liz asked me, "Do you want to join us on a visit to Kigali market?" As much as I really wanted to go and hang out with people closer to my own age, I knew I couldn't possibly join them. The Keeslings wouldn't have approved. And I knew which side my bread was buttered on. I looked at Liz and shrugged.

Ruth and I would spend a lot of time together in the coming days. In between opening a sterling account at the Bank of Kigali so funds could be sent directly to the field from the UK, meeting park authority officials to discuss the Karisoke visitation policy, and attaining the airway bill for the anesthetic machine that had been shipped on British Airways and was now at the airport, we managed to track down every gorilla carving in town and buy all the available silver products to use as decor for the twenty-fifth anniversary dinner at the hotel banquet room on Wednesday night. "It's going to be one hell of a shindig, friend," said Ruth. "All the bigwigs will be there." I also helped her with her speech. Later, on a phone call with Jillian, I told her that Ruth was as fond of her as she was me, and that she had told me, "If the UK board gives you any flack about Jillian, you tell me." Jillian advised me to treat Ruth and Tom like Mom and Dad.

––––––––––––

"Seems you're her poodle now," said Dieter.

"I'm just going with the flow, amigo," I laughed. We were in my room, drinking and talking about Ruth's relentless power brokering.

"She's a human bulldozer," said Dieter, "and her intransigence could ultimately destroy the fund." He spoke clearly and concisely, using precise diction and idioms. Born in Germany, he had come to the States as a refugee when he was a teenager. Like me, a hidden immigrant, he'd taught himself to blend in. I told him the UK Fund wanted to pay Dr. Louis Nzeyimana's salary. He agreed. I also told him I was surprised that the new education plan had been commandeered by Ruth.

"No one was consulted," said Dieter. "Ruth and Pat McGrath, lifelong friends, have become sworn enemies over the issue. The McGraths and the Kesslings are a-feudin'!"

"Jesus Christ! The politics in this charity are incredible," I said. "I saw it in Indianapolis with all the backroom lobbying. Not sure what they were scheming. But I *can* tell you this: not every US trustee is wholly supportive of Ruth. Some are prepared to challenge her."

"Right," sighed Dieter, "but as we've seen, with Ruth, it's all or nothing. She'd happily bury the fund if we tried to take it away from her."

"It's not a personality cult," I said, refilling our glasses. Ruth believed her meeting with Dian Fossey just months before she was murdered had anointed her with a higher power to carry out her duties for the gorillas.

"It's like that old adage," said Dieter. "The founder without whom you could not have gotten this far and with whom you can go no further." But for all our inebriated grandstanding, it seemed not even we were prepared to find a way to loosen the woman's iron grip on the charity.

"If we can agree on a unified message," I said, sipping my bourbon, "follow a set of communication standards instead of some egotist's whims, and do not stray from the plan, we can more effectively engage the public. This one-woman show has got to change."

The US board meeting kicked off at the hotel at eight thirty the following morning. The trustees were surprisingly perky after their interminably long flights. Those who arrived minus their luggage, not as much. They hadn't quite arrived yet. Tom made introductions, ran

us through the itinerary, and then shuttled us off to the US Embassy
to meet Ambassador Robert Flaten, who delivered an extensive briefing
on the history of Rwanda, leading up to the present civil war. He
described the remarkable attempts that had been made in Arusha to
negotiate a peace settlement between the Rwandan government and
the Rwandan Patriotic Front (RPF), otherwise known as the rebels.
The rebel RPF, it seemed, was largely made up of Tutsi soldiers whose
families had been exiled to neighboring countries in the 1960s, when
Hutus, the other dominant tribe in Rwanda, had driven them out.
They had returned with a vengeance in 1991, launching the country
into civil war. The politics of the thing made my ears bleed, but if
I ever hoped to do my job properly, I needed to understand the situation on the ground as best as I could. It was Star Wars in Africa.

I called Rosemary Godfrey in London and asked her if she could
fax up-to-the-minute figures before our board meeting reconvened in
the top-floor conference room of the hotel. It was a chance to show
off the efficiency of the London office to the US trustees. In a room
that boasted panoramic views of Kigali's countless hills, I delivered a
lively report on our activities to date. I don't think anyone on either
side of the Atlantic dreamed the UK fund would grow quite so quickly.
Indeed, for the first seven years of operation we would enjoy annual
growth of 30 percent. Association with the Dian Fossey Gorilla Fund
was an attractive prospect for many companies. I was flooded with
inquiries from the moment I started, and I wrote many more replies
than appeal letters. (Always reply to personalized letters, no matter
who they're from.) In the end, I found I had the luxury of choosing
the best among many good proposals.

"And after I meet gorillas in the wild this weekend," I said to the
gathered trustees, "there will be no stopping me. I'll be just as inde-
fatigable as Ruth." They all laughed. There was no attempted coup
by the US trustees. Ruth held her position as president international.

She also delivered a glowing tribute to Jillian and me. I was chuffed. She knew what buttons to press.

———————

Veterinarian Liz Macfie was at the wheel of a Ford pickup. The drive from Kigali to Ruhengeri was winding and precipitous. It was a crystal-clear day. I rode in the back the whole way with one hand on the anesthetic machine. An hour out of Kigali the road ascended to a hogback where the views were spectacular. The volcanoes were plainly visible in the distance and breathtaking to behold.

Liz pulled over. I couldn't believe how perfect they looked. I remember reading Edgar Rice Burroughs's *Tarzan of the Apes* when I was a child and thinking the illustrations of the chain of volcanoes where Tarzan lived was fantastical, unlike anything I'd seen in Africa. Nowhere could you find six perfectly conical volcanoes all in a row like that, I thought. And then I saw Virunga. "There be gorillas!"

Climbing back into the back of the pickup, I told Liz that we should probably hurry up if we wanted to reach camp before nightfall. But before driving to the park, she insisted we divert to her house, a bungalow on the outskirts of Ruhengeri. She wanted me to meet the two infant apes she was looking after, a chimp and a gorilla. "They were confiscated from poachers a few months ago," she said as we pulled up outside, "and, because reintroductions are rarely successful, we're sending them to zoos in Europe."

From the look in her eyes, I knew Liz was terribly unhappy about that outcome. The infant apes' little faces bobbed up and down in the window as they tried to catch a glimpse of the new arrivals. Once inside, I was their tree. Each ambled up a side of me. The chimp flung his arms around my neck while the gorilla hung on to my shoulder. Although roughly the same age, the gorilla was considerably heavier than the chimp. They both gave off an earthy odor, the smell of a living, active ape. Holding them in my arms, I felt a strange surge of emotions that I imagined, being childless, were similar to how a father feels when he holds his baby for the first time. And I was filled with determination to do right by these sweet, innocent creatures.

From the park boundary we continued on foot. Mount Bisoke rose up steeply before us. The climb was steep but not as strenuous as I feared. My motivation to get there gave me wings. We reached Karisoke after dark. Guards carrying lanterns met us on the path and guided us into camp. Hurricane lamps hung outside the cabins, faintly illuminating the corrugated tin walls and surrounding foliage. Jungle sounds were everywhere. So far, I had only known Karisoke in the dark and rain, but it was already working its magic.

We gathered for a candlelit dinner in the new building: barbecued chicken, mashed potatoes, carrots, and salad. It was the best meal I had ever eaten in such a remote location. Charlene then took me on a moonlit walk through a Hagenia meadow beside a rambling stream near camp. She said she couldn't stay there any longer unless her husband joined her. I didn't feel that way about my wife. I was too consumed with my own personal triumphs to want to share the moment with anybody else.

Dieter had told that one of the streams near camp fed into the Nile, and another, the Congo. I took a pee and wondered if it would flow into the Med or the Atlantic. The aura in the mountains at night was haunting. I'd never experienced that kind of cool and time-less ambience. The past and the present billowed together and were bound by a natural ensemble of nocturnal cries. A wistful paradox of time enveloped me at Karisoke, like I was listening to an iconic sixteenth-century symphony or standing before the murals of a master impressionist. Dian was there too. During the night, the cries of tree hyraxes, like witches, invaded my dream. I saw Dian standing on a bluff above me with a pistol in her hand, yelling, "Get off of my damn mountain!"

Even though we were close to the equator, it felt like winter. Halfway up a volcano, visibility was low and beard lichen hung eerily from the trees, stroking the mist. A chill wind enveloped my fellow trekkers and me as we climbed a steep, overgrown, and slippery trail alongside the Kazi River on the eastern slopes of Mount Karisimbi. With every encumbered footfall, decay and new life blended and oozed beneath my boots. The smell was intoxicating.

I stopped to catch my breath. Gorilla trekking tests the limits of even the most able bodied and brave. My hangover didn't help. The night before we had celebrated twenty-five years since Dian Fossey set up the research center. Drinking banana beer and dancing and drumming with the rangers in the big house after the American trustees had gone to bed was refreshingly primal and reminded me of the unbridled tribal fetes of my youth. We kept everyone else in camp awake. My head was still pounding from the experience.

It began to rain heavily. Wheezing and gasping, I struggled on. Raindrops splattered on broad leaves, which, along with my labored breathing, was the only sound I heard. African soldiers skulked nearby. We didn't see them but we knew they were there, patrolling the park, looking out for rebels making incursions from neighboring Uganda. Leading me to the gorillas was Loni, an American researcher; Nemeye, one of Fossey's favorite trackers; Dieter; and Bob Campbell, the Kenyan *National Geographic* photographer who was sent to photograph Dian Fossey in the late 1960s. It was his first time back since filming *Gorillas in the Mist*, in which he was credited as both crew (special photography) and character (played by Bryan Brown).

"I'm curious to see if any of the silverbacks recognize me by my hiking gear," Bob said softly. "I've worn the same outfit every time I've visited them."

"Silverbacks, plural?" I gasped. "I thought it was just one silverback per group, you know, the alpha male."

Dieter shook his head and chuckled. "My friend, Group 5 has four silverbacks: Pablo, Shinda, Cantsbe, and Ziz. Ziz is in charge. Wait till you see the size of him."

We walked for an hour at a fast pace through what seemed like a hallucination—a primordial rain forest thick with giant lobelia, Hagenia dripping with lichen, Hypericum, and thick mist. The journey was as arduous and trying as it was mystical and fascinating. It was as if we'd traveled back to a prehistoric time to commune with our shy and hairy cousins in the mountains.

"Bloody hell," I gasped, standing with my hands on my knees. "How much farther?"

"Virunga is merciless," said Bob. "Who knows where the gorillas are today. They range all day long." He and I were sharing a cabin at Karisoke. I couldn't have asked for a more sociable roommate. When I came in drunk the night before, he was still awake. We lay on our cots and talked for an hour. He told me how Dian used to make him sleep in a tent, even after they became lovers. The next morning before dawn, Vatiri, a ranger with whom I'd been drumming and dancing and drinking, came into our cabin with a shovel full of burning coal and stoked our potbellied stove, warming up the cabin before Bob and I got up. Vatiri had also carved me a bamboo flute that he placed next to my cot. I was deeply moved by this gift. He and I now had a profound connection.

The wind blasted a hole through the mist and for a moment we could see Lake Kivu and the town of Gisenyi a few thousand meters below us. We then found Group 5's night nests. A forward tracker assured us over walkie-talkies that the gorillas were not far. We descended into a saddle and were surrounded by giant lobelia plants. There was an unusual odor in the air, like a workman's armpit after a hard day's toil. Bob told me it was a fear odor that gorillas give off when they sense danger. I imagined they could smell us too. They probably knew I had drunk a barrel of banana beer the night before.

A gorilla was sheltering from the rain beneath a Hagenia tree. But for a faint reflection in his dark eyes when he briefly glanced at us, his form was barely discernible in the faint light. He sat perfectly still. He would not move until the rain stopped, or until I crossed a line. Bob made a well-rehearsed guttural sound with his throat, known as a *belch vocalization*, which in gorilla language means "Everything's cool."

More gorillas appeared. I was relieved that we had found them. Rainfall facilitated our entry into their world. Around us the foliage glistened. Despite the high average rainfall in their habitat, by all appearances gorillas did not much like the rain. They remained stock-still, shabby black forms huddled together, hardly even looking up.

After a few careful steps we were almost beside Ziz—the largest silverback in the Virungas—who was straddling a mossy log. He looked like a bouncer on a smoke break. Careful not to make any sudden movements, I sat down slowly on the undergrowth near him. As the dominant silverback of Group 5, Ziz tenuously tolerated three other silverbacks in his group who were utterly frustrated at not being allowed to copulate with the females. This had made them dangerous to researchers, who were regularly dragged and beaten. Shinda bit one researcher on the back of her knee, and she needed surgery. But Loni assured me they were calmer today. When the rain stopped, the gorillas began cavorting. I was thrilled to be among them. Hearing gorillas hum as they ate, taking in the smell of their body odor and shit, and seeing the look in their reflective brown eyes, I felt at home. Every hair follicle on my body had gossamer wings and was ready to fly. It was total bliss.

Ziz was barely two meters away from me. Weighing around 220 kilos, he was enormous. It was touching to watch such a large and fearsome beast sweetly play games with his young, letting them climb on his back and roll down his belly. Occasionally, with breast-beats and grunts, he warded off his horny adjutants from his females. He paid no attention to us bald apes. Suddenly, he rose to his full height and beat his chest. I swallowed my heart.

"Was that intended for me?" I cried.

"No," said Loni. "He's demonstrating for a female."

Ziz led the group eastward along the slope in search of leafier provender. This drew the three peripheral silverbacks closer to where we were sitting. Shinda walked up and gave me a fearsome look. I rose to my feet and cowered behind Loni again. But on Ziz's command, the junior silverback begrudgingly moved on. I sat back down and removed my journal from my backpack. I was about to write in it when Pablo, the group's rear guard, approached me threateningly. I quickly rose again and stood behind Loni. Had I not, I'm sure he would have grabbed my leg and dragged me through the lobelia and nettles like a rag doll, or worse, run off with my journal.

A handful of curious females came near and began examining me. Mtwali, an adolescent female, rolled onto her back and touched my knee with her hand. She then started fondling the lapel of my raincoat, then slowly reached up and touched my cheek. My heart soared. I was deeply flattered by her advances. Meanwhile, Effie, the group's matriarch, who was helping a new mother wean her infant, glanced at me with dark, cognizant eyes. No other wild animal had ever looked at me with such presence of mind.

I burned off a roll of 200 ASA film and, as the sky darkened, I loaded a roll of 400 ASA. Before it was too dark, as planned, Dieter posed with his Macintosh PowerBook. I took a dozen shots of him sitting next to Mtwali as she looked up at him. By this time, we had been with Group 5 for more than two hours. Dieter decided it was time to head back.

It began to rain heavily, so we picked up the pace on the Porter's Trail. In a daze of après-gorilla bliss and grinning from ear to ear, I tramped on ahead, my Yashica camera swinging from my neck. As well as the pleasure of having met gorillas in person, I was proud to have gotten the money shot, the image we'd been hoping to get, a shoo-in for donations from Apple.

Suddenly, I was face-to-face with a battalion of Rwandan soldiers heading in the opposite direction. Not a word was spoken, but the air was pungent with perspiration as they marched past me. Slowly, I moved my finger to the Yashica's shutter button and squeezed off a shot of the soldiers. After they were gone, I put the camera in my backpack and forged on.

I was determined to get dry and drink a cold Primus beer. But when I reached camp, I discovered my backpack had been unzipped the whole way and now the camera was gone. "Oh shit!" I cried, anxiously setting off to retrace my steps. Terrifying thoughts rushed through my head. *What if the soldiers find it? When the film is processed, their commander will see that I photographed his troops on patrol, and I'll be truly fucked. I could be thrown in jail, like that time in Yemen, for photographing near a naval base, or worse. I could be killed.*

I met a smiling Dieter on the trail—he was holding my camera. "Found it in about ten inches of mud," he said. "Must have fallen out of your pack."

I was relieved the camera did not fall into the hands of the military, but by all appearances it was ruined. Bob Campbell, a Magnum photographer, said it would cost as much to repair as it would to buy a new one. I was devastated; it had photographs in it that were irreplaceable.

Bob assured me the film was salvageable. In our cabin, he painstakingly cleaned off the mud, put the camera under a blanket to keep out the light, opened the back, removed the film, and then carefully wound the roll of negatives back into its cylinder. Later, when I got the film developed, among the photos of gorillas was a single image of the soldiers, surrounded by flora and emerald gloom, staring blankly from lopsided helmets, their sullen black faces rendered more haunting by the traces of water damage around the edges.

5

CREATING A CONSERVATION CULTURE

"WHAT WE NEED is an all-singing, all-dancing, gorilla-loving nation," I told Ruth as I paid for a postcard in the hotel gift shop. It was a tourist postcard illustrating Rwanda's attractions. Dotted around a map were a zebra, lion, chimpanzee, and buffalo, but no gorilla. Gorillas were nowhere to be seen, nor was their habitat among the green areas on the map—the country's national parks. It was a shocking omission that I would make it my life's work to correct.

"Hurry!" said Ruth. "We're leaving now." The rest of the US board was piling into a minibus parked in the hotel forecourt. I was the last to get on board, reducing the average age by half a decade. It was like a bus full of giggling understudies for *The Golden Girls*. "Everyone here?" asked Ruth. "Yes," we all replied. We then sped off in the direction of the presidential palace to meet President Juvénal Habyarimana.

A seasoned travel expert, Tom Keesling had such extensive connections and influence that no matter where he took his high-end clients, a private meeting with the head of state was on the itinerary. It was Tom who made all the arrangements for Richard Nixon to go to China in 1972. I would learn a good deal from watching him work.

I showed the president the postcard I had just bought in the hotel gift shop and asked if he thought it strange that gorillas were excluded. He was nonplussed and smiled uneasily, no doubt wondering, *Who the hell's this upstart?*

Dieter asked him what measures were being taken to ensure the gorillas were kept safe in the midst of his country's ongoing war. "Peace talks," he smiled. "We are making progress in Arusha."

I was surprised to hear the UK was not involved in the peace process. Upon my return to London, I would write to foreign secretary Douglas Hurd and ask why not. And he would reply, saying he had largely bowed out of the talks and was leaving it up to the European Commission to do the UK's bidding. It sounded like a cop-out and a missed opportunity. Indeed, he would soon eat his words and seriously regret his country's lack of involvement in the search for lasting peace in Rwanda. Ruth then presented the president with a picture of an American buffalo and slapped him condescendingly on the knee.

After we left the presidential palace, we were driving through the city when we discovered we'd made a very grave mistake. In our haste, we'd forgotten Ken Musgrave, a judge on the US Court of International Trade, at the hotel. He threatened to resign from the board over the gaffe. "How dare you treat me with such disrespect," cried the judge, who was on his third large bourbon and branch water when we found him at the hotel bar. "I've donated enough money to this cause to put every one of those goddamn mountain gorillas up in Claridge's for a year."

Tom was extremely apologetic. "How can I make it up to you, judge?"

"You can't," he growled. "The damage is done!"

The trustees left the next day. We were relieved to see them go. As their plane ascended into a cloud-filled sky, we celebrated with a "wheels-up" party.

"They can do no more harm to this small but dignified country," sighed Liz.

"I don't mean to be ruthless," quipped Dieter, "but it feels better to be Ruth-less."

We drank and laughed and cursed the Keeslings. Later I stood on the veranda with a glass of Mützig beer in my hand, and again wondered how I might get back to living where the nights were so balmy. "All I wanted to do was get back to Africa," wrote Ernest Hemingway in *Green Hills of Africa*. "We had not left it, yet, but when I would wake in the night I would lie, listening, homesick for it already." That was me, already missing the place before I'd even left. Part of me wished I could stay and never leave. It was good to be back tapping into the global consciousness. The job had gripped me. It was hard to imagine a more dramatic career change or one that suited me better. I was curious about what direction Jillian and I might take the fund in. Never, in my wildest dreams, could I have imagined where the fund would take us.

On Christmas Day 1992, the *Sunday Times* published a photo of a newborn mountain gorilla on its front page. I was mightily proud of Jillian for placing the image in such a major newspaper, but she was appalled by its quality. It had been taken by a Karisoke researcher. "We've got to be able to get better shots of newborns," she said. The *Times* color supplement featured an interview with Sigourney Weaver and an appeal endorsed by her, on behalf of the mountain gorillas, which ended up raising a heap of money and public awareness of our cause in Britain. To end a year punctuated by so many triumphs on such a high note was more than we could have hoped for. Jillian and I were proud of our achievements.

The celebrations were short-lived. At the start of 1993, peace talks in Arusha between the government and rebels stalled and Rwanda began drifting back into civil war. In February, believing that the government was giving too much away in Arusha, hard-liners went on a six-day killing spree in northern Rwanda. Many houses were burned and hundreds of Tutsi were killed. The RPF rebels responded by invading from Uganda again. Their forces encountered little resistance from the army, which they outgunned six to one. The rebels cited hard-liner violence as the reason they'd invaded, but the offensive may actually have been an attempt to increase their bargaining power at the peace talks. They took the town of Ruhengeri and then advanced unchecked, moving steadily south and gaining territory without opposition, a violent onslaught that alienated the RPF from their allies in the Rwandan opposition parties, as well as in the West.

Meanwhile Louis Nzeyimana, our education coordinator, and his pregnant wife Agatha were trapped in their house in Ruhengeri. When we spoke on the phone, I could hear shelling in the background. I contacted the local commander of the UN peacekeepers and asked if he could evacuate them to Kigali, where I believed they'd be much safer. All our foreign staff—Dieter, his wife Netzin, Charlene, Liz, and the researchers—were evacuated back to their passport countries. At least they were safe. Louis and Agatha made it to Kigali. Then, as it became clearer that the army was losing ground to the RPF, Habyarimana requested urgent military assistance from France, which sent four hundred soldiers. The arrival of French troops in Kigali significantly changed the military situation on the ground. The RPF now found themselves under fresh attack, French shells bombarding them as they advanced southward. By February 20 they were within thirty kilometers of Kigali, and many observers believed an assault on the city was imminent. *Oh, Christ*, I thought. *What kinda nightmare must Louis and Agatha be going through?* The assault never took place, however. The RPF declared a cease-fire.

The invasion knocked the stuffing out of all of us at the fund. Granted, the civil war had begun shortly before my wife and I got involved in this work, so we had yet to see peace in Rwanda. However, until now the fighting had not disrupted our work to any extent. But as a consequence of the RPF's military campaign invasion, all our activities in Rwanda ceased and the Karisoke Research Center was ransacked and looted by errant soldiers. Although crushed to see our work wantonly destroyed by armed belligerents, and for having to go back to square one, at least we'd been thoroughly disabused of our foolish naïveté.

Jillian obtained broadcast-quality video footage of the sacked research center, made multiple copies of it, and then dashed around Soho dropping off the cassettes with the news editors of as many broadcast outlets as she could find. It was later shown on BBC, Sky, CNN, ABC, NHK, CBC, and CBS—to an estimated worldwide audience of 140 million viewers. She had a talent for public relations.

In the spring, after it was deemed safe enough for visitors, Jillian traveled to Rwanda with Harvey Mann, a photographer from *YOU* magazine, and Ruda Landman, a South African journalist and cohost of M-Net's documentary show *Carte Blanche*. It was Jillian's first trip to Africa. I was concerned about her going alone. It was one thing to venture into a war zone myself and quite another for her to do the same without me. She confronted me on my hypocrisy, so I stopped objecting. It would have been extravagant for both of us to go. I had just been, and PR was her thing. By all accounts, the fighting had ceased and it was safe. I saw her off at Heathrow. There was something liberating about the role reversal.

Escorted by a convoy of UN peacekeepers, she and her media team drove from Kigali into the demilitarized zone around Ruhengeri. Her intention was to meet up with park authorities and restart conservation activities. She would not visit the gorillas. Meanwhile, I was in London biting my nails, waiting for a phone call confirming she was safe. I waited hours for her call. The phone never rang. Eventually I went to bed, somehow managed to banish awful thoughts from my head, and slept.

In the middle of the night, the phone rang. "Hello," I said drowsily.

"Hello, love. It's me. Just got into Gisenyi. Couldn't call you before now."

"Are you OK?" I asked anxiously.

"Yes, but you wouldn't believe the ordeal I've been through. In the middle of bloody nowhere, Greg, our Land Rover ended up on its side in a ditch and all the petrol drained out. Harvey and I had to walk into town to get petrol while the M-Net crew organized a work party of local farmers to get the Landy upright again. We eventually got the thing started, but it was so badly in need of repairs and kept stalling that it took us six hours to reach the Meridian Hotel in Gisenyi, which is where I'm calling you from now, darling. It's so good to talk to you."

"Such a relief to know you're OK, Jillie," I sighed. "I feared the worst."

"Fucking hell, it's been a hell of a day. And when we finally got here we were so tired and hungry, Harvey insisted they wake the chef and get him to cook us all a steak dinner. You don't know how good it feels just to be in this hotel room talking to you now. Tomorrow, we're going to meet Rosamond Carr on her flower plantation outside Gisenyi."

"That will be a tonic," I said. "You'll love Ros."

"I love you," she said.

"Me too." As I went back to sleep, I imagined Jillian making herself comfortable at Ros Carr's flower farm, a splendid relic of the colonial era, complete with black wooden beams, open stone fireplaces, and dusty bookcases. On the walls hung black-and-white pictures that Bob Campbell had taken of Dian Fossey and the gorillas, and every book ever published about mountain gorillas. Ros, a former fashion illustrator from New York, had copies of *Marie Claire* and *Vogue* scattered across her antique coffee tables. Sembagari would serve tea. A wood fire would crackle and spit, its iron grill preventing the sparks from setting fire to the hyrax skin rugs and cushion covers. After a cuppa, they might wander outside and explore rows of blooming flowers, smell the aroma of frangipani and volcanic soil, and look up in awe at the majesty of Mount Karisimbi, maybe feel a strong sense of nostalgia for the pioneering days of Dian, as I did. No doubt, her afternoon at Ros's house would not be as I imagined. But I knew she'd love it.

When they returned from Rwanda, Ruda Landman broadcast a report on *Carte Blanche* in South Africa and Harvey Mann ran his pictures in *YOU* magazine, launching our "Pal of Pasika" fostering program. Pasika was an endearing infant female gorilla with an eye-catching hairdo, artfully photographed by Harvey. It was a life-changing trip for him, whose commitment to the cause remained strong for years. Jillian teamed up with Care for the Wild to manage the fostering scheme. Pals received a glossy poster of Pasika, a T-shirt, a certificate, a copy of her family tree, and an update on her progress every six months. It was a very popular adoption scheme. Along with our regular appeals, a merchandise catalog, and *Digit News*, Pal of Pasika helped bolster our brand and raise public donations from an ever-expanding donor base. In just a few months, the Pal of Pasika program raised over £10,000—another string to our bow.

Jillian came home inspired. She had a sparkle in her eyes that I had not seen in a while. Getting her hands dirty at the coal face of conservation, racing across town in all manner of transportation to get from one meeting to the next, and making a difference where it really mattered, had awakened a fighting spirit in her. And seeing the level of poverty in the villages next to the gorillas' pristine Volcanoes National Park ignited her sense of social justice. She sought a way to elevate those people out of poverty while, at the same time, ensuring the survival of the endangered mountain gorillas. This would be her calling.

"Hampstead Heath is only pristine," said Jillian, "because the people who live next to it enjoy a level of economic prosperity that allows them to care about the well-being of trees." It was time for the fund to step up for Jillian. I agreed to petition the UK trustees to employ her full-time. Harrumphing and humming and dragging their heels the whole way, the board reluctantly agreed to appoint her as director of development. In North America, her new title implied fundraising. In Europe and Africa, it implied economic development. Hence, she got the best of both worlds.

From then on, Jillian would attend board meetings and do her own bidding, albeit with my support. In time she and I would be equally paid codirectors. I was unsure about this arrangement at first. No question she was carrying as much of the workload as I was for the fund, but I liked being top dog, head honcho, a big fish in a small pond. My wife ridiculed me for my sense of superiority, said it was unjustifiable. She was right. This was not an apish hierarchy. I wasn't a silverback. She was my wife and codirector. Besides, I needed her. We were a team. At the end of our working day, we sat on our living room couch to decompress, drink wine, and analyze the day's events. We were each other's sounding board, counselor, cheerleader. It was a symbiotic arrangement. We told each other we'd do this for no more than ten years. Many stresses were inherent to being married to the job, living and working together, day in day out, but we would succeed so long as we continued to support each other.

––––––––––

One of my remits was zoos. Britain was home to a multitude of zoos. And although I was, and still am, wholeheartedly against the keeping of captive wild animals, whether in cages or vast enclosures designed to resemble their natural habitats, the zoo-going public accounted for the second-largest leisure activity, after movies, in Britain. Zoos were an interface between ordinary people and wildlife conservation organizations like ours working in remote parts of the world. Many of the larger zoos were directly involved in conservation, but smaller regional facilities, which also drew large crowds, sought ways to channel their support. I had written to those zoos whose ape enclosures had received a high rating in John Ironmonger's *Good Zoo Guide*, and offered to visit them and give a talk to their supporters in exchange for them installing a collection box outside the ape enclosure. They were happy to have my endorsement.

Twycross, which scored highly for primates, was among the few zoos I visited, as well as Longleat and Durrell Wildlife Park. I also visited Belfast Zoo. The city was still under siege and had been retro-engineered to provide security to ordinary citizens and to maintain a modicum of peace amid all the trappings of conflict in Northern Ireland. Every police station, for instance, was enclosed in chicken wire to prevent belligerents from lobbing Molotov cocktails onto it. And most roundabouts had a military post in the middle manned by an unsmiling soldier who was holding a high-caliber weapon. Everything—the trees, the garden walls, the soldiers—seemed to be colored in the same shade of cadmium green, not shamrock green.

Situated on a wooded hill overlooking the city, Belfast Zoo was a refuge from the Troubles. Zoo director John Stone, a stocky, cheerful, red-cheeked man, welcomed me warmly to his facility. As we toured the grounds, I asked him why the ring-tailed lemurs were allowed to roam free. "Because they're reliably good natured," he said. "And they know where the food is. Occasionally one will go walkabout, but when hunger strikes, it comes back." I told him I used to have one as a pet when I lived in Madagascar. "Really? What were you doing there?"

"I spent three years in a boarding school in the south of the island, the American School in Fort Dauphin. It was out of this world."

"I imagine it was," he smiled. "So you know what I mean about ringtails."

Stone's zoo was well maintained and clearly well funded. "It is one of the few places where people can come and feel good," he said. "And because of this, the Belfast City Council throws ample amounts of cash at us."

When we arrived at the gorilla enclosure, without hesitation, the silverback charged us and slammed his fists against the plexiglass. "Oh, he always does that when I come around," laughed John. "He can't bear that I'm the boss, he resents my implied dominance over him."

The Regent's Park zoo, which was close enough to our office that we could hear the elephants trumpet, never put out a collection box for us. They had their own conservation program in the field and saw no value in cooperating with us. Nevertheless, I became friends with Mick Carmen, the head apekeeper. He encouraged the fund to use the facilities at the zoo and to hold meetings or events there. We also recruited two trustees from the zoo community: Jeremy Mallinson, director of Jersey Zoo, and Professor Roger Wheater, OBE, director of Edinburgh Zoo. Jeremy was keenly interested in primates and renowned for his attempts to reintroduce lion tamarins back into the wild in Brazil. A spirited bon vivant who drove a Jaguar, his first love was N'Pongo, a female gorilla at his zoo. He used to take her into Jersey with him to raise money. Roger Wheater, who was director of the Uganda National Parks in the early 1970s, was a funny fellow with a sparkling personality. He and I got on well. Our shared background in East Africa gave us commonality.

"I was five when I first visited Murchison," I told Roger during a break for sandwiches and wine at his first board meeting. "One night I was stalked and almost eaten by a hyena."

"Really, what year was that?" asked Roger.

"1967," I replied.

"Good Lord," he laughed, "I was chief warden then. Why didn't anybody tell me a *mzungu* boy almost got eaten by a hyena? You look as if you survived." He then told me a story about an alcoholic elephant that used to show up at the rangers' quarters and rip the place apart if he couldn't get his daily dose of local brew. "In the morning, we'd find him lying on his belly, legs splayed out, and with his trunk curled round the inside of a barrel. He eventually became so troublesome that we feared he might kill someone, so sadly, in the end, we had to shoot him."

Rosemary Godfrey brought levity to our board meetings. She had begun attending to keep minutes. She was intelligent, attractive, and had a wonderful sense of humor. And her acuity and bubbly character were a tonic to the seriousness of our agendas. How serious could they be? Let's face it, gorillas are hilarious. Why not be more like the gorillas? Rose's witty antics put a smile on all our faces. If I received an important call at the office and others were eavesdropping on my end of the conversation—watching my eyes widen with delight as I listened to a donor announce that they were sending a five-figure donation—Rose would stand nearby holding an unplugged phone wire and, to the others, mouth the words, "It's not even plugged in." We also hired Lian Simmons, a bookkeeper, who came in to the office once a week to do the books. She, too, attended our quarterly board meetings to sign off on finance. Lian was like Scotty on *Star Trek*, telling us, "We canna give it anymore, captain," when Jillian and I aimed too far beyond our means. She gave the trustees confidence by doing terribly sensible things like setting up an escrow account into which we would put £1,000 a year to cover any future legal fees that might come up. If Lian looked calm, as she usually did, all was well.

The UK board tried to maintain good relations with the US board, but the politics were debilitating and the US board never—*never*—accepted the sovereignty of the UK, that we *had* to be masters of our own affairs. This caveat exists in most countries. Directors of other international NGOs I met confirmed it. Greenpeace had to create an oversight body, a charity based in Amsterdam whose board was comprised solely of Greenpeace directors from around the world. The World Wildlife Fund had a similar setup. The only way to direct a unified global effort is to delegate portions of the overall mission to individual countries. To do that, the US and UK fund set up an International Coordinating Committee (ICC), comprised of trustees from both boards who delegated duties to a global executive director: Dr. Dieter Steklis. The ICC met biannually. It worked for a while, until the US board felt its power slipping away.

At any rate, apart from paying our education officer's salary, the UK did not have much of a field program to call its own in Africa— yet. Conservation education was a good bet. From the outset, we had actively promoted gorillas in UK schools. Ian Redmond wrote a talk for primary school students titled "If I'd Been Born a Gorilla." It was a simple, illustrated lecture about a day in the life of a young gorilla. Rose took on the challenge and visited schools across the country to deliver it. She also participated in the annual British Association of Young Scientists (BAYS) exhibition at Imperial College, which was organized by Ted Porter, Jillian's ex. An array of whiz-bang exhibits and demonstrations were meant to grab young people's attention and inspire the next generation of engineers, physicists, and scientists, or in our case wildlife conservationists. In addition, Rose coordinated an army of volunteers who were scattered across Britain—individuals or groups of people of all ages and backgrounds who organized small-scale events in their communities or neighborhoods to raise money for the fund. Shortly after their event, Rose would show up for a photo op holding up a giant check alongside the organizers. She was responsible for organizing Gorilla Week, which we timed to coincide with the anniversary of Karisoke in September. It made sense to have a week in the year when everyone could concentrate their volunteer fundraising activities and events and take advantage of the PR Jillian generated for Gorilla Week. "August is a good month to place stories in the media," she said, "because stars and politicians are on their hols."

Jillian and I were invited to a few weddings that summer. Peter Elliott invited us to celebrate his union in York. It was a lively event. Many of the guests were Peter's fellow ape actors, some of whom had disproportionately long arms. Jillian and I got high and thoroughly enjoyed ourselves. While talking to some guests, I could remain seated while they stood and still maintain direct eye contact. Back in London, Peter got an opportunity to show off his talents in Covent Garden. His animatronic gorilla costume had many believing that there was a real live gorilla roaming through the market. The gorilla's face was animated through remote robotic control. And Peter's performance was so authentic that the police had to be there to reassure the public. Some people couldn't help but take a few steps backward when Peter approached. Even after he had climbed into a chauffeur-driven convertible VW Beetle and driven off, the crowds swarmed after him determined to catch a final glimpse of the gorilla. It was clear why they called Peter the industry's "primary primate." Our public relations stunt did not impress everyone, though. A Belgian woman accosted me in the market and demanded how we could be so concerned about wild animals when the people in Rwanda were being killed by rebel soldiers. I explained that it was our charity's remit to protect the gorillas regardless of other needs but that the UK fund was looking at ways to improve the lot of poor Rwandans as well.

We received another wedding invite, this time from Barclay Hastings, who was marrying his partner Richard Lloyd-Morgan, an opera singer. The ceremony was held in a Methodist church in Knightsbridge that permitted such unions. It was the first gay marriage that Jillian and I had witnessed and one of the most intimate weddings I've ever seen. Not long afterward, Barclay was diagnosed with knee cancer. It seems the brilliant veterinarian was unable to face the prospect of never again being able to tramp through wildernesses to treat wildlife in distress, so at an international wildlife veterinarian symposium in San Francisco he administered a fatal dose of rhinoceros tranquilizer to himself and took his own life. So . . . fucking . . . heartbreaking!

In June, Ziz's remains were found in the forest. I was devastated. Not him, not that big beautiful ape. I'd only met him once but he'd really got his hooks in me. He inspired me. That "mama's boy," as Fossey called him, had grown up to be one of the largest of the world's mountain gorillas, a king of the silverbacks. The last time park rangers saw him alive was in April. It was difficult to determine the cause of death, his body was so badly decomposed. Dr. Louis Nzeyimana, a qualified veterinarian and the only member of the fund's staff who was in situ at the time, carried out the necropsy. He concluded that the twenty-two-year-old Ziz had died of pneumonia.

Following February's attack in Rwanda, fearful that hostilities might resume again, our foreign staff, researchers, and veterinarians had all remained in exile for three months. During that time Louis continued working alone. He conducted a feasibility study with the Rwanda parks authority and the education and environment ministries. The study found a compelling need for environmental education. In Ruhengeri, it was seen as an essential aid for a region that had endured the worst fighting in the country's three-year civil war.

In July, I arranged for Louis to come to England and help us design a winning bid to the European Commission for an environmental education project in Rwanda. To work on the proposal, we decamped to the Cotswolds. Guiting Power, a village dating back to AD 780, is set in a small valley amid rolling grasslands, and every house, pub, and shop in the village is made of Cotswold stone, a yellow oolitic Jurassic limestone rich in sea urchin fossils. Nearly all the buildings were owned by the Guiting Manor Amenity Trust, a charitable body. To qualify to live in one of its properties, some of which were affordable housing, tenants had to work in the village. The International Centre for Conservation Education (ICCE) was located in Guiting Power and ICCE's director of training, Adam Adamou, and his wife Emma lived in a little two-story stone cottage on the village high street. They kindly agreed to put Louis and me up in their home.

Mr. and Mrs. Mu, as I liked to call them, enjoyed smoking hashish and drinking beer. Louis disavowed the hash but could put back the pints. I recall him coming down for breakfast one morning in his best shoes. He put one foot on the top wooden step, lost his footing, and then fell down the stairs, or rather skied down—an avalanche of lanky limbs, jolting each time his shoes hit a slippery step—remaining upright the whole way down, never toppling. Whenever I play that scene over again in my head, it still gets a laugh.

One sunny afternoon, David Rogers, who lived close by, invited the three of us to join him for a pie and a pint at his local pub. He wanted to check on our progress and to meet Louis and Adam. We sat outside. Ale, sunshine, and a common cause quickly gave rise to solidarity.

"It must have been terrifying for you and your wife," said David, speaking to Louis, "being trapped in Ruhengeri when the rebels attacked."

"Hearing those big guns was frightening, yes," said Louis. "But we did not actually see so many soldiers in town and those we did see did not give us any trouble. It was as if the RPF was saying, 'Now that you see what we can do, you will take us more seriously.'"

"Well, it's jolly brave of you nonetheless to carry out your duties under such grim circumstances. We owe you a debt of gratitude for your dedication on behalf of the gorillas."

"I feel much safer now in Kigali," said Louis, glancing at me.

"I gather you three have been working hard," said David.

"Louis makes sure the proposal fits Rwanda's school curriculum and system," I said, sipping my pint of Abbot Ale. "I make sure we meticulously meet all the EC's requirements. Meanwhile, Adam here's the man with the vision. Ain't that right, Mr. Mu?"

"Um, thanks," said a moonfaced Adam as a warm summer breeze blew his thick black mane around his head. He was shy and self-effacing, and he spoke with a lisp. "The environment is something I feel quite passionate about, and this is a very important opportunity to get the message out there," he beamed. I cannot remember how our paths crossed, but I knew no one better to help us design a cutting-edge conservation education proposal than Adam. A creative thinker, excellent teacher, and an environment savant, he was amazing to work with. He saw everything in green. His big Cypriot heart was forever in the ferny foliage. His passion for jazz fusion brought us closer as friends. He turned me on to Fourth World, a Brazilian jazz band led by husband-and-wife legends Airto Moreira and Flora Purim. Adam had befriended them and knew they wanted to do something for wildlife. But he stopped short of putting me directly in touch with them. He saw me as a bit of a used-car salesman when it came to that sort of thing and wondered if I'd handle them poorly.

Five days of brainstorming and hard work in the Cotswolds produced a polished proposal that I delivered by hand to Brussels. Two months later, the EC approved €720,000 over three years. Starting in August 1994, a series of teacher training courses would be held at a new conservation education center in Rwanda, to be built on donated land. We would train resource teachers selected from the 350 primary schools located near the park, and they in turn would teach their pupils during the school year about how to make ecologically sound decisions. The center would also act as a hub for environmental education, attracting students, nature clubs, and ecotourists. Within three years we aimed to establish a national conservation education strategy in Rwanda. Agenda 21, the centerpiece of the 1992 Earth

Summit in Rio de Janeiro, said governments should strive to integrate environment and development as a crosscutting issue into education at all levels. Because of us, Rwanda was set to be among the first nations to do so. I called Louis in Kigali with the good news.

"Tonight I will drink a Primus in celebration," he said.

Finally, the UK fund had a project, designed from scratch, that we could boast about. The learning curve was steep, but the result was also deeply satisfying. This was our first step outside the gorilla habitat. With an education program designed to reach a quarter of a million primary-school children in the war-torn area surrounding the park, we were one step closer to realizing my vision of an all-singing, all-dancing, gorilla-loving nation. We had our stride back.

I loved my job and always strived to do better. I got into full career mode, stopped counting the hours. I worked most weekends and never had trouble sleeping at night. Being involved in something bigger than me where my efforts had a lasting, positive impact on the world, was satisfying. The gorillas had captured my psyche. And after Dieter returned to Rwanda to engineer the reestablishment of the twenty-six-year-old research center, Karisoke was once more up and running.

6

MISSION TO PLANET EARTH

"GORILLAS FROM SPACE?" I laughed. "How awesome is that?" A fax had just arrived from Dieter Steklis informing us that NASA intended to obtain high-resolution radar images of the Virunga volcanoes, as part of its Mission to Planet Earth. The Remote Sensing Center at Rutgers University was working with the fund to develop a geographic information system (GIS) of the gorillas' habitat in Rwanda, and NASA had agreed, tentatively, to include Virunga on a list of sites to be "imaged" by a Spaceborne Imaging Radar aboard the space shuttle *Endeavour* in April 1994. The radar images taken from the space shuttle would augment the GIS—a vital tool for protecting parks where human encroachment is intense. So far satellite "spot" imagery of the Virungas had been unreliable because, as the title of Dian Fossey's book suggests, the habitat is continuously shrouded in mist. Consequently, this was one hell of a breakthrough for the gorillas.

A week later, when the lights came up at Ronnie Scott's Jazz Club in Soho, after a performance by Fourth World, Peter Elliott came over to where Jillian, Adam, Emma, and I were seated. Grinning from ear to ear, he said, "Hey, guys, I've got some good news for you. They're doing a new gorilla movie. Kennedy/Marshall, who made *Jurassic Park*, is making a film based on Michael Crichton's *Congo*." Of course, Peter would be the guy Hollywood called when the script

demanded an ape. The next day I bought the book and began reading it. The story featured space-borne satellite images of gorilla habitats in central Africa, and there was an uncanny parallel between the
high-tech ERTS expedition into central Africa described in Crichton's
book and our use of space technology. "At ERTS, we deal mostly in
remote sensing, satellite photographs, aerial run-bys, radar side scans,"
wrote Crichton. My heart raced as I read on. Serendipity! I called the
number in L.A. that Peter had given me and spoke to Sam Mercer,
the movie's producer. I told him all about our space shuttle mission.
"We like real," said Sam.

Jillian and I were beside ourselves with all this good fortune. First
the EC grant, then the space shuttle, and now another Hollywood
movie. We began tooling up for what we imagined would be a major
PR coup. We had three months before launch day. Then a letter
arrived from Dr. Ellen Stofan at the Jet Propulsion Laboratory (JPL)
in California. "Unfortunately, we are unable to acquire data over
the Karisoke area in Rwanda, nor does it appear that the site will be
covered by other data-takes in the area." Citing an oversubscription
of peer-reviewed scientific experiments on the shuttle, NASA had
bumped us off the mission. We had crash-landed back down to Earth.

"Who do we know that could influence NASA?" asked Jillian as
we sat on the couch that evening drowning our sorrows.

"I think I know just the person," I said.

Arthur C. Clarke owned the first computer I ever saw, a Commodore
PET 200. It had a plastic trapezoid-shaped monitor fixed on top of a
white plastic box, an integrated keyboard, and a cassette recorder for
mass data. "Greg, meet Junior HAL," he said. He had named his PC
after the onboard computer on the Jupiter-bound spacecraft that goes
mad in *2001: A Space Odyssey*, a film that he cowrote with Stanley

Kubrick. Some of the PET's design features were inspired by *2001*: its brand-name font and its shape, which was similar to the space phone.

I was sixteen years old, visiting my parents in Colombo, Sri Lanka, for the first time during a break from boarding school in Madagascar. I had been struggling with a lesson on sidereal time in my astronomy correspondence course. So, I looked up Arthur's number in the phone book and called him to ask if he could help me.

"Sure, come around," he said. "I'm at 25 Barnes Place." That was barely a kilometer away from my parents' house on Gregory's Road. As I walked the tree-lined route, I felt like I was floating in space, striding across the planets.

Growing up during the Apollo missions, I became obsessed with rockets, astronauts, and space. When I was a kid, my mother took me to an exhibition of the Apollo 11 moon mission in Lagos, Nigeria, which included a life-size model of the lunar module and an actual moon rock. I was eight when I first saw *2001: A Space Odyssey*, at the Scala Cinema in Ibadan. My mother had innocently taken me to see the latest "space movie." I was terrified by it and yet fascinated by the movie's far-reaching vision. It was the most mind-blowing experience of my young life. I could not shake the image of astronaut Frank Poole forever tumbling through space.

Thereafter I read all of Arthur's books and became a lifelong fan of his science fiction novels. And on the day I met him at his house, I brought a copy of *Imperial Earth* with me, which he gladly auto-graphed. He also gave me a handful of glossy promotional brochures that the Jet Propulsion Laboratory had sent him, filled with photo-graphs of the planets taken by the Voyager missions.

Arthur's office, or "ego chamber" as he called it, was stuffed with his published works. Every bit of wall space was taken up by tokens of his central role in the Space Age. Although best known for science fiction classics like *Childhood's End*, *Rendezvous with Rama*, and *Fountains of Paradise*, Arthur had also written books promoting real space travel.

And there were as many photos of him posing with cosmonauts as astronauts, as he sought to transcend Cold War politics by reminding us of the awesome potential of the cosmos.

"What's this?" I asked, pointing to a framed black-and-white picture of a pockmarked crater on the lunar surface.

"That's Earthlight," smiled Arthur, "a crater on the moon. On the Apollo 15 mission in 1971, astronauts Scott and Irwin drove past it in their moon rover and named it after my novel."

His broad accent was often mistaken for American, but he was from Minehead, Somerset. We went over the complexities of sidereal time and I think I got it. "Now," he said, "let's see if Junior HAL knows what he's doing." Blue text scrolled across the computer screen, giving us the exact position of Venus at that very moment. Arthur wrote the coordinates on a piece of paper and then stepped outside to a second-story terrace inlaid with terracotta tiles. A pageantry of aromas wafted in on the warm, humid air: sandalwood incense, coconut oil, and orchids. Blaring from a nearby radio was the high-pitched wail of a Hindi woman singing songs from the hit parade. The sensory overload was all so new to me—I had only been in Asia for two days.

Arthur's tropical garden was superabundant and lush and fragrant and crowded with an array of satellite dishes. In 1979 he probably had the most advanced privately owned comms system in the world. He was, after all, a far-seeing space race utopian who in 1945 dreamed up the idea of the communications satellite. He picked up his Celestron C8 telescope from the corner of the terrace and moved it to the center, away from anything that might have shaded us from the midday equatorial sun.

"These tiles were laid out in line with the celestial equator," he said. "Makes it easier to position the telescope." He punched in the coordinates for Venus. The telescope's built-in motor drive whirred, and the instrument swiveled into a new position. "Here, see for yourself." I peered into the eyepiece. Venus was dead center, quarter phase.

"The motor drive will stay locked on the planet's position for days," he said. "Now let's see if we can find it with the naked eye."

I looked at him with surprise, but he just smiled. He got me to stand in the shadow of a wall, making sure the sun was blocked out. "Now scan the sky behind the sun," he said. "You're looking for a tiny white crescent." It was like trying to find a fingernail clipping at the bottom of a swimming pool, but I succeeded in the end. I found Venus with my naked eye.

Meeting Arthur was a high point of my youth. He inspired me to embrace amateur astronomy, learn more about space travel, and become a writer.

———————

I called international directory enquiries, obtained his home number, and dialed it. "Hello," said a voice.

"Arthur C. Clarke?" I asked.

"Yes," he said. I hesitated. I couldn't believe the great man would answer his own phone. "Who's this?" he asked.

"Greg Cummings," I said, "You may not remember me, Mr. Clarke, but fifteen years ago at your house in Colombo, you showed me how to find Venus with the naked eye."

He hesitated for a moment then said, "Yes, of course I remember you."

I suspected he was merely being polite. I told him I was now working with mountain gorillas and then explained our dilemma.

"Gorillas from space?" he roared. "How perfect. I'd be happy to help. Wildlife conservation is a cause close to my heart." He then sent a fax to Dr. William McLaughlin, his most senior contact at JPL, saying, "Gorillas in the Mist—Help! Please contact Ellen O'Leary of SIR-C Mission Planning/Radar Data Center re correspondence with Scott Madry of Rutgers concerning planned survey of Rwanda. It's vital to the Dian Fossey Gorilla Fund but now looks like being cancelled. I hope it can be re-instated, it would be wonderful publicity for JPL/NASA!"

The strategy paid off. The gorillas were reinstated. I wrote an impassioned letter to Arthur thanking him for his prescience and described how I imagined the silverback Ziz had seen out his final day on Earth, as the sun set against Mount Mikeno casting a triangular shadow through the mist. I said I imagined the king of the silverbacks had a few final thoughts about his own mortality before, "like Moonwatcher reaching up to the monolith," he reached up to the stars with hope and then died. Arthur sent back a handwritten card: "Dear Greg, Thanks for letter and enclosures of 7th February—am circulating! Very touched by your 2001 flashback!"

———————

In late March Jillian and I traveled to New Jersey. It was our first business trip together. In a leafy courtyard outside the student dorm at Princeton, we sat down with Dieter Steklis and his wife Netzin, a Princeton grad student, and went over the new environmental education project. Dieter was of two minds: grateful for a six-figure grant but unsure of our intentions. He was surprised to learn I was the sole signatory to the agreement with the EC. "Now, I'm not saying there's anything wrong with your project per se," he said. "But we're in the middle of applying for a grant from USAID to pay for *our* education project, and I don't want this getting in the way." He saw us taking territory away from him.

We then went for a drive in his sports car, which had a personalized license plate: SLVBCK, for silverback. "Not everyone gets it," said Dieter. "I once had to deal with an irate driver who thought I wanted to bring slavery back."

We toured the revolution battle sites near Princeton, saw where the Mercer Oak once stood, not far from the spot where General Hugh Mercer fell during the Battle of Princeton. "OK," said Dieter. "Let's move forward with the EC-funded education project."

The next day the four of us attended a meeting at Rutgers University's Remote Sensing Center, convened by Dr. Scott Madry, who was developing a GIS of the mountain gorilla habitat. Joining us was a gaggle of influencers: Dr. Robert Sullivan, assistant environmental scientist at the Argonne National Laboratory, John Rubin, a producer at National Geographic TV, and Mike Backes, associate producer of the movie *Congo*. The meeting only commenced after one of Dr. Madry's research assistants turned up in a pink gorilla costume.

John Rubin said he was keen on a live broadcast. Mike Backes wanted to know about using the radar image. He said they were still in the early stages of adapting Crichton's *Congo* and looking for authenticity to enhance the movie's production design. Mike had swooped into Hollywood from Silicon Valley on a wave of new technology to become an industry player. He had a gaming company called Rocket Science, cowrote the movie *Rising Sun* with Michael Crichton, and supervised display graphics on *Jurassic Park*. Capturing the zeitgeist of the age of new media, he wore chic rimless eyeglasses and a black silk shirt, and sported an ultrahip chrome dome that glowed with unusual brain power (he won three times on *Jeopardy*). And he was funny. After meeting Dieter, he said, "He looks like the kind of guy who could pull an arrow out of his thigh with his bare teeth." Before flying back to L.A., he said he'd tap his friend and collaborator, Michael Crichton, for a gift, and would put in a good word for us with the *Congo* team. Mike seemed to like us. The feeling was mutual.

On Sunday, Jillian and I took a train into Manhattan. She had never visited New York City before. As we pulled into Penn Station, I panicked. I had visions of us getting mugged the moment we surfaced on the street. Needless to say, that didn't happen. But when I asked a police officer to direct us to our hotel, he said, "Do I look like a travel agent to you?"

Skulking across Midtown without further incident, we began to feel safer and relaxed our strides. My wife and I were both townies at heart, the product of a few short years we each spent among the tall buildings of Manchester and Montreal. We were turned on by Midtown's lavish storefronts, the bustle on the sidewalks, and the skyscrapers. I had visited Manhattan a couple of times as a kid, connecting to Pan Am's West Africa flight. My uncle Bob had a corner office on the forty-fifth floor of the Chase Manhattan Bank downtown. From there we watched the tall ships sail into New York Harbor to mark America's Bicentennial in 1976. On my last trip, after some college buddies and I had driven down late at night from Toronto on a drunken whim, we arrived on the morning after the great blizzard of February 1982. We got stuck in a snowdrift in Spanish Harlem and had to be helped out by some surly locals.

This time Midtown manifested the way I felt: tough, dynamic, and lucky. At 350 Fifth Avenue stood a famous gorilla landmark: the Empire State Building. "That's where King Kong fell to his death," I said.

"It was beauty killed the beast," added Jillian, quoting the final line of the movie.

In the East Village, in a bijou garden lighted with fairy lights at the back of an elegant restaurant, we ate a steak dinner. It was a warm evening for March. Excited about the prospect of the space shuttle launching in a fortnight, we couldn't stop talking about its PR potential. "I see a connection between *2001* and the shuttle mission—the apes reaching up to the unknown, the Space Age . . . Arthur suggested I get in touch with Roger Caras, president of the ASPCA, who was vice president of Kubrick's company, Hawk Films, when they made *2001*. He's also keen to collaborate with Sigourney. He said he met her when she was a little girl."

"Really?" asked Jillian. "Small world!"

"Yeah, Pat Weaver, Sigourney's father, was president of NBC, and Arthur used to visit their home when he was in New York in the fifties."

"We've got a lot of interest from the broadcasters," said Jillian. "As well as John Rubin, I spoke to Keenan Smart at Nat Geo. And Michael Bright at BBC Natural History said he's interested in doing something around it. But what?"

"How about a live feed during the shuttle mission, with Arthur C. Clarke in Sri Lanka, Sigourney Weaver in New York, astronauts on *Endeavour*, and gorillas in the Virungas?"

"Sounds too complicated," said Jillian. "We haven't got time to set all that up."

"Sigourney's company, Goat Cay, said it would be fine to use her name in conjunction with the NASA flyby of the Virunga Mountains, but impossible for her to commit to any kind of interview or satellite hookup because she didn't know where she would be."

"Exactly," sighed Jillian. "So we cannot rely on her. But Arthur's willing."

"I can't believe all the amazing people we're working with right now, Jillie," I said as I reached across the table to touch her hand. "The fund's growing so damn fast. Seems the sky's the limit with this cause. We are really starting to go places."

"It certainly has been a busy two years. And we're moving office again next week."

"That's the second time we've upgraded our workplace in the business center."

"I know, and finally, I'll have a bloody desk to work from."

Back in London a week later, on a Wednesday night, at around 10:30 PM, we received a call at our flat from Dieter. He was not in the habit of calling us at home. "What's up?" I asked.

"It's not good news, I'm afraid," he said solemnly. "This afternoon a surface-to-air missile shot down a plane outside Kigali with the Burundian and Rwandan presidents on board. There are no survivors."

"Oh God, that's terrible news," I gasped. It was grave and had the potential to restart the war. "What now?" We discussed the effect this could have on our work, whether to evacuate staff, and what to say publicly about the incident.

"It could soon blow over," said Dieter. "So far, there have been no aftereffects per se. And as you know, Habyarimana was blocking the peace process. Now that he's gone, maybe we'll see some movement toward peace in Rwanda. Still, the RPF might get blamed for downing the aircraft, which could lead to new reprisals from those loyal to the president."

The assassinations dominated the BBC World Service news at 11:00 PM: "A plane carrying the presidents of Rwanda and Burundi has crashed. All on board have been killed. . . . They were in Dar es Salaam attending a summit of regional leaders, chaired by President Museveni of Uganda. . . . RPF say they were not involved. . . . Sporadic gunfire was heard in Kigali. . . ."

My heart began to beat like a drum circle of djembes. I was not ready for this. *Endeavour* was scheduled to launch the next morning. Would NASA even radar-scan the gorillas' habitat now? It wasn't the first time fighting had skewed our plans, but it was all happening too fast.

Bad weather forced *Endeavour* to delay its launch by two days. By then, all interest from the broadcasters in Gorillas from Space had melted away. At 7:05 AM on April 9, the space shuttle blasted off from Kennedy Space Center. Once it was in orbit, we were able to follow the spacecraft's progress via hourly reports sent by the shuttle crew to a newsgroup on the Internet. And then, as planned, on its fifty-eighth orbit of Earth, the shuttle aimed its radar-imaging equipment at the Virunga volcanoes and acquired the first "data set" of the gorilla habitat. Astronaut Rich Clifford, who was on board at the time, recalls how the imaging radar could "see" through the obscuration, the gorillas in the mist.

But there was little to celebrate. While *Endeavour* orbited above the country, our expatriate staff were being airlifted from Rwanda to Nairobi. Led by Dr. Pascale Sicotte, the new Canadian director of the Karisoke Research Center, the evacuated conservationists then held an emergency meeting to decide on a plan of action. Jillian sent a Channel 4 crew in with Dieter Steklis to film the meeting in Nairobi. Pascale said she had left money and supplies for the thirty antipoaching rangers who, against the worst odds, chose to remain at Karisoke and continue tracking gorillas and cutting poachers' snares in the forest. The fund would maintain a supply line to the rangers through Zaire. Setting up an interim base in Zaire would allow some scientists to return to the Virungas to continue monitoring the gorillas from the other side of the volcanoes. Meanwhile, education officer Dr. Louis Nzeyimana and his wife and baby were trapped in Kigali, amid all the killing. No one had heard from them in days.

7

GORILLAS FROM SPACE

"Dian Fossey Gorilla Fund," said Rosemary. "How can I help you?"

"Hello, yes. May I please speak to Greg Cummings?"

"Who's calling?" she asked.

"It's Louis Nzeyimana in Kigali."

"Oh my God, you're alive," she cried. "Hang on, Louis, let me go get him."

Miraculously, the Nzeyimanas were alive and well. Now we had to find a way to get them out. Three days later, Louis, his wife, and his baby managed to drive out of Kigali in a donated Suzuki jeep plastered with gorilla logos.

I called the British consul in Nairobi. Given that it was a Saturday, he was loath to accept my urgent phone call, but he listened to what I had to say. "My Rwandese colleague, his wife, and their eight-month-old baby are on their way by car to the Zaire border as we speak," I said. "If he manages to cross into Goma, there's a plane waiting to take them to Nairobi. It's imperative that they then continue on to London. British Airways has donated their flights. Will you please issue him and his family visas to the United Kingdom?"

"I'm terribly sorry but I hardly think—"

"Look," I said, more forcefully than a young upstart working for a wildlife NGO in London should probably have addressed a man

92

of his distinction. "I'm not asking for refugee status for them. Louis is enrolled in a course at the International Centre for Conservation Education in the Cotswolds, one of the best facilities of its kind in the world. The training is essential if he is to fulfill his role as our education officer in Rwanda after the fighting ends."

"I see. So, you're saying it's simply fortuitous that this conservation education course in the Cotswolds happens to coincide with his country's collapse into anarchy?"

"I know it sounds dodgy, but you can check on it, sir. Please ask someone to call Brussels. Last month they approved a quarter of a million–pound project that Louis and I designed with the ICCE. You have my word, he's coming to England for professional reasons, and he will return to Rwanda when he's completed the course. And it's imperative for the safety of his family that they do not get left behind. They've been through seven kinds of hell, sir."

"I can only imagine," said the consul. "Right, then. Best we act accordingly. I'll personally make sure that they're issued visas when they arrive at Jomo Kenyatta."

"Thank you so much, sir. The gorillas are grateful."

The following Monday, Jillian and I stood outside Heathrow Terminal 4, anxiously awaiting the arrival of the Nzeyimana family. "What's the baby's name again?" I asked.

"Francesca," replied Jillian (Francesca is not her real name). She smiled calmly, though I knew she was just as worried as I was. What was taking them so long? Every other passenger on their flight had already come through. It seemed Immigration was not convinced about Louis's reason for visiting the United Kingdom, and we had no way of communicating with them. It was two hours before they stepped through the terminal door. Agatha was holding Francesca in her arms. Louis towered above them. After an outpouring of tearful relief, we piled into our compact and drove to our home in Child's Hill.

"If it hadn't been for the mountain gorillas," said Louis, as he drank a beer on our balcony overlooking West London, "I don't think we would have made it out alive. The drive to the Zaire border normally takes three hours, but after three hours on the road we were still not very far from Kigali. Every few kilometers there was a roadblock manned by Interahamwe. Rifles and machetes were thrust in our faces. The militants demanded to see a governor's writ of safe passage. They refused to believe I was a Hutu until they saw my identity card. But when I told them my job, showed them the gorilla stickers on the side of the jeep, and told them we were on our way to Karisoke to protect the gorillas, their mood suddenly changed. The militants knew Karisoke, knew the importance of the gorillas to Rwanda, and were genuinely pleased to hear I was going back to the Virungas. My only regret was that I was *not*, but escaping my country."

"Well, we're very relieved that you made it, my friend," I said. I then told him that the EC had shelved our education grant and USAID had done the same. Louis was not surprised.

"I guess that means I won't be going back anytime soon," he sighed.

Before Louis began his course in the Cotswolds, the Nzeyimana family lived with us in our two-bedroom council flat for three weeks. During that time, I never saw Agatha once put her baby down. The child was forever in her arms. NBC interviewed Louis at our London office for *Now* magazine but did not use the interview in the end. The international press was generally reluctant to cover the plight of gorillas in the context of the horrific human tragedy in Rwanda. Louis never returned to Rwanda. He and his family moved to Vienna, where they've lived ever since.

Endeavour was still in orbit. But we got only silence from NASA/ JPL on the Virunga image. Rumor had it that they were worried about being accused of spying on Rwanda.

Arthur again contacted Bill McLaughlin to ask for his help. On April 19 Ellen Stofan faxed Arthur, "We are happy to report that data were successfully acquired on two passes over the site, on Orbit 58 and Orbit 171. Images have been processed at JPL for the first data take and will be transmitted to the research team at Rutgers for analysis. . . . We look forward to attempting to image the Karisoke site on our second flight in August. . . . Thank you for your interest in our mission—we are very excited about our successful flight." At least we would soon have something to show for all our efforts and overinflated hopes. It was the least we deserved.

Over the course of a hundred days, nearly a million people were killed in Rwanda. The scale of the human tragedy that unfolded overwhelmed us. We could not unsee or unhear what occurred during that time. People we knew lost so much, loved ones by the score. Things would never be the same again for the country. At such a time, who could champion wildlife? But we had no other remit. Detractors challenged us for caring about gorillas, but what else was a gorilla charity meant to do? The Rwandese people were desperate just to survive, and certainly had little reason to care about their wildlife in these times. Still, we firmly believed that in the future, Rwanda's rare apes could be an important source of revenue that could help rebuild the country.

In May I sent out an emergency appeal letter, launching a campaign to raise £100,000: "Amidst the terrible human tragedy in Rwanda, the survival of the last 650 mountain gorillas in the world once again hangs in the balance. . . . DFGF and other gorilla conservation groups are now taking emergency steps to return to the Virungas and gain access to the mountains from Zaire. A joint conservation task force will take essential supplies and equipment for the antipoaching rangers and trackers, set up an interim base, and continue to protect the endangered mountain gorillas." My letter did not immediately raise the target we were aiming for, but by galvanizing a fresh wave of supporters, it opened up a new chapter in the mountain gorilla conservation story.

Mercifully, the movie *Congo* was still in the cards. Five days after *Endeavour* landed at Edwards Air Force Base in California, completing a successful eleven-day mission (NASA added two more days), Jillian and I sat down to dinner at Primates restaurant in Camden Town with Hollywood producer Sam Mercer and his location manager Paul Pav. It was our first official meeting with the Kennedy/Marshall Company, producers of *Congo*.

"Mike Backes had nothing but good things to say about you two," said Sam as we pulled up our chairs.

"He's a cool dude," I said. "Sounds like he's involved in some cool projects."

"Yeah, we like Mike." We then ordered our meals. There was no question who would pay the bill. Sam was on an expense account.

He asked how things had been affected by the massacres in Rwanda. I told him we had evacuated all our staff, including Dr. Nzeyimana and his family. "The bottom's dropped out of our world," I sighed. "We're still processing what happened and trying to figure out what's going on. We've never had to deal with anything like this before. I mean, last year we had to evacuate because of the war, but it was a battle with armies and big guns, nothing like the bloodthirsty machete massacre we're now witnessing on the nightly news."

"Paul here barely escaped with his life," said Sam.

"Well, that's an exaggeration," said Paul. "I never got closer to the trouble than Nairobi. But, until the shit hit the fan, we had been considering filming *Congo* on location in Virunga."

"Instead, we've decided to shoot in Costa Rica," said Sam. "They've got volcanoes and jungles and nothing more threatening to contend with than vipers and monkeys."

"Do the volcanoes look anything like what NASA radar-imaged for us?" asked Jillian.

"Mike said the GIS he saw at Rutgers looked great. Now, is the space shuttle image still on?" asked Sam. "I heard NASA was stalling."

"Oh, they were." I said. "But Arthur Clarke changed their minds, again."

"Good to hear," smiled Sam. The waiter then brought us our meals. My lamb shank with garlic and creamed potatoes was mouthwatering.

"Well," said Sam, "depending on the quality and duration of use, Paramount is prepared to make a donation to your organization of between $25,000 and $50,000 for your image." Sam and Paul watched us as they let the news sink in.

"That's bloody generous," said Jillian. She looked at me and grinned. We were thinking the same thing: there was no reason for them to pay us a dime for it, as all of NASA's images were public domain.

"Mmm, this lamb is delicious," I said. We were cool.

Congo was a big-budget action-adventure movie featuring mutant, ravenous gorillas. Lucky for us, the lead role was a normal gorilla called Amy, who spoke sign language. Jillian had already sent the studio a stack of promotional material to hang in Amy's playhouse. And there was more to be had: a plush toy, the premiere, an on-pack video promotion for the fund. *Congo* gave us hope during that dark time.

In June we met Gerry Lewis, a hard-nosed cockney with decades in the movie business. He was Steven Spielberg's salesman in Europe, and *Congo*'s UK distributor. We discussed the possibility of a UK premiere and a licensing deal to benefit the gorillas.

"I don't give a fuck about your cause," said Gerry. "Get me celebrities on the front pages of the tabloids and I'll be 'appy."

Mike Backes called the next day to say he was concerned that the Rutgers GIS, which was still lacking the April shuttle image, was too low in resolution. The heat was on to get Kennedy/Marshall the Virunga image before its mid-June deadline. JPL was having difficulty translating the space shuttle tapes.

I contacted Ellen Stofan directly and tried to speed up the process. She was keen on the Hollywood connection, so I connected her with Mike. Kennedy/Marshall then extended its deadline to mid-September. In the meantime, Karisoke researcher Alastair McNeilage visited the Remote Sensing Center in New Jersey to help fine-tune the details of the Virunga GIS.

At Le Caprice in Piccadilly, Jillian and I dined with Sam Mercer, Gerry Lewis, and Jill Fullerton-Smith, who was making a doc to go with *Congo*'s release. Gerry apologized for his abruptness a few days before. Sam told us we shouldn't worry about the fund's involvement with *Congo*. "All will be fine," he said.

Upon returning to L.A., he then confirmed that Mike was now working directly with JPL, which was "regenerating a higher definition/clearer image for Mike and Silicon Graphics to review. Perhaps this will help to settle/resolve Mike's concerns."

———————

In July Dr. Pascale Sicotte flew to Zaire. She had only just begun setting up temporary operations in Goma when fighting in the northwest of Rwanda forced a mass of people to flee to Zaire. The RPF was trying to put a stop to the genocide.

Fearing the worst, Karisoke rangers joined the exodus of millions who crossed the border into Goma. With supplies from Oxfam and the help of local businessmen, Pascale was able to set up a separate camp for the men at Bukima on the edge of the park, and she got assurances from the Zairean authorities that the men would be given preferential treatment. "The situation we now face is different," she said. "The Rwandan gorilla workforce is in Zaire simply struggling to survive. Helping them survive means that we protect the knowledge they have accumulated on the forest and on the gorillas."

The men brought with them the sad news that Effie, the oldest female gorilla, had been found dead. For twenty-five years Effie had presided over a secure family of gorillas that, by the time of Ziz's death, numbered thirty-seven individuals. She was the fourth gorilla to die since war began in 1991. Incredibly, she died of natural causes. "Effie's death marks the end of an era," said Ian Redmond, "because she was such an important character in the group, she was the Queen Mother of the Virungas."

In mid-August, as the situation in Rwanda began to improve, Dieter Steklis traveled to Rwanda with Ian Redmond and a BBC Natural History Unit crew (at the expense of the BBC) to meet officials in the new caretaker government, assess the condition of the gorillas, and negotiate the safe return of our men from Zaire. Dieter also met the new Rwandan prime minister, Jean Kambanda, who assured him we could quickly return our rangers to Karisoke and resume work.

On August 18, Dieter and Ian arrived at the research center accompanied by twelve rangers. The rest of the men, who were given fresh supplies and medicine (courtesy of Bayer Pharmaceuticals) would travel from Zaire in a UN convoy a few days later. Karisoke had been badly damaged by looters, again. Furniture and roofing had been removed or broken, and research data was scattered everywhere. They also found cow dung in the middle of camp—the first time in more than twenty years that cattle had been herded so far into the Virungas. Meanwhile, the BBC got the entire scene on film.

A week later the UN convoy taking the remaining rangers back to Rwanda from Bukima was ambushed in Zaire by extremists, and one of the Karisoke rangers was severely injured. We heard he was recovering and that the fund would soon make another attempt to return the men from Zaire to Karisoke.

It was a testament to their bravery and dedication that the men still wished to return and resume their work at Karisoke. And it was clear to us then that without the commitment of those antipoaching rangers who kept vigil for three months during the conflict, we may have lost our closest relatives in the natural world.

Everyone involved in the fund was on tenterhooks as peace slowly crept back to Rwanda. But there would be many more setbacks before things returned to normal in the field. It would never be the same again.

———————

August 18 was also the day the space shuttle *Endeavour* was due to launch again from Kennedy Space Center in Florida on its second Mission to Planet Earth. With just weeks to go before launch day, three sealed envelopes arrived at the London office, addressed to Arthur C. Clarke, Sigourney Weaver, and me. Inside was an invitation card embossed with the space shuttle on a launchpad that read, The National Aeronautics and Space Administration Cordially Invites You to Attend a Launch and Landing of the Space Shuttle at the John F. Kennedy Space Center, Florida.

I faxed Sigourney Weaver with news of her invitation and asked her to consider coming to Florida to help us promote the event. I told her how difficult it had been these past few months, in light of the terrible human tragedy in Rwanda, for us to secure any media coverage of the plight of the mountain gorillas. "The situation now, however, is changing," I said. "The space shuttle story is an extremely positive angle, and we've been generating increasing interest in the media around the project. While your attendance at Cape Canaveral would largely involve watching the shuttle take off from a VIP box, if you were willing to give a couple of brief comments to the press we would be sure to get the coverage the gorillas so urgently need. Please let me know by phone, if you have time before you leave for Paris this morning, whether or not you think this is something you would like to do."

Goat Cay faxed back with Sigourney's regrets.

Yet by a stroke of luck, Arthur, who was seventy-seven, confined to a wheelchair, and hadn't left Sri Lanka in years, had already planned to be in Florida on that day. "I'm trying to keep my visit secret from the media as this is a holiday with my family, and I'm also saying goodbye to dozens of old friends I won't see again. However, I have alerted JPL, and the astronauts know I'll be there. If all goes well, I'll certainly be at the launch, so we'll play it by ear."

Twenty-five years earlier, Arthur had coanchored CBS's televised coverage of the historic Apollo 11 moon mission at Cape Canaveral with Walter Cronkite and Orson Welles. But he had never seen a shuttle launch.

NASA was glad to have a Space Age legend attend the liftoff and asked if he would take part in a postlaunch press conference. They invited me to participate as well. Jillian took exception to this. She and I quarreled on our Virgin Atlantic flight to Orlando. She insisted, given her role as the fund's PR spokesperson, that I give up my place at the conference panel for her.

Netzin Steklis flew in from Princeton and met us at the Orlando airport, where Jillian and I had rented a car. Driving the Bee Line to Merritt Island, we continued to argue until Netzin settled it. "Neither of you are going to be on the panel," she said. "It'll just be me and Arthur."

On the day of the launch, Jillian and I awoke at 2:00 AM. You could cut through the humidity with a knife. I found a palmetto bug the size of a toad in the shower. We drove to a breakfast reception hosted by the JPL: sweet muffins and juice. At 3:30 AM, we transferred to Cape Canaveral. The traffic on Highway 1 was bumper-to-bumper, as locals headed to the beach in time to see another rocket blast off. In the distance, powerful searchlights were trained on *Endeavour*. Up-lighted in that way, its imminent departure looked ominous. At Spaceport

USA, our bus pulled up next to the Rocket Garden: a display of Mercury, Gemini, and Apollo rockets.

It was 4:00 AM when I walked into the guest center, Room 2001. Apropos of its name, there was Arthur C. Clarke, seated in his wheel-chair, a pair of large spectacles on his smiling face and a navy blue space shuttle baseball cap on his bald head. His T-shirt sported an image of the Milky Way galaxy with an arrow pointing to an outer spiral arm, with YOU ARE HERE written next to it. The Space Age legend was surrounded by NASA officials. He had a boyish, pinch-me-I'm-famous regard for his greatness, as though he couldn't quite believe it.

"Great to see you again, Arthur," I said, shaking his hand. I wanted to hug him. "After all the faxes and phone calls, it's so good to meet you in person again."

He looked at me with magnified eyes. An element of doubt lingered in his mind. Still, lights on and everyone at home. Valerie and Hector Ekanayake remembered me. They managed Arthur's diving company, Underwater Safaris, and had taught me how to scuba dive when I was eighteen. Hector put his hand on Arthur's shoulder and said, "Remember when you got so mad at Barracuda for taking Greg down to 120 feet on his first ocean dive in the Maldives?"

Arthur's face lit up. "Oh yes," he cried, "I *do* remember you now."

Security officers checked our passes and tickets before we boarded the bus to the viewing site, which was a few kilometers away from Spaceport USA. To get anywhere near the launch complex at Cape Canaveral, we had each been subjected to thorough background checks. Our predawn journey across the space center took us past disused gantries lined up alongside a runway so wide you could land a small plane sideways on it. The horizon was beginning to glow as we arrived at the viewing site, a grass clearing on the banks of a wide lagoon that separated viewers seated in rows of bleachers from the launchpad. Arthur sat in a section reserved for VIPs. Jillian and I found our place among the mere mortals.

First light revealed a lagoon teeming with waterfowl. Seeing the space shuttle—a vehicle built for titans—lit up against the horizon made my heart race. The morning was warm and humid and suffused with salty air from the Atlantic. A large digital clock on the grass kept track of the countdown. Occasionally it would stop as technicians went through a series of checks, and then resume. We could hear their chatter over the PA system. So far, August 18 was shaping up to be the most exciting day of my life.

When the countdown reached twenty seconds, the chatter escalated as the shuttle prepared to blast off. Jillian and I squeezed each other's hands. Astronaut Tom Jones, who was in the spaceship at the time, recalled the seconds before launch in his 2006 memoir, *Sky Walking*: "At T-6 seconds, *Endeavour*'s three main engines rumbled into life. I was strapped into my center seat on the middeck, just to the right of classmate Jeff Wisoff, as we felt the orbiter rumble and shake under the thrust of a million pounds of liquid-fueled thrust. Out the hatch window I could see the gantry apparently sway—it was actually *Endeavour* 'twanging' under the thrust. I mentally counted: 5 . . . 4 . . . 3 . . . 2 . . . 1 . . . waiting for the giant kick from the boosters' ignition. Instead, the Master Alarm blared in our headsets as the three main engines fell silent. Instead of liftoff, we were left swaying atop the orbiter as the launch team announced an abort—an automatic shutdown due to some as-yet unknown problem."

All we heard over the PA was, "We have main engine cutoff!" Then a gasp from the crowd. Launch control soon verified that the engines had automatically shut down at T-1 second, due to an overheating turbopump. "Its discharge temperature had violated redline limits," recalled Jones. "Had we launched with that violation, we might have lost an engine right after liftoff, sending us into a very hairy Return to Launch Site abort."

"Well go on, then," said Jillian. "Fix it."

A Texan in the row behind us said, "That dog ain't gonna hunt."

People began to climb down from the bleachers and head back to the bus. A puff of white smoke—solid rocket fuel exhaust that was momentarily emitted by the boosters—drifted across the lagoon on an offshore breeze. We watched it drift slowly by. All our aspirations were hitched to that tiny white cloud. We just couldn't catch a break.

After the aborted launch, Jillian rallied the media, told them the granddaddy of the Space Age was at the center. We both agreed that Netzin, a scientist and Princeton grad student, was a better gorilla spokesperson than either of us. Unfazed by the launch abort, Arthur gave a masterful presentation to the gathered press, championing the fusion of his two great passions: space and wildlife. And as the superb radar coverage of the Virunga habitat captured on *Endeavour*'s April flight was shown on a big screen, the audience let out an audible sigh.

Jillian and I then flew to Naples to spend a couple of days with Tom and Ruth Keesling. The climate was far less humid on the west coast of Florida. The Keeslings lived in the affluent neighborhood of Port Royal, named after the infamous seventeenth-century Jamaican city where privateers and smugglers spent their spoils from the looting of ships at sea. Port Royal's street names exemplified the pirate theme: Rum Row, Spyglass Lane, and Buccaneers Roost. Tom and Ruth lived on Cutlass Lane in a luxurious waterfront house. They took us to the Port Royal Club for dinner. To be a member, you had to have letters of advocacy from five people who lived in Port Royal. People bought the nonwaterfront lots just so they could have a membership at the club. They used to call them dinner lots.

As the sun dropped into the Gulf of Mexico with a rush of beautiful light, our hosts treated us to an exquisite seafood dinner. Tom and Ruth had an unshakable bond that I greatly admired. No matter the gaffes that tumbled from his wife's lips, Tom never offered anything less than total support for Ruth. They could see Jillian and I were becoming a power couple in gorilla conservation, like them, and had invited us to Naples so they could schmooze us. If we had to make a choice between the Keeslings and the radical, Birkenstock-and-Afro-print-skirt-wearing naysayers who wanted them out, Jillian and I were in no doubt about where our allegiance lay. Ruth and Tom had devoted more resources to gorilla conservation than anybody else we knew. It would have been irresponsible of us as fundraisers to alienate such important donors in any way. Besides, we could always play both sides against the middle, as was our wont. "I'll have another margarita, please, Tom."

8

VIRTUAL AFRICA OFFICE

HAVING SUCCESSFULLY BLASTED off five weeks after its aborted launch, the space shuttle was again in orbit and nine days into its mission. "Delighted *Endeavour* is doing its thing!" wrote Arthur.

That Sunday, Jillian and I were at home watching *Equinox*, a science documentary series on Channel 4. The week's episode, "The Rubber Universe," was about the Hubble constant, which determines the rate at which the universe is expanding. Visually intriguing and narratively far out, the doc captured our imaginations, especially the final scenes where an astronomer explains that when the universe finally contracts it will be no bigger than an orange. And as the credits rolled, I saw that it had been written and directed by Storm Thorgerson.

"Hey, I know that name," I said. The next morning, Jillian called the production company and told them we wished to contact Mr. Thorgerson to discuss making a film about gorillas from space. He called back the following day. We arranged to meet.

In the late 1960s, Storm Thorgerson cofounded Hipgnosis, an art design company that had produced the covers of some of the greatest rock albums of my generation. His work with Pink Floyd, for which he'll likely be best remembered, involved conceiving and photographing elaborate "events" that were often extrapolated from a single lyric on the record. His most iconic design, *The Dark Side of the Moon*, is a beam of light through a prism on a black background.

"I've been a huge fan of your work since I was a teenager," I gushed when I met him. "You opened the door to great music for me. When I first started collecting LPs, browsing the secondhand record store bins in Toronto, you were my guide. I soon learned that 'Designed by Hipgnosis' was a hallmark for quality rock albums, man. And you never let me down."

"Thank you for your flattering remarks," smiled Storm, raising his wineglass. "We don't get many groupies in graphic design." Storm, Jillian, and I were having lunch at Primates. It was a sunny autumn day. Diagonal shafts of sunlight tumbled through the restaurant. "So, tell me about this film you want me to make," he said.

We briefed him on the details and told him we had plenty of material for a documentary. He was perplexed to learn that the second of two space shuttle missions had just landed in California. "Wouldn't it have made more sense to come to me before your rockets had launched?" asked Storm sardonically. A middle-class Cantabrigian, he spoke with the air of a thespian, scoffing and sneering at every folly. He was fifty and graying, and looked like he was about to sneeze. At first, I thought he was being contemptuous, but as I got to know him better, I realized this was just his resting bitch face. "Seems pointless to make a film about gorillas from space after the radar shuttle has gone and come back—twice. *Doesn't it?*"

"But there's more to this story," said Jillian. "Space technology is beginning to play a more substantial role in gorilla conservation. Greg and I were just in Guildford, meeting with Professor Martin Sweeting at Surrey Satellite Technology. An article in the *Sunday Times* alerted us to his work making low-orbit satellites at a fraction of the cost of most space-bound craft."

"We plan to use this technology for our own fieldwork," I said. "Equipment, training, and setup of a satellite base station cost no more

£10,000, which the David Shepherd Wildlife Foundation has agreed to fund. Soon we'll be able to communicate with our Karisoke staff on a daily basis. And the best thing of all is there's no operating cost."

"Following the massacres in Rwanda, unrest is likely to simmer in region for some time, so we need new strategies," said Jillian. "We need to find ways to protect the gorillas remotely."

"Don't you think this would make a compelling documentary?" I asked Storm.

"Who'll pay for it?" he replied. "Where's the money going to come from?"

"Um . . . we hadn't really got round to thinking about that part yet," I said sheepishly. "But you must know a few wealthy individuals in the music business we could ask."

"Don't expect me to ask Pink Floyd for money," sniffed Storm. He was ambivalent about our cause, one of the few people we'd met who knew virtually nothing of the plight of the mountain gorillas, nor of Dian Fossey, and had no interest in knowing more. "If gorillas need saving, then it's up to governments to do something," he said. "That's why I pay taxes." Nevertheless, he was plainly intrigued by our Gorillas from Space pitch.

"What about getting *Equinox* to produce?" asked Jillian.

"It's a possibility," said Storm. "Have you got something I could show them?"

"I'll send you a proposal this afternoon," she said.

———————————

The following Saturday, I was alone at home in Child's Hill. Jillian had gone to visit her mother in Salford. Outside it was cold and gray and I was preparing to settle in for the evening of television viewing and navel viewing with a couple of beers when the phone rang. It was Storm.

"Is it true you've never seen the Floyd in concert?" he asked.

"Nope," I said. "Never seen them live."

"Well, tonight they're playing their final performance at Earl's Court—their last performance of the tour, in fact—so I've arranged for a backstage pass for you. Who knows if they'll tour again. The pass will be waiting for you at the stage door on Old Brompton Road."

"No way!" I cried. "For real? Thank you so much, Storm."

"Yes, well, you better hurry up, because the concert begins in forty minutes."

I hung up and punched the air. Had I really just been invited into the inner circle of one rock's most successful bands, one that famously walled itself off from its fans? My elation increased as I rode the tube down to Earl's Court. Images from the band's discography came to mind—every one a Storm creation. The rear end of a cow standing in the English countryside. A man diving into a lake without causing a ripple. Hundreds of beds lined up in rows on a wide-open beach. Two men shaking hands and one is on fire.

When I emerged from the Underground station, I expected to see a giant inflatable pig floating above the venue. Masses of people were queuing outside. After Pink Floyd's record-breaking thirteen nights at Earl's Court, tickets for the band's final performance were hard to come by. I located the stage door where Storm told me to pick up my pass and stood in line with Mike Rutherford, the bassist from Genesis, and his wife.

"Loved your album, *Smallcreep's Day*," I told him, smiling. "But then I'm a huge prog rock fan."

An official asked me for my name, checked me off a list, and then slapped a sticker on the lapel of my blazer. Uncertain at first what AAA signified, I quickly discovered that it meant I could go any-where I damn well pleased. Steel barricades manned by surly bouncers were no match for my Access All Areas pass. They simply waved me through. I could have walked out on stage if I wanted. Instead, I was backstage watching a roadie hand-spool a seventy-millimeter film onto the projector so it could be back-projected on a circular screen onstage behind the band for their opening number, "Shine on You Crazy Diamond." I was on the inside looking out. I felt so fucking privileged. This was every Floyd fan's dream.

After a set of songs, mostly from their new album *The Division Bell*, which had been a balm in those dark days when the massacres in Rwanda had dumbfounded me, the band broke for an intermission. Utterly beside myself, I wandered around the vast arena holding a plastic pint glass full of beer in my hand. A fleet of gleaming 18-wheelers was parked inside behind the stage. I then heard a heartbeat followed by voices and machinery. I hurried back to an unexpected delight: *The Dark Side of the Moon* performed in its entirety. After that, I failed to make it to the sound console to meet Storm and his mates. I spent the rest of the concert standing in front of the stage, mouth agape, surrounded by some twenty thousand enthralled fans, every one of us transfixed by rock's supreme live act. And as the band performed each song, surreal films depicting the tune's theme were projected on the circular screen behind them—"Breath," "Time," "Money"—every film a Storm creation. I didn't take drugs. Didn't need them. I was high on serendipity. Until the cloudburst thundered in my ear and the band started playing different tunes, I was just fine.

Later at the backstage party, I chatted with Kate Bush and Nick Mason, Pink Floyd's drummer, about our NASA missions, Gorillas from Space, and Storm Thorgerson's plan to film the project for *Equinox*.

Having an AAA pass to the Floyd's final night was a tremendous boost to my morale after months of grief. "This is an experience I will pass on to my grandchildren," I wrote in my journal the next day. I never had children, therefore no grandchildren. I guess back then I thought there was still a chance. I wished Jillian had been there too, if only to be on the same page as me afterward.

When she returned home from Salford, she was livid. Notwithstanding that no one but me is allowed to write in my journal, she wrote a bitter addendum to my entry about the concert, underlining words for emphasis: "And *I'm* pushing my way into *your* space? *I'm not* letting *you* do *your* own thing? Whose hands have you taken *Equinox* out of? I'm really *glad* you enjoyed the gig. I hope all this gets you what you *really* want, and advances *your* career still further. Your loving wifey (remember me), Jillie B Bean."

Her tone and words were symptomatic of a battle we'd been engaged in from the start. Jillian was outraged that, despite being nine years my senior and more experienced than me, she struggled to equal my status at the fund. I took the brunt of her resentment for that, even though I had little control over it. She cast me as a coconspirator in the whole misogynistic mess.

After the concert I was supercharged. I became drunk with my own successes. It began to go to my head. I had to remind myself that however much my charm and grasp of the subject matter allowed me to make good use of the opportunities, it was gorillas, with their long arms and opposable thumbs, that opened those doors for me. When in doubt, think like a gorilla.

———————

The year began with an audible gorilla chest beat. On New Year's Day 1995, the BBC nature special *Gorilla* was broadcast on the BBC and narrated by Sir David Attenborough. It told the story of Dieter and Ian's return to Rwanda in August, a month after the genocide. Over three million people watched, and thirty-five hundred viewers wrote in. At the end of the broadcast, Sir David made a personal appeal to viewers to donate to our cause. We hired Personal Telephone Fundraising, a Brighton-based telemarketing company, to get on the phones and solicit donations during the broadcast. The fund raised £32,000 that night, as much as it raised in the first six months of operation. We were so impressed by the results that we would subsequently use PTF to back up future campaigns. While telemarketing costs are high, the return on investment makes it worthwhile.

In January, Sam Mercer confirmed that Kennedy/Marshall had the image and would send us $15,000 now and "an additional $15,000–$20,000 upon evidence of the image appearing in the final cut of the picture." The next day Sam sent another fax, backing out of this deal: "After speaking to Mike Backes, we felt that a total donation of $15,000 was appropriate for the image." (Thanks a lot, Mike.) Sigourney Weaver faxed Arthur C. Clarke, thanking him for his support for the fund: "You probably don't recall meeting me at my parents, Pat and Liz Weaver, when I was eleven. I took a *Playboy* magazine out of your briefcase and read it. I'd never seen a *Playboy* before so your visit is indelibly recorded in my memory!" Goat Cay said Arthur's reply was too personal to relay.

Celebrities were coming out of the woodwork, and Jillian and I were bouncing from one glamorous event to the next. Sigourney Weaver invited us to the London premiere of *Death and the Maiden*, where we also met Ben Kingsley. Mike Oldfield invited us to the launch of his new album, *The Songs of Distant Earth*, at the London Planetarium, where we met the artist and told him about Gorillas from Space. His album was beautiful and haunting. He later donated £25,000, "in recognition of the inspiration and contribution of Arthur C. Clarke to my last album." We met Lana Topham, producer of Pink Floyd's films, to discuss Storm's involvement. We decided the film would be called *650: A Gorilla Dilemma* and include Arthur C. Clarke, Douglas Adams, and the music of Pink Floyd, what Storm called our "dream team." Lana suggested advertising it in *WIRED* magazine and on the Internet, to help boost sales cheaply. We decided we needed an event at which to launch the film.

Ricci Rukavina, head of new media at Kennedy/Marshall, wrote asking us to submit a sponsorship proposal that he could pass on to Paramount Pictures. The studio wanted to know what we needed. Sigourney agreed to endorse our bid and said she would personally telephone Kathleen Kennedy, whom she held in very high regard. We asked for the moon. The pace was quickening.

In March Sigourney spoke to Kathleen on our behalf, making a strong case for the fund. She also offered to pitch the CEOs of *Congo*'s primary sponsors: Pepsi-Cola and Taco Bell. Somewhat ruffled at being "blindsided" by Sigourney, Sam Mercer called to tick me off and then ask what the fund's program priorities were. He said Kennedy/Marshall had decided to make mountain gorilla conservation "a headline in the promotion of *Congo*," and Sam was going into a meeting with Paramount executives to personally endorse this approach. Blindsiding worked.

In early April, my wife and I flew to Los Angeles for meetings with execs from the movie and space industries. Neither of us had ever been to California before. With so much business to conduct, we rented a car—a red Mustang convertible. As we drove along Melrose Avenue in a jet-lagged daze, soaking up movieland's silver-screen dream vibe, nothing seemed quite real. But the superficiality was countered by all the great art that had been created in Hollywood.

Our first appointment was at Kennedy/Marshall. A guard at the Paramount studios gates checked our names against his appointment log and then let us through. The production company was in a one-story, palm-shaded adobe building with terra-cotta roofing, in an area away from the soundstages. Its interior design was nostalgic: big windows with wooden blinds, a large fern in each corner, and oversized movie posters from the golden age of Hollywood on the walls. Producers Sam Mercer and Kathleen Kennedy and director Frank Marshall were all locked into postproduction duties and could not meet us. Instead, we met Ricci Rukavina. Ricci smiled, offered us drinks, clapped his hands, and confirmed everyone at the company was keen to support the gorillas and needed no convincing, but that it was Paramount that would approve any deals. Our meeting was short. He managed to stoke and douse our enthusiasm at the same time.

We then drove northeast to Pasadena at the foot of the Sierra Madre—still snowcapped in spring—and navigated our way through town through the campus of the California Institute of Technology to the Jet Propulsion Laboratory. JPL was a hive of brainy activity. Rocket scientists busied themselves in sophisticated research rooms of vastly different sizes. Warrens of blue corridors connected them, with exhibits of every unmanned interstellar spacecraft traveling through our solar system at that time. JPL was mission control for them all. "It's like the Apollo 11 exhibition I saw as a kid in Nigeria," I said to Jillian, "only on a much grander scale."

Dr. Ellen Stofan and Dr. Bill McLaughlin welcomed us to the facility. Dr. McLaughlin had an asteroid named after him—they don't come much geekier. They enjoyed being involved in the fund and vowed to continue promoting the gorillas. "The Virunga image is the science team's favorite," said Ellen. Bill read us an excerpt from a piece in *Spaceflight* magazine that he'd written, which included our address. Ellen told us she would be in London for a year from June and would like to work closely with the London office to continue promoting our Gorillas from Space project in her lectures. They both seemed to like Jillian and me. We had a knack for popularizing science, even with our lack of academic credentials. We got it and they valued that.

"How many cutting-edge space technology centers have we visited in the past year?" I asked my wife as we drove along Highway 110 on our way back to L.A.

"I count at least five," smiled Jillian.

"*Who does that*—even in our line of work?"

We were checked into the Radisson on Wilshire Boulevard. It had a rooftop pool. The view of the downtown skyline was spectacular. Blurring the lines between movies and reality, I played Vangelis's *Blade Runner* soundtrack on my portable CD player—one of the best soundtracks ever. Even as a standalone album it evokes distant future times and gives the listener an ethereal sonic bathing, washing away the here and now so as to become transcendent with tomorrow's world. It's also wicked to listen to at night while watching helicopters land on skyscrapers in downtown L.A., one after the other, like a plague of replicants importuning the Tyrell Corporation. "I could get used to this town," I said. "I should have been an actor."

Driving through Beverly Hills the next day, sunlight strobing through the tops of lanky palm trees lining the shiny streets, we were on our way to Guttman Associates, a publicist. Mike Backes persuaded us to consider them. He joined the meeting and introduced us to Dick Guttman and Beverly Magid. Beverly had visited gorillas in the wild and was already a supporter of the cause as well as an avid Afrophile. Dick had represented everyone from Cary Grant and Paul Newman to Elizabeth Taylor and Barbra Streisand. We explored how they might help the fund.

Beverly suggested we meet for lunch the next day on Rodeo Drive to work out the details of our Paramount pitch. We found her and Mike already seated at a table. They received us like a pair of big-time industry players. A galaxy of movie stars dotted around tables near us. Then Dick Guttman paid us a surprise visit. "I'm not dining with you," he said, glancing back at a table where a woman was reading the menu. "I'm dining near you." The woman looked familiar.

Over lunch, the four of us discussed all the possible angles we could take with the studio. "Paramount has decided," I said, "that they want their support to be directed toward a mountain gorilla census, costing $150,000, and the Virunga Management Plan, costing

$90,000. But so far, they've failed to commit to any promotions to go with the movie's release."

"Like a gorilla plush toy," added Jillian. "Or the movie's premiere."

"Because, I mean, where's the funding going to come from?" I asked. "It's not like we've got points on the movie. I cannot imagine the studio will pay us out of its own pocket."

"You're right," said Beverly.

"Just remember," quipped Mike, "Hollywood people are carnies with good teeth."

When the meal was over and we were preparing to leave, Dick returned to our table and introduced us to his lunch date. "Greg and Jillian, I'd like you to meet Patricia Hearst. She needs a ride home. Would you mind driving her? She's staying near you."

"I'm at the Wilshire," said Patricia. "Dick says you're at the Beverly. We're close." Where else but in Hollywood would Patty Hearst, granddaughter of newspaper tycoon William Randolph Hearst, ask to hitch a ride with a couple of nobodies like my wife and me?

"Sure," said Jillian, "we'll drive you."

Jillian got behind the wheel and I sat in front. Patricia insisted we roll up the windows and turn on the air conditioner. "I avoid breathing L.A. air whenever I can," she said coolly. She had a radical backstory. It was all over the papers when I was a kid. In 1974 she was kidnapped by the Symbionese Liberation Army, and then turned up two months later as "Tania," wielding an M1 carbine and holding up a bank in San Francisco. She claimed she had been brainwashed during her captivity. She got thirty-five years for her crimes, but President Jimmy Carter commuted her sentence after she'd served twenty-two months.

We avoided the subject as we drove down Wilshire Boulevard. Instead, as was our wont, Jillian and I pitched her on behalf of the gorillas. Our double act was well honed by then and we delivered a seamless pitch. By the time we dropped her off, she had agreed to approach the Hearst Foundation on our behalf. Result! Dick Guttman knew what he was doing when he asked us to give her lift. He had set her up on our behalf. And we'd all been Hollywood schmoozed.

"Can't promise anything," she added. "My family's not exactly flavor of the month with environmentalists, since we own most of the Californian coast."

The fundraising and public relations lessons were coming in fast. The effect was dizzying. Back on the Paramount lot, we had one more meeting before flying back to London. A half dozen studio executives and producers gathered in a plush conference room to hear our presentation. They were dressed smartly in designer pastels, silks, and off-white linen. If we'd passed around a hat, the combined value of their jewelry could have saved the gorillas. They were all smiles and said yes to everything without committing to anything. Basically, every sponsorship opportunity for the movie *Congo* had been auctioned off before production began, before they even knew of our existence. Pepsi and Taco Bell promotions were all sewn up the previous year. Plush toys too. We left there empty-handed, but when we returned home, we found a fax from Sam: "Good news at last. Paramount has responded favorably to your request for a UK Premiere!!"

———————

"What's the point of having a dream team if you're not prepared to fucking listen to them?" yelled Storm. We were making a short film, a goodwill message from Arthur C. Clarke to be shown at the London premiere of *Congo*. It was not the film I had envisioned Storm making, but there wasn't any money for that. Storm had enlisted the services of a cameraman in Sri Lanka to film the science fiction author's speech: "I am very happy that I was able to play some part in persuading NASA's Jet Propulsion Laboratory to use the space shuttle *Endeavour*'s radar to produce the first map of this hitherto uncharted terrain. And I think you'll agree that the result is visually stunning . . ."

With Arthur's greeting in the can, Storm now wanted to shoot a close-up of his books, but I objected to the additional cost. Storm didn't back down. After thirty years of having to explain his visions to music industry cynics, he was hardly going to yield to a graphic design groupie. Every suggestion I made was met with hyperbole and sarcasm. "OK!" I said, "We'll do it your way."

The next morning, I carried my collection of Arthur's science fiction paperbacks down to King Studios in Soho. Storm was at the controls of a 35 mm rostrum camera, designed to animate still objects. Silently, between sips of tea, he arranged the books on a table beneath the camera, then rolled the film and slowly panned the books. Moving diagonally and capturing every tear, scuff, and dog-eared corner, he then told an unexpected story, different from what was written in the books, or from what I had envisioned. It was a kind of visual alchemy.

He and I soon became friends. His studio in Belsize Park was a stone's throw from my office, and I'd often visit to watch him work. He cared little of the gorilla cause. No matter. His mordant sense of humor was an antidote to the chaos in my world. I was happy to drop my fundraising act and listen to his stories about rock-star photo shoots. For my birthday, three weeks before it was officially released, he gave me a CD of Pink Floyd's *Pulse*—a live album recorded at Earl's Court on their last tour. The cover came with a flashing red LED on the side of the case.

"It's a third eye," said Storm. The light kept on flashing for another three years.

In the run-up to the *Congo* movie premiere, everyone in the London office was on the phones trying to drum up support from companies, asking them to take a page of advertising in the premiere program: a glossy, twenty-page booklet whose sole purpose was to generate advertising money and goodwill messages. We raised over £8,000 selling single and half-page ads. MPL, Paul McCartney's company, was too late getting its ad in but sent us £1,000 anyway.

Congo producer Sam Mercer was back in town. He invited Jillian and me to join him and his wife for dinner. We met them at Pont de la Tour, a restaurant on the South Bank next to Tower Bridge. It was a welcome treat. Over dinner, we recalled the roller coaster ride of the previous two years. And when it was time to leave, Jillian and I suggested they share a cab with us, as it was pouring rain outside.

"No need," said Sam, "we've got a limo waiting for us." We climbed into the back and, as we drove across London, we sang "California Dreamin'" by the Mamas & the Papas, which was part of the *Congo* soundtrack. We were pretty good on the harmonies too.

"What a load of shit!" yelled Douglas Adams, throwing open the lobby doors of the Empire Leicester Square. The author of *The Hitchhiker's Guide to the Galaxy* had just sat through 109 minutes of *Congo* and was clearly unimpressed.

Not surprising. The movie stank. I was amazed he stayed until the end. As planned, before the start of the movie, and to a packed auditorium, Arthur's message was shown and then followed by a joint speech by the director, Frank Marshall, and my codirector and wife, Jillian. Rod Stewart was there, which would put the fund on the front page of a few tabloids the next morning and make Gerry Lewis very 'appy.

At the premiere after-party, in the basement of the Royal College of Art on Kensington Gore, I caught up with Douglas Adams, Storm Thorgerson, and David Gilmour, lead guitarist of Pink Floyd. Drinks in hand, the three talented Cantabrigians were standing side by side next to a scale model of a volcano spewing dayglow lava from its summit. Douglas introduced me to David, and of course I already knew Storm. Douglas and David were mates. The previous year at Earl's Court, the night before I went, David had invited Douglas onstage to play guitar with the band in front of twenty thousand fans.

"Sorry if I was a bit vocal back there at the theater," said Douglas. He was an imposing man, both in stature and imagination. "But, I mean, the movie really was shit . . ."

"No, you're right," I laughed. "But the charity did well out of it. The studio paid us five figures for our radar image, even though it was in the public domain. And they used our literature in their set designs, and gave us a glamorous premiere, which greatly raised our spirits after a dismal year. At the end of the day, the gorillas made some serious money out of it."

"So it was good for something," said Storm.

"Did you see the message I sent Peter today?" asked Douglas.

"Oh my God, yes," I said. "Thank you!"

That morning, after he learned that our guest of honor had had to bow out of the premiere at the last minute, Douglas wrote to musician Peter Gabriel: "Peter, please excuse this last-minute thing—I've been asked if I can help out so I'm trying. There's a big Charity Premiere tonight of the new Michael Crichton movie, *Congo*. It's in aid of the Dian Fossey Gorilla Fund, which is a pretty good thing. The Guest of Honour was to have been David Attenborough, but his wife has just fallen seriously ill. So here's the flattering offer—would you be prepared to be the last minute substitute Guest of Honour? I know you will practically swoon with the thrill of being honoured in this way, but . . . What can I say. It's all in a very good cause. Hell, it's two free tickets to the movies and a party. Go on, say you will. Please let me or Greg Cummings at the Dian Fossey Gorilla Fund know one way or another as soon as you possibly can."

"Shame he couldn't do it," said Storm.

"A bit short notice," smiled Douglas.

I was in awe of it all. Equally a fan of Peter's work as I was of Douglas's work as I was of Arthur's work as I was of Storm's work as I was of Pink Floyd's work, I was in star-fucker heaven. It was a dream to be working with them all at once.

"I thought Arthur's greeting looked great up on the big screen," I said to Storm.

"Really?" he replied, casually surveying the room for familiar faces. "I thought it was corny. . . . God, it's hard to imagine I earned a master's here. RCA used to be so much groovier."

"Douglas," I said enthusiastically, "I sent an appeal out this week to coincide with the movie's release, and I was wondering—"

"Another one?" asked Douglas. I looked at him aghast. "Don't you ever tire of writing appeals? Nothing wrong with them, as such," he added. "It's just this tendency to continually put Band-Aids on the problem that bothers me. I mean, you put all that effort into asking for donations, but only ever raise enough to keep the gorillas safe for a few more months. What would it take to draw a line under the issue? I know some wealthy people. How much money do you need to make sure, as much as is humanly possible, that the mountain gorillas are saved . . . forever?"

"Now there's a challenge," I said, jingling my iced bourbon. "Actually, it really would not take so much to save them. Some lateral thinking, a lot of hard and careful work, and a creative campaign involving a few choice celebrities and billionaires just might engender the kind of popular support that our hairy mountain cousins need to ensure their place in the wild."

"Yes, but how much? What's the figure?"

"Let's see, the annual cost of gorilla protection is around a quarter of a million dollars."

"So you'd need an interest-bearing lump sum to pay for that in perpetuity," said Storm. "Say $5–$6 million?"

"To save a species?" scoffed Douglas. "A bloody bargain."

The prospect of raising a sum large enough to ensure I never had to fundraise again was very appealing. It seemed that after gathering the patrons we needed, we were entering the realm of big-gift fundraising. "We should continue this conversation at my office," I smiled.

Douglas's involvement began as a result of the emergency appeal letter I sent the year before. "Dear Greg Cummings," he wrote. "Your letter arrived just as I was about to take some foreign currency to the bank so I thought I'd just ship it straight round to you instead. Included is also a cheque from my wife. I'll try to prize some money out of some other friends as well. I'll also apply my mind to ways of spreading the word. Please give me a call to confirm you received this. Good luck. Best, Douglas Adams." His foreign currency added up to around £3,800. I called him immediately to thank him. We hit it off and spoke at length on the phone. He told me he was a keen supporter of wildlife conservation and had had recently climbed Mount Kilimanjaro dressed in a rhinoceros costume to raise money for rhinos. He was happy to become more involved with the gorillas and said he would ask his musician friends to send donations too.

A week after the premiere, he came to our office in Primrose Hill, along with Richard Harris, CTO of The Digital Village, an online entertainment company where Douglas was chief fantasist. "With TDV, we're heading into new territory in digital media," said Douglas, "adapting *Hitchhiker*'s worlds into interactive forms." We had never had such an illustrious visitor.

We sat at a large circular table in the carpeted basement next to a wall-sized map of central Africa. Douglas knew the territory. He had met wild gorillas in Zaire while researching *Last Chance to See*, his nonfiction book about the world's most endangered species. We were lucky to have his support. Writing no more than a dozen books, he had sold upward of fifteen million copies. He was well loved in Silicon Valley. Tech moguls were in awe of his scientific wit. He was tech's Monty Python, a darling of the digerati, a surfer on the cyber tidal wave, an icon of new media.

We discussed tapping new sources of funding. I asked him what he personally could contribute. He said theater groups often staged amateur productions of *Hitchhiker*. "I'd be glad to send you those royalty cheques when they come in. Meantime, I'm meeting people who are sitting on pots of money. When I'm with them, you'll be the parrot on my shoulder." I smiled at the Pythonesque image of a gorilla that thinks it's a parrot, sitting on Douglas's shoulder, watching him glad-hand moguls. "So, tell me," he boomed, "how does $250,000 a year save gorillas?"

"Bananas. Lots of bananas," I quipped. "Actually, most of the money gets spent on antipoaching patrols, equipment, salaries of the park rangers, and running the research facility."

"Do you have researchers out there now?" asked Richard.

"No," said Jillian. "They were all evacuated. That's twice in two years we've had to fly our foreign staff out of Rwanda. Security's not likely to improve anytime soon, either."

"We're exploring alternatives," I said. "A virtual Africa office."

"What we envision," said Jillian, "is a network of resident conservationists, in Rwanda, Zaire, and Uganda. If we can identify those people who are committed to protecting the environment, we can engender a local gorilla conservation effort—a front line for protection."

"Ultimately, we're aiming for an all-singing, all-dancing, gorilla-loving people."

"OK, so what you need," said Richard, "is an information resource that can be accessed from anywhere—a digital hub." He looked at our network of desktop PCs all running Windows 95, then shook his head in dismay and added, "And you're going to need some Macs too."

"I should be able to get those donated," said Douglas.

Before leaving, Douglas signed a copy of *The Hitchhiker's Guide to the Galaxy* for Jillian and me with the inscription, "Looking forward to working with you." He then sent an email to Apple Computer: "We are planning to do a major TDV website with them and in the long term have even more ambitious plans—real-time gorilla tracking in virtual models of the Virungas on the Web. The Fund already has use of a satellite for transmitting data back from Africa. They desperately need equipment right at the moment, and I have been strongly advocating Apple to them." As a result, Apple donated about £5,000 worth of high-end desktop gear to the fund. Our virtual Africa office was beginning to take shape.

From then on, Douglas defined the role of patron. He was determined to save this species by any means necessary. As a result of his networking, donations came pouring in, from David Gilmour, Michael Palin, Paul McCartney, Terry Jones, Hugh Laurie, and Christabel Holland. One day Rose answered the phone at the office and a voice on the other end said, "Hello. John Cleese here . . . from Monty Python. I'm sending you a cheque for £3,000. May I please know the exact spelling of your charity, and your address?"

One of my most cherished gifts, which came in during this heady time—not as a result of Douglas's networking nor even of Arthur's, who had tried in vain to put us in touch—was a modest £250 donation from Stanley Kubrick. He sent it in response to one of our newsletters. I later learned the illustrious film auteur was an avid reader of trade papers, and I guess *Digit News* fit the bill. Forget the size of his gift—I was simply happy to know we kept the great Stanley Kubrick informed about mountain gorillas.

———————

In his book *Being Digital,* Nicholas Negroponte talks about an early prototype of a machine that pushed back at you, a force-feedback device. I wrote to him to ask if such a device might be used to support our antipoaching efforts: plotting poaching activity on the 3D map we had made from JPL's data set of the gorilla habitat, to determine the path of least resistance for the gorillas.

My letter prompted an invitation in September 1995 from Michael Hawley. I wasted no time flying to Boston. In 1985, Negroponte founded the Media Lab at the Massachusetts Institute of Technology in Cambridge, Massachusetts. It is one of America's foremost research facilities. The Media Lab's building E15, or the Wiesner Building, was designed by renowned architect I. M. Pei. On the outside it resembled a shiny new gift box, or the packaging to a futuristic game console. Inside the four-story building was a warren of studios and workshops. Professor Michael Hawley, who had studied under Marvin Minsky, gave me a tour of the facility. Things That Think, Toys of Tomorrow, and GO Expeditions were all projects he was working on at the time.

He showed me a large room that had been entirely blacked out and was lighted only by LEDs. "Nike are sponsoring this project," said Hawley. I cannot recall exactly what they were working on in there, but the scene reminded me of backstage at the Floyd concert. As we toured the lab, I told Michael all about our Gorillas from Space project and showed him digital illustrations and a Virunga fly-through on my Palm Pilot. The Media Lab seemed an ideal partner for the conservation education center that we were planning to build somewhere between Bwindi and Virunga. (The two mountain gorilla habitats are only thirty-five kilometers apart.) And such a facility would be an ideal naming opportunity for a donor to Douglas's once-and-for-all fund. I also told him about SatelLife, the other people I'd come to meet in Cambridge. "It's an initiative of the International Physicians for the Prevention of Nuclear War, to put remote doctors and health workers in touch with medical specialists in the US," I said. "They operate a fridge-sized low-orbit satellite with a 386 computer on board and a UHF radio receiver that can link to anyone who has the right equipment. The satellite passes overhead twice a day, whereupon our staff at Karisoke can send and receive digital packet radio signals and connect to the Internet. It's a cumbersome means of communication, but reliable and cheap. And it helps save gorilla lives."

"The future of spaceflight is low-cost rockets," said Michael.

"You reckon?"

"This is a haptic device," he said, grasping a shiny metal pen attached to a mechanical arm, "the technology you asked about in our letter to my boss. It takes advantage of my sense of touch to simulate objects, applying forces, vibrations, or motions to my hand. Here, give it a try." Floating next to the device was an invisible and inflexible cube. I could feel its presence by moving the pen over its surface, or knocking it against it. But I couldn't see it. Magic!

"Come, let me show you something else you might like," he said, leading me down the hall to another workshop. "A couple of colleagues have built a holography research group here." Suspended from the ceiling were full-color holographic portraits encased in glass. And on an optical bench full of lasers there was the holo-video system used to make 3D videos.

"Not exactly Princess Leia beaming her SOS message back to Obi-Wan Kenobi," laughed Hawley, "but you get the picture. Have you thought about making a hologram of a silverback?"

"Wow," I gasped. "Now that would be amazing."

"There's a lot of equipment involved," smiled Hawley. "How would gorillas react to having lasers in their midst? Also, the silverback would have to stay perfectly still, if only for an instant. Any movement by more than a millionth of a meter is enough to ruin a hologram."

"That's a tall order," I laughed. "But we could create a soft mock-up of the equipment out of foam rubber and give them a few weeks to get used to it. Then, when we're sure it's OK, we introduce the real equipment, wait for the big fella to meditate, and then shoot our hologram."

"OK, here's what we can offer you," said Hawley. "At the Media Lab your charity will enjoy the same privileges as our corporate sponsors. That's a benefit worth $120,000 a year. You can look in on any of the technologies we're developing and see what suits your conservation efforts."

Wow! Another exclusive door had swung wide open. Was it me or the gorillas or both? He then invited me to attend Ten Ten Ten—the Media Lab's tenth anniversary celebrations on October 10. I declined as I needed to return home to Jillian and prepare for our forthcoming trip to Africa. We were heading down there in a week, our first trip since the genocide. I did, however, contribute to his project, *A Day in the Life of Cyberspace*, with a piece I had written, "A Day in the Life of a High-Tech Gorilla Tracker":

Nemeye has spent all morning leading a handful of trackers through the muddy forests of the Virunga volcanoes in search of Beetsme's group. They find them on the slopes of Visoke and there is a newborn amongst them. Jenny is the mother. Nemeye and the trackers take a reading on their GPS unit, and make a few notes.

On returning to the Karisoke Research Centre in the early afternoon, Nemeye downloads his data directly from his data logger into a portable PC and writes a quick e-mail report to go with it. A few mouse clicks and the data is ready to be relayed to the low orbit satellite, Healthsat II, as it passes overhead. At 2 PM local time, the satellite is directly overhead and the data is automatically transmitted, using a simple VHF/UHF Transceiver, to the low-orbit satellite and stored in its onboard 386 computer.

By 9 AM Eastern Standard Time, Healthsat is within range of Cambridge, Massachusetts, and transmits all post and data to SatelLife's ground station there. SatelLife relay Nemeye's e-mail message and GPS data directly through the Internet to Rutgers University in New Jersey.

As Dr. Dieter Steklis reads Nemeye's e-mail report that morning at Rutgers, Dr. Scott Madry is already plotting the GPS coordinates from his data package on the 3-D model of

the Virunga GIS that is stored on a computer at the Remote
Sensing Centre at Rutgers University. Within six hours of
Nemeye finding Beetsme's group on the slopes of Visoke,
their position is accurately plotted 7,000 miles away on the
Virunga GIS in New Jersey. All this without having to radio-
tag the gorillas in the way most conventional wildlife satellite
tracking systems work.

Dieter, Netzin and Scott meet at the Remote Sensing
Centre mid-morning to discuss Nemeye's report. They run
through the past two weeks of Beetsme's positions in quick
sequence and closely follow the group's movement. The fortnight's poaching records are also run in sequence simultaneously. A distinct pattern emerges and it appears increased
human activity in the area has been affecting Beetsme's ranging
patterns.

Dieter then sends an e-mail message back to Karisoke
suggesting the antipoaching rangers target the problem area.
He also faxes Peter Clay in Kigali with details of suggested
action with the park rangers. Within 24 hours of Nemeye's
report being sent, Peter and Karisoke's antipoaching rangers
are already taking corrective action in the Virungas.

9

CONGO

THE AMERICAN MUSEUM of Natural History is spread out across two blocks on the Upper West Side of Manhattan, next to Central Park. Like turrets in a hunting chateau, the museum's pink stone rotundas protrude from the wooded grounds. It offers a serene asylum from the urban hubbub of humanity, turned up to eleven. As I roam through the museum's dimly lit corridors, poring over its menagerie of mummified beasts, fossils, minerals, meteorites, and artifacts, I feel I'm in familiar company. Like me, they come from all over the planet.

At the heart of the museum is the Akeley Hall of African Mammals, a two-story exhibition hall of wildlife dioramas that draw the viewer from relative darkness into the brightness of distant worlds. The first time I saw the gorilla diorama, I was struck by its accuracy and attention to detail, but also by an anomaly. The silverback's pose is wrong. His habitat is faultless. Genuine geographic features are painted into the scene.

"But he's beating his chest with his fists," I sighed. "Akeley got it wrong, just like everyone else." Apparently, in the hundred-odd years that his gorilla diorama had been on display, no one had spotted the mistake. Because people think gorillas beat their chests with their fists. It is how they're portrayed in the movies. But gorillas do *not* beat their chests with their fists. They slap the indentations beneath their pectoral muscles with cupped hands, thereby making a sound loud enough to be heard miles away by rival gorillas, in particular, silverbacks.

Next to the Old Man of Mikeno, I feel strangely at home. The stuffed silverback bridges my worlds. Could there be anything more diametrically opposed to a living creature ambling freely in nature than one stuffed and displayed in a static diorama in a far-off city museum? And yet, face-to-face with a gorilla, even one that's long since breathed its last, you see how special the animals are. Nobility and gentleness shine through. Sure, not being shot and stuffed would have been a far more favorable outcome, but it beats being a zoo animal, where not only are you condemned to a life in captivity but so are your progeny, until the day the zoo closes. I've met the wild descendants of the gorillas in Akeley's diorama, which in my book makes it a more fitting tribute to the species than the most wildly resonant zoo enclosure. Mercifully, there are no mountain gorillas in zoos.

In January 1996, I arrived at the exact spot depicted in the gorilla diorama. It was as if I'd stepped through a portal on the Upper West Side and arrived in Zaire, thirty-six hundred meters up the side of a volcano, from where I could see Mount Nyamuragira and Mount Nyiragongo, two of Africa's active volcanoes, and Lake Kivu. Between them, a million refugees were camped. With their tin-roofed shelters laid out in rows and reflecting the equatorial sunlight, the camps resembled vast solar farms. The refugees had come from Rwanda, in the wake of the genocide in which many had participated, and as the result of the RPF advancing south and ending the massacres.

My trekking companions were Dr. Trinto Mugangu, a Congolese scientist, and Popol Verhoestraete, a Belgian entrepreneur, both in their late forties. To join the expedition, Trinto had flown in from Kinshasa and I from Uganda. Popol lived in nearby Goma. Trinto was a UNDP (United Nations Development Program) consultant, expert in wildlife ecology in protected areas, and visiting professor at the University of Maine. A portly, mild-mannered, intelligent man, he smiled a lot and looked out of place in his city duds and shoes. Popol said my brilliant white sneakers were no better suited to the territory. "Not only can your shoes be seen from space," he said, "but they look like space shuttles." Since moving to Zaire from Brussels in the early 1970s, Popol had become an old Africa hand (usually a euphemism for bigot), and a hell of a character. He had fingers in many pies: wildlife, coffee, import-export, refugees.

We were hiking on the opposite side of the volcanoes to where I'd previously trekked in Rwanda, albeit in the same ecosystem. After Congo gained independence from Belgium in 1960, the park was renamed Virunga National Park, the local word for volcano. A few metal signs demarcating the "Albert National Park" remained and were riddled with bullet holes. From north to south, Virunga NP extends approximately three hundred kilometers, along the borders of South Sudan, Uganda, and Rwanda in the east, and covers an area of roughly eight thousand square kilometers. It's not easy maintaining the integrity of such a large protected area, especially when it was hemmed in by dense human population and, since the Rwandan genocide, by rampant insecurity. More than 3,000 faunal and floral species have been recorded—including 218 mammal species, 706 bird species, 109 reptile species, 78 amphibian species, and 22 primate species—of which around 10 percent are endemic. Because of its extraordinary biodiversity, Virunga was declared a UNESCO World Heritage site in 1979, the first national park in Africa to be so designated.

The park is a geological roller coaster. Elevations range from 680 meters in the Semliki River valley to 5,109 meters in the Rwenzori Range (Mountains of the Moon). It includes five main biomes: lowland forest, savanna, swamp-edged lake, and the forested massifs of Rwenzori and Virunga, granitic and volcanic, respectively. The Virungas comprise eight volcanoes: Mounts Karisimbi, Mikeno, Bisoke, Sabyinyo, Gahinga, Muhabura, Nyiragongo, and Nyamuragira. Still very active, the last two have erupted dozens of times in the past one hundred years, greatly impacting the park's habitats and wildlife, as well as the surrounding communities. Nyiragongo, a stratovolcano, has a wide liquid lava lake that glows at night and ceaselessly spews toxic gas that can be seen from the town of Goma.

It was not my first time in Zaire. In October, Jillian, Adam Adamou, and I had traveled in by road from Rwanda, crossing the border at Gisenyi. Straightaway, we saw a noticeable difference in people's behavior, dress, and attitude. The men wore loud shirts and shades. The women wore tight dresses in loud prints and had fantastic hairdos. People laughed a lot and got off on Congolese rumbas that constantly blared from their radios. Zaire was Africa's Brazil.

Jillian and I were on our first trip to Africa together, and it was our first time back since the genocide. In Rwanda we trekked gorillas—my wife's first and only encounter—and held meetings with officials to explore the most pressing needs in gorilla land. All the Karisoke rangers had returned home from Zaire, and the Karisoke Research Center was now being run out of a bungalow in the suburbs of Ruhengeri. Wherever we went, a pall of sorrow hung in the air. In Kigali, at the Novotel where we stayed, we could still smell blood in the carpets. One night Adam, Jillian, and I stood on the roof of the hotel and watched heat lightning on the horizon flash through the belly of a distant storm and illuminate the thousand hills of Rwanda. There was only one question on our minds: How could it have happened?

The first time I visited Rwanda, the country was already in the midst of a civil war, but "civil" was the operative word. Every outbreak was handled with restraint. Then something flipped. Some say they saw it coming. I never did. What was it that the murderers so desperately feared that made them so ruthless, so merciless with their neighbors? We were shown the spot outside the Hôtel des Mille Collines where children were systematically decapitated and dismembered by machete-wielding Interahamwe.

Despite the gloom of the aftermath of the genocide, and the paralysis that remained in the country as a result, we managed to accomplish a few things in Rwanda. Dieter was in line with the UK fund's thinking, and he helped us present our plans to the relevant ministries. We were well received by all whom we met. They were grateful for our optimism in reestablishing our gorilla conservation program, now pivoted to provide benefit to the impoverished communities living adjacent to their habitat. They appreciated our new perspective, and our adaptability.

In Goma, Popol Verhoestraete put us up in his home. He had married an Esselen, the owners of TMK, an air charter, which afforded him some stability. He and his wife Natalie lived in relative luxury on the shores of Lake Kivu in a prefab Japanese bungalow with sunken living room and lush, resplendent grounds where a dozen rescue dogs ran free. When Jillian awoke that first morning, it was to the sound of ceaseless drumming. "They're preparing for war," said Popol in an attempt to wind her up. She took the bait. Later that day, he insisted that we test a donated bulletproof vest by firing at it with an AK-47. Needless to say, the vest wasn't worn by any living thing at the time, but rather strung on a washing line in his garden. It passed the test.

Popol was full of fun facts about the local environment. For instance, as a result of its location above a rifting fissure, the 400-meter-deep Lake Kivu was highly volatile. "Don't be fooled by these calm waters lapping against the shore there," he smiled as we sat drinking Primus beer in his garden at sunset. A bubbling storm cloud rose high into the stratosphere, and the sky was an epic mural of purple, indigo, and red. "You know what a mazuku is?" he asked. "It's a pocket of air so rich in carbon dioxide that it can kill. *Mazuku* means 'evil wind' in Swahili, and they are plentiful on Lake Kivu and they are invisible. Children out for an innocent swim suffocate and drown as a result of getting caught in one. And there are places onshore where you can put a match to a methane vent and light a perpetual fire."

He told us Lake Kivu is a limnic lake. Dissolved in the stratification beneath the surface are vast quantities of carbon dioxide and methane. The amount of methane is estimated to be sixty-five cubic kilometers. Normally, these gases remain dissolved in equilibrium at the bottom, but if disturbed sufficiently by, say, an earthquake, they could suddenly rise to the surface in what is known as a *limnic eruption*. Its powers of devastation are beyond imagining. Evidence from sediment cores indicate that every thousand years or so a limnic eruption has asphyxiated every living creature in the lake basin. Scientists agree that a long-anticipated limnic eruption could happen any day now. Some two million people and their livestock live in the lake basin. Within minutes they would all suffocate to death. I was so taken by this phenomenon that I wrote a novel about it. The main plot device in *Gorillaland* is Lake Kivu's woeful volatility. Never mind asphyxiation, what would happen if Mount Nyiragongo's lava ignited Lake Kivu's methane?

Following our twelve-day tour of the mountain gorilla range states, in which Adam, our consultant, played a vital role in identifying a sound conservation methodology, Jillian and I presented a package of proposals to the US and UK boards, the likes of which they'd never seen before. We proposed hiring a regional development coordinator to be based in Rwanda, and building a conservation center on the edge of the park in Zaire. Our plans were unanimously approved, providing we could raise the money to fund them. Hence, three months later, I was back in Zaire, looking for a spot to build a conservation center, fearfully proud and confidently worried about our prospects. Where would we find the money? If we built it, would they come?

Popol was the Zaire representative for IGCP (or PICG in French). "I work for PIG and you work for D-FUCK," he liked to tell me.

"Except that now we're called DFGF Europe," I retorted.

"So you are just the same as all the others," he scoffed. He was a cynical fellow, but nothing enraged Popol more than the incompetency of Zairean bureaucrats. Once, after being falsely accused of corruption, he had placed his head on a block in front of President Mobutu Sese Seko and told him to chop it off. His deep affinity to the country's natural beauty was matched only by his aversion to those who'd let such an environmental disaster unfold around it.

"Come, I'll show you the damage," he said as we set off from Goma by road. Trinto and I sat in the back of his Toyota Land Cruiser 4x4. George, his handyman, drove. He and Popol argued like an old married couple. When Popol ridiculed my Swiss Army knife, George came to my defense. It was all in good humor, I thought, caressing my trusty penknife. The road rose higher as we left Goma and entered the Virunga massif. To reach the park, we drove north on the RN2. The RN2 is statistically Africa's most dangerous road; travelers on it have been knocked down by sleeping truck drivers, ambushed by thieves, shot at by snipers, and mauled by wild animals. A few months before we drove it, five Italian aid workers were killed when their car was ambushed and robbed on this road. "It's safe now," said Popol, nodding slowly.

With my camera at the ready, I took a few passing "potshots" of interesting scenes. Mostly, I shot the mass of humanity walking along the road. Flying in the face of its own policy guidelines, the UNHCR (United Nations High Commissioner for Refugees) had chosen to locate the camps right next to a highly endangered ecosystem, indeed a UNESCO world heritage site. Amazing how the stroke of one bureaucrat's pen can cause irreparable damage. Every day, for fuel, the refugees consumed a section of parkland forest the size of a football field. Adding to the havoc, there were armed groups in the camps, Interahamwe and ex-Rwandan army officers responsible for the genocide. The camps acted as their bases in Zaire, from where they launched repeated attacks against Rwanda's new government. The war may have been over, but the belligerent forces in exile posed a constant threat to a fragile peace. And as the situation worsened, aid donors began to abandon what they called "the messiest humanitarian quagmire ever."

I asked if we could stop so I could photograph the deforestation on Nyiragongo's slopes. George obliged. I leaped from the vehicle, squeezed off a few frames of a denuded hillside, and then leaped back in again. We hadn't driven a kilometer up the road when we were aggressively overtaken by a truckload of heavily armed soldiers who demanded we pull over, shouting about illicit photos. A bus full of refugees stopped alongside us and the people inside began shouting in French, *"Prenez la caméra! Prenez la caméra!"* ("Take the camera! Take the camera!")

The soldiers yanked open the doors of the Land Cruiser. They confiscated my camera and ordered Trinto and George out of the car, as they were Zairean, then force-marched them into a roadside Nissan hut. Popol and I swiftly followed. Once inside, Popol demanded to know the reason for our arrest. The commanding officer, who was holding my camera in one hand and a 9mm pistol in the other, said it was because of the photos I had taken of the camp.

Popol became enraged. "How dare you?" he yelled at the officer in French. "I work for IGCP and UNDP, and we pay your fucking salaries. We are documenting the destruction that *you* have done to your fucking national park, you moron!"

"Popol, chill out," I said worriedly. "The guy's got a gun."

"I don't fucking care!"

What followed was an adrenaline-charged negotiation. My suggestion that they develop the photos to prove our innocence was dismissed on the basis of cost. After I promised I'd take no further photos, they let us go. No bribes were paid. We drove on in silence, through the Virunga corridor, a steeply forested valley separating the five dormant volcanoes located within the mountain gorilla habitat from the two active volcanoes located without. A coucal's rapid-fire descending call echoed off the dank primordial forest. For a moment it seemed we were in a different cool place where trees and animals thrived. The forest ended abruptly, and we were then flanked by what had once been swift and deadly flows of lava from Nyamuragira, long since cooled and solidified. Several kilometers wide and tens of kilometers long, these lava fields are clearly visible in the radar images that NASA obtained for us on board *Endeavour*. In person, it was an otherworldly sight. Popol said they once found an elephant carcass encased in the lava.

Our Land Cruiser was overheating. We had to stop a few times to refill the radiator. Then the radiator blew its cap off. As much as we searched along the road, we could not find it. George borrowed my Swiss Army knife and carved a wedge out of an ear of corn, then substituted it for the cap. "You see," he said, glaring at Popol. "What would we have done without his knife?"

"Look at these idiots," said Popol as we passed two men cutting down a tree on the side of the road. "The Belgians planted those eucalyptus trees on the side of this road so it would not erode. Now, they're almost all gone."

"Like the Belgians," I said.

"Cretins! They cut off their nose to spite their face. You see those holes they've dug beside the milestones. They think that's where the colonials hid their gold. Unbelievable, these people sometimes . . ."

First stop, park HQ at Rumangabo, where we were greeted by an honor guard of the Institut Zaïrois pour la Conservation de la Nature (IZCN) park rangers, led by Warden Wathaut. The warden then gave us a tour of the main building, an oversized edifice with a grand portico entrance, columns, and four large arches above which 1926 was engraved in the masonry, the year the park was gazetted. We were shown a mural depicting the eternal battle between ranger and poacher, and all the endemic animals were gathered around the combatants, looking on with dread. Too close to call at this point, folks. Outside, I photographed the warden's four daughters and son, who were all smiles as they huddled together at their garden gate. We published the photo on the cover of the next edition of *Digit News* with the caption THE MOUNTAIN GORILLAS' SURVIVAL DEPENDS ON THE GOODWILL OF THE LOCAL PEOPLE. I only mention this because one of the girls in the photo, Alexandrine Wathaut, would later become the administrator of our Goma resource center.

From park HQ we headed to Bukima gate, where the Karisoke rangers had spent a brief exile, and drove a winding dirt road rutted with cut-glass volcanic rock. The vehicle could go no farther, so we grabbed our supplies and, with the aid of porters, continued on foot. Popol instructed George to meet us in Djomba in five days. Climbing up a steep slope, about sixty meters high, through the buffer zone to the park's edge, I nearly died from exhaustion. No matter how fit you are, altitude can break the unacclimatized. By nightfall we were settled in the Bukima gite, a three-bedroom wooden cabin on the slopes of Mount Mikeno that slept six and was self-catering. I was amazed by the relative luxury and coziness of this remote Congo station.

Gapira, a senior park ranger who had joined our expedition, briefed us on the situation in the park. In the last year, the number of snares recovered had tripled. They had confiscated over four thousand machetes. The human carnage was untold, even by bloody Zaire's standards. Gapira said that at one time there were so many dead bodies scattered across the countryside that feral pigs began to feed on them.

"Man-eating pigs? Really?" asked Popol, doubting the likelihood of his account.

Gapira then leaned in closer and said in a whisper, as though the hills had ears, "Not only pigs, *afendi*, but man-eating ducks too."

For supper, we ate broiled chicken and potatoes and drank Primus beer. Seated by the fire, Popol, Gapira, and I then sipped neat Wild Turkey bourbon (Trinto was a teetotaler) and talked about gorillas and Dian Fossey.

Mikeno was lit by a moonless sky so full of stars I worried they might fall on our heads. A million flickering lights from the camps in the valley glowed with a tranquility that belied the suffering and bellicosity therein. As our fire died down and the others retired to their rooms, it was just Popol and me. The conversation turned to the quality of the local marijuana. "All the rangers grow ganja up here," he said. "It's my job to confiscate it from them. So when we get back to Goma, I'll let you try some."

We were both keen on astronomy and thereafter wandered through the equatorial constellations that, along with a number of well-known stars, asterisms, and deep-sky objects, were dominated by Orion and Taurus, the hunter and the hunted. At eleven thirty, I was the only one awake, sitting in a little wooden room writing in my journal by candlelight. Inspiration came so thick and fast I couldn't transcribe my thoughts quickly enough.

The next morning, we set off to find Luwawa's group, whose silverback had recently been shot by soldiers. Subsequently, after Luwawa's death, a wild, unhabituated silverback had assumed leadership of what was a group of already habituated gorillas (those familiar to human presence). As we approached, the new boss became quite agitated and refused to allow us to come any closer. And yet, no matter how much he screamed and beat his chest and thrashed about the vegetation like a demon, he couldn't convince the other gorillas in his group to flee. In the end, we gave up our pursuit and sat down in a dried-up river-bed nearby, a sunny, meandering rift through the otherwise pristine Afromontane forest.

All at once, about twenty meters upstream from us, the gorillas began to emerge from the woods and cross the dry riverbed: large, black, shaggy, charismatic mammals that moved fluidly and stoically, each glancing curiously in our direction. It seemed they wanted to see us. It was the first time that I truly felt their kinship.

We trudged on through the forested plateau that separated the park from the flanks of the volcanoes, searching for a spot to build our conservation center. There was an air of blissful ignorance about our quest. Were we insane, expecting to build a "media lab" in Zaire, in the middle of all this havoc? Don Quixote came to mind. But there was nothing whimsical about the cause. The center would be a resource that local people could use to find out more about the rare and valuable ecosystem in their backyard before it disappeared. If I was out of my depth, I didn't realize it at the time. The stakes were very high. To some extent (more than we knew then), the future of Zaire's gorillas depended on us.

We found Rugabo group in the bamboo forest. In August, over the course of two weeks, three gorillas (two silverbacks and one adult female) were killed, including Rugabo. Poachers from the Djomba and Bukima communities carried out the killings. They were motivated by a mysterious exotic animal dealer who wanted to buy a baby gorilla. The consequent poaching caused severe disturbances in Zaire's gorilla groups. Four gorillas disappeared. Despite investigations by the IZCN and conservation NGOs, no traces of the animals were ever found. We assumed that they fled and were integrated into a wild gorilla group. Rugabo group was now run by a blackback. Within a fortnight, the family had gotten over the shock of seeing two of its group members killed and began accepting visitors again. Among gorillas, you enter a world where all human constructs dissolve like fast-decaying detritus. Tranquility in the midst of havoc.

Half a dozen soldiers were hanging around a makeshift camp in the forest, their grenade launchers and assault rifles propped up against a tree while they laughed among themselves and smoked weed. We introduced ourselves as gorilla conservationists, and they welcomed us. They were part of a battalion of paratroopers sent by President Mobutu to the Virungas to protect the great apes after the recent spate of killings. One of the paratroopers posed for a photograph. Dressed in camouflage fatigues and a pair of flip-flops and holding an RPG and an AK-47, he cut quite the figure of a jungle combatant. I didn't know if I should feel reassured, worried, or cool.

———————

Congo's allure was understandable, given that human beings originated there. And while there's no evidence to support the theory because acidity in the jungle soil destroyed all fossil records, anthropologists believe that seven million years ago, at the end of the Miocene epoch, the common ancestor to gorillas, chimpanzees, bonobos, and humans was forced by climatic changes in the Congo basin to migrate eastward. Our ancestor may have been bipedal and even more humanoid than gorillas: something of a "humarilla." Eventually the jungle came to an abrupt end, and the land dropped away into a vast inland sea. The humarilla had reached the western escarpment of the Albertine Rift Valley and the 550-kilometer-long Lake Obweruka, an ancient great lake fed by the Katonga and Kagera Rivers. As she made her night nest on the high ridge, she may have watched the shadow of the escarpment move slowly eastward across the lake and into a distant forested land that faded into adumbration in twilight. To her, the Rift Valley must have seemed as impassable as outer space is to us: the first frontier. Eventually, brachiating and palm-walking with their families in tow, our hominid ancestors began to conquer the continent's geological obstacles. Whether they passed north or south of Lake Obweruka is a matter of speculation, as they were certainly unable to swim across it, but in due course they left Congo's rainforest for the savannas of East Africa's high plateau.

The gorilla's story is more sobering. It has more to do with rising escarpments, rain shadows, and changing river courses. Confined to specific forests, as a result of a reduction in suitable habitats, gorillas got hit hard by climate change and almost became extinct. Around half a million years ago, two land bridges emerged across the Rift: the Rwenzori Mountains and the Virunga volcanoes. Meanwhile, the eastern escarpment began to rise, eventually cutting off the flow of the Katonga and Kagera Rivers, which diverted northward into Lake Victoria. The rising escarpment also created a rain shadow that allowed the forests to thrive again. The once vast Lake Obweruka broke up into Lakes Kivu, Edward, and Albert, and the Albertine Rift turned arid. To the gorillas, the lush rainforests on the eastern side of the Rift must have seemed inviting.

Genetic data confirms the mountain and lowland subspecies of the eastern gorilla diverged 380,000 years ago. Presumably the mountain gorillas of Bwindi and Virunga, the only gorilla populations found east of the Albertine Rift, used the Virunga land bridge to cross it. By 10,000 BC, at the end of the last ice age, all eastern and mountain gorilla populations had settled into their present habitats, though the forests were then much larger and more interconnected than now. Still, never again would mountain and lowland meet.

Between 1000 and 500 BC, the second Bantu migration saw humans begin to move southward from the shores of Lake Victoria into the Congo basin. The natural path for them to follow was the Albertine Rift, where they grew bananas, which brought them into direct conflict with the gorillas in the forests, which had hitherto only seen the occasional Twa Pygmy. After that, the gorilla populations went into steady decline.

But when did mountain gorillas settle on the cold, wet slopes of Virunga? Until around one hundred thousand years ago, the volcanoes were too active for this to have been a viable gorilla habitat. It's possible that when they settled there, the mountain gorillas were on their way *back* to the Congo basin from the impenetrable forests of the eastern escarpment. In which case they could, in fact, be the descendants of Bwindi gorillas. We may never know, but it sure is fun to speculate.

"Are there any leopards on this side of the volcanoes?" I asked as we tramped through the Afromontane forest. Until humans came along, leopards were the gorillas' only predator.

"No," said Popol. "They left long ago. There are no more 'dangeroos' in Virunga." ("Dangeroos" was his word for dangerous animals.) "The *mutus* [local people] have eaten them all.'

"President Mobutu Sese Seko Kuku Ngbendu Wa Za Banga," said Trinto, "whose name means 'the all-powerful warrior who, because of his endurance and inflexible will to win, goes from conquest to conquest, leaving fire in his wake,' claims that when he was just a teenager, he barehandedly killed a wild leopard near his village on the Congo River."

We were nowhere near the Congo River. That great confluence snaked through the jungle some five hundred kilometers west of our position. And yet we could feel its presence. Whether arising from the onomatopoeia of its forceful flow or from the rhythm of a battle drum, the name Congo is etched deep in our subconscious. And the river characterizes its eponymous nation. Timeless and yet immediate, eras are intertwined, here and now and then. Primordial memories linger in our minds.

Until the explorer Henry Morton Stanley, the "Breaker of Rocks," stomped through the interior in 1874 at the behest of King Leopold II of Belgium and opened the door to its exploitation, the Congo jungle had remained relatively untouched by outsiders. Since then, however, it had been open season, and plundering the Congo, whether literally or figuratively, has become old hat. King Leopold II of Belgium lusted after her ivory and rubber. In the name of rubber production, tens of millions of Congolese were tortured and killed by his agents in the Congo Free State—so we could have fucking tires. How far did we travel on that gruesome trade in human hands? And when it was still a young nation, not yet formed, Congo was raped of its innocence. Like raping a child.

Thereafter, Belgium and the successive governments of an independent Zaire only had eyes for minerals—diamonds, gold, tin, cobalt, zinc, tourmaline, copper, uranium—each with its own inherent horrors. It is never-ending. After a century of mining, there are still $24 trillion worth of minerals in the ground, more than anywhere else on Earth. And aboveground, there's enough peat to power America for ten years, driving a final nail into the coffin of the planet's rapidly warming climate. Many more surprises have yet to be discovered in the heart of the Congo. One thing's for certain: Congo the place was nothing like *Congo* the movie. Seems we added the only touches of verisimilitude to that movie.

Trinto and Popol were good listeners. Grateful for willing ears, as we tramped through mist, I babbled on, remonstrating about my fellow conservationists and the scientific community who, regardless of what Jillian and I achieved for the gorillas, dismissed us as dalliers for our lack of academic credentials and resented our successes. "Few of them appreciate what we're doing," I sighed, my gaze fixed on the lead tracker's footfalls as he stomped through the putrid, dank undergrowth. "Some despise us for it."

"Academics are used to having their wings clipped," said Trinto. "But you and Jillian, you are free agents. And PhDs take exception to that."

"You want a PhD?" asked Popol, slapping me on the back. "I can get you one from the University of Kinshasa tomorrow!" We had a good laugh about that and other Congo truisms as we continued on our merry way through the park. After a long silence, Trinto asked me if I knew about the Mount Tshiaberimu gorillas.

"Which volcano's that?" I asked, looking to see how many peaks were in view. None.

"It's not in Virunga," said Trinto, "but eighty kilometers north of here, next to Lake Edward. Tshiaberimu means 'mountain of spirits.'

It's a forested mountain, about three thousand meters high, in a small enclave on the edge of the park."

"Huh," I said. "And it's got gorillas?"

"A tiny population. They're very special. They may even be a unique subspecies."

"It's true," added Popol. "Tshiaberimu is an area of great importance. The relative isolation of these gorillas makes them a vital reserve in the gorilla gene pool."

"So what needs to be done at the mountain of spirits?" I asked.

"A census, to understand how many gorillas we're dealing with," said Trinto.

"Can we involve the local population?" I asked.

"*Bien sûr!*" smiled Trinto.

"OK. I'll find a way to fund it. Also, Trinto, how'd you like to be our man in Congo?"

"What do you mean?"

"Our representative in Zaire."

"I would be very honored to work for DFGF UK."

"Europe," I said. "We changed our name to the Dian Fossey Gorilla Fund Europe."

"And the US?" asked Popol.

"They changed their name to DFGF International. It's all one-upmanship with them. But they lack talent, creativity, and finesse. And they're too far up their own asses to see it."

On day four, we began our trek from the Djomba gite, once the site of the most luxurious lodgings in the Virungas. Djomba Lodge was the jewel in the crown of Governors Camp properties in Africa—its construction was overseen by founder Aris Grammaticas himself. No wonder—the view was exceptional. On a clear day you could see the

Mountains of the Moon. Lately, however, it had become a base for the Zairean army, which eyed us suspiciously as we set off down the slope. A great blue turaco was perched in a tree next to the ramshackle wooden lounge. Its call, a rolling staccato, echoed off the slopes. We were headed to the buffer zone to find Oscar/Rugendo group, so named because some Zairean mountain gorillas that were first given a "colonial" name and then got a local name were allowed to keep both—hence, Oscar/Rugendo. What made tracking this group of twelve gorillas so intriguing was that the week before, they'd left the forest altogether and traveled some five kilometers into the adjacent farmlands. It was the largest single exodus of megafauna from the ecosystem since the forest elephants left in the 1970s.

What could prompt a silverback to vacate the ecosystem where he was born? Some say he did what any sane primate would have done: he busted, escaping the havoc in his habitat. Or had he simply gone bananas? Oscar/Rugendo had a penchant for banana trees. (Contrary to popular belief, gorillas are not drawn to the fruit as much as they are to the stalk of the tree.) Consequently, park rangers had been trying to dissuade farmers from planting banana crops next to the park. No surprise then that we found Oscar/Rugendo in a banana shamba far away from his habitat. Fortunately, the land belonged to a local chief who didn't mind having a dozen mountain gorillas camped in his backyard. A poorer farmer might not have been so obliging. Still, the chief was seeking damages of $5,000 a day from IZCN, the wildlife authority.

As daylight faded, the gorillas began fashioning night nests from the leaves of the surrounding banana trees, blithely bending and weaving them into springy bedding. Banana is not endemic to gorilla habitats, so the gorillas' dexterity with it was a wonder to behold. Curious villagers watched from a safe distance. But there was no safe distance. We needed to get those gorillas back into the park.

That evening, back in Goma, I called Ian Redmond in London, who had previously worked with Dian Fossey, and told him about the situation. He said that to ward off gorillas from areas that were heavily trapped by poachers, Dian had used bells.

"*Les cloches*?!" laughed Popol. "But where the fuck are we going to find bells in Zaire? They've all been stolen."

A week later, after I'd returned to London, I heard Popol had rallied the Zairean park rangers at Djomba. Wearing civvies rather than their usual green uniforms—so the gorillas would not associate their distress with the guards—they formed a horseshoe around the group and used boom boxes to drive them back into the forest. No one got hurt. A little while later, Oscar/Rugendo again strayed from the forest. This time he was shot and killed by armed men.

———————————

I have been impressed with the work of the Dian Fossey Gorilla Fund. . . . While encouraging those who can to support such efforts, as a simple Buddhist monk I offer my prayers that peace will soon be restored throughout this troubled region and that harmonious relations will assume among the people, the animals, and the environment.

—A letter from the Dalai Lama

How to succor beasts in the wake of such epic human tragedies as the Rwandan genocide and Zairian refugee crisis? How could we not? Not only are they sweet and innocent but they are among our closest relatives in the wild. We share 97 percent of our genetic makeup with gorillas. If we can't save our closest cousins, then what hope for the rest of wildlife?

Gorillas were dying like flies. Every day we heard another sad story. Land mines in Karisoke. Rangers in firefights with poachers. Gorillas getting shot. The only hopeful story at the time was that of Mugurusi, a silverback in Bwindi Impenetrable National Park in Uganda, who died of old age. The park on the Rwandan side was better protected now, but security remained an issue. I don't know how I maintained my composure on that trek in the wake of so much death, but I knew this was not the time for hesitation. I think I was so determined to realize the vision that we—Jillian, Adam, and I (and, to some extent, our chairman David Rogers)—were implementing for the gorillas that I conquered my negative feelings. Optimism and our conservation vision had to prevail, against all odds.

———————

Much had happened in the twenty-four months since the president's plane was shot down outside Kigali. Virunga's horrors caused a paradigm shift. Reevaluating our conservation methodology, Jillian and I had conceived of a new way to save gorillas through economic development by including local stakeholders. As a husband-and-wife team attempting to bring about social change in one of the world's most dangerous regions, we faced some serious challenges. So we hired an expert to be our regional coordinator for development. Luiz Fabbri was a Brazilian development economist with experience in Mozambique and Angola, though he'd never worked in wildlife. Luiz first conducted a survey of people living next to it to see what value they put on the park. "Zero," he told me. "They think it belongs to European royalty."

"Maybe that's because it used to be named after the prince of Belgium," I said.

"No, they think all wildlife parks in Africa are owned by European aristocrats."

"Right, so how are we going to do this? We may soon have an opportunity to pitch our cause to the world's wealthiest philanthropists."

"I'll do my best," smiled Luiz. "Once they see the benefits, there'll be no turning back." He identified what activities precipitated encroachment of the park—medicinal plants, water collection, honey collection, and bushmeat—then found local grassroots organizations that were focused on mitigating those activities and struck up a partnership. The aim was to take pressure off the park through training in alternative livelihoods while increasing local income from those livelihoods. The result was a long-term, war-resilient, gorilla conservation program.

In October 1996, fed up with the surprise attacks emanating from its refugee camps, Rwanda invaded Zaire to fight alongside a Congolese alliance of anti-Mobutu rebels led by Laurent Kabila. They systematically shelled the camps and committed massacres with light weapons, which cost the lives of up to eight thousand refugees and forced the repatriation of half a million back to Rwanda. George, the handyman, later described the scene outside Popol's walled compound to me: "I got up on the wall to see what was making this strange shuffling noise, and it was Rwandans, thousands of them, saying nothing as they walked past our gate. The Tutsi army had come and told them, '*Allez*! Your home is in Rwanda. Go now. *Toka hapa*!'"

The assault escalated quickly to what became known as the First Congo War. Uganda, Burundi, Angola, and Eritrea joined the invasion and by the end of the year, Kabila's AFDL (Alliance of Democratic Forces for the Liberation of Congo) had captured a wide swath of territory along the border with Rwanda, Uganda, and Burundi, which temporarily satisfied Rwanda because it gave it power in eastern Zaire and crippled the former *génocidaires'* ability to use the camps as a base for attacks. According to President Paul Kagame, the campaign strategy comprised three elements: (a) destroy the refugee camps; (b) destroy ex-Rwandan army and Interahamwe, based in and around the camps; and (c) overthrow the Mobutu regime. Following the acquisition of this buffer territory, there was a pause in the AFDL's advance. Peace had returned. But this relative calm belied the horror that was unfolding in the Congo jungle basin, with the 130,000 refugees at Tingi-Tingi camp who had not repatriated.

In the midst of the fighting, the fund's newly appointed Zaire representative, Trinto Mugangu, visited the UK and spoke to DFGF Europe's local groups in London, Stafford, Northampton, Sussex, and Bristol. Dressed in the same attire he wore trekking, Trinto spoke of the plight of the rangers who continued to work in adverse conditions, of our plans to build a center at the park, and of the mission to save an isolated group of gorillas on Mount Tshiaberimu, or "Mt. T." as he called it. Due to the hostilities in the region, Jillian and I could not visit the mountain then. So we hired a Zairean biologist, Vital Katembo, to begin managing the project *in situ*. When I finally did visit, seven years later, I fell in love with the mountain of spirits and its rare pygmy gorillas. More on that later.

I then received a call at home from Michael Crichton, the author of *Congo*. Mike had given him my number. Surprised and wholly unprepared for his call, I tried to engage him about *Congo* the movie and all the success it had brought to the fund, but he dismissed it. "They made a movie of my book," he said. "That's all." Years before, Crichton had visited mountain gorillas in Rwanda and was deeply moved by the experience, which he describes in his book *Travels*. Having witnessed the conservation challenges firsthand, he understood what we were up against. He'd read my proposal for Mt. T. We discussed the project and the fact that no one else was funding it, which seemed to please him. It was a refreshingly frank conversation. He then pledged $25,000 in start-up funding for Mt. T.—$10,000 now and $15,000 in a year's time.

10

A ONCE-AND-FOR-ALL FUND

DOUGLAS FINALLY GOT a chance to present his idea for a once-and-for-all fund to save the gorillas forever to a suitably wealthy person. He wrote to tell me about it: "I saw Paul Allen at the weekend, and did broach the subject, saying that it was within the power of somebody, for $250,000 a year, to ensure the survival of an entire species. He definitely registered the information, but what he will choose to do about it is anybody's guess at the moment. I will next see him in May and I will then explore how far into his mind the idea has percolated. I'm on the case!"

As it turned out, the idea hadn't percolated very far into Paul Allen's mind, so we turned our attention to Microsoft's other founder, Bill Gates. He was an excellent prospect. Not only was he the richest man in the world, hence a safe bet when trying to raise an enormous sum of money, but he had also previously stated, in an op-ed piece in the *New York Times*, that he regarded mountain gorillas as one of the "natural wonders of the world."

Douglas had tried without success to put me in touch with his friend Nathan Myhrvold, Microsoft's chief technology officer (CTO), so he wrote to Linda Stone, VP of special projects: "Everybody seems to have gone silent at Microsoft! Among the things I talked to Nathan about was a plan to raise a large fund from the computer industry to permanently underwrite the conservation of mountain gorillas, and he responded warmly to the idea and even mentioned that it was something that Bill 'might' respond to since he was pretty impressed by his own trip to see the gorillas. My friend Greg Cummings is currently in Seattle as part of a trip round the west coast in pursuit of this goal and, in spite of intercessions from me and Mike Backes, is having no luck in reaching Nathan. I gave him your address too, but he has not managed to reach you. If you are in town, please could you give him a call? Even if you aren't able to help, he's feeling a bit stranded!"

The polar jet stream can be cruel on the Pacific Northwest in April, like a prison guard with a hose. Rain fell endlessly, transforming the rugged landscape into a giant water feature. I was staying at the Edgewater, the only waterfront hotel in Seattle. Elliott Bay was humming with maritime activity—impossible to see or hear through the torrential downpour, but I could feel it in the force of the waves against the wooden stilts below my room.

"Front desk? Hi, this is Mr. Cummings in room 330. Any messages? I'm expecting an important call." Of course, there were no messages. They would have called. The red light on my phone would be flashing. I hadn't left my room since I had arrived, not even to eat. I'd been holed up for days with room service, waiting for someone at Microsoft to return my calls.

I grabbed a Rolling Rock from the minibar, sat down in a soft chair in front of the gas fireplace, flipped open my donated PowerBook, and logged on to my donated AOL account. The computer screeched and groaned interminably like the death throes of a Japanese movie monster, then said cheerily, "You've got mail!"

It was a week-old email from Douglas Adams to Nathan Myhrvold that I'd marked as "unread" to remind me of my mission: "You remember the conversation we had about gorilla conservation, and the plan to put together a once and for all fund to ensure (as far as is humanly possible) their future survival? The author of that plan

Greg Cummings, is flying over to the West Coast very shortly, and I wonder if you could find the time to see him. He's the head of the UK end of the Dian Fossey Gorilla Fund. He's a good guy and I'm sure you'd enjoy talking to him, and if there's any way you could help us further the plan, we'd be grateful." Although the email was never answered, I'd nevertheless booked my flight on the strength of its author's reputation among America's well-heeled nerds. Nathan was bound to schedule a meeting. How could he turn down an introduction from the inventor of the Infinite Improbability Drive? ("You're never sure of where you'll end up nor what species you'll be when you get there.")

"You've got mail!" It was from Mike Backes in Hollywood: "Nathan was in a spectacularly pissy mood today. I tried valiantly to pitch him, but he was having none of it. I think the guy's a bit overextended."

After shutting my PowerBook, I slowly rose to my feet and walked to the window. Visibility was zero but my vision was clear. I'd come to the Emerald City to tap the largesse of America's economic miracle. But I hadn't been able to arrange a single meeting. As I listened to the tranquil knocking of waves against the hotel, I imagined a ship hidden in the dense fog out there carrying a mysterious cargo: an enormous ape that was shackled below its decks in the hold, his great side heaving as he breathed. Gorillas played a big role in my imagination. I was under their spell, a double agent commingling with Homo while covertly advancing gorilla's agenda.

It was the next day. Sunbeams cut through the Edgewater's smoke-filled lobby. "Cannot fuck this up, Greg," I told myself as I wiped my clammy hands on my chinos and strode toward a waiting car in the forecourt. "The big fellas are counting on me." Driving to Redmond in a black town car, I was filled with trepidation. I'd finally scheduled a meeting with Dr. Nathan Myhrvold, who held a postdoctoral fellowship at Cambridge under Stephen Hawking and was a dinosaur hunter and a master French chef who won first prize several years running in the world barbecue championships in Memphis, Tennessee. He was, by reputation, the smartest polymath in tech. "I don't know anyone I would say is smarter than Nathan," Bill Gates told the *New Yorker*. "He stands out even in the Microsoft environment."

Microsoft, or "the campus," bustled with young, entrepreneurial brogrammers who looked fresh out of college. Blossoms lined the leafy pathways that connected the maze of low-rise buildings. I signed in at Building 9 and was led up to Dr. Myhrvold's modest office on the first floor, a two-module corner office. The smiling thirty-seven-year-old bespectacled expert with ginger-blond hair was less intimidating in person than on paper. "Come in. Sit down," he said merrily.

"Sorry for doorstepping you," I said.

"No, that's OK," he laughed. "You were only doing your job. I apologize for not being more forthcoming to begin with. I didn't realize at first why you wanted to see me." Rocking in his swivel chair, he spoke in a high-pitched, melodious voice that bubbled with wit and enthusiasm. The technology wizard seemed to be chuckling incredulously to himself about the amazing epoch we were living in. We talked about Douglas's books and his involvement with the gorillas. I recounted my recent trip to Zaire, leaving out the gruesome bits. He then told me that not only had his boss met mountain gorillas in the wild but so had his mother. "She got caught in Rwanda just as the genocide began, and she barely escaped the mayhem by crossing into Tanzania on a camel."

"A camel?"

"Yup. What's the population density of Rwanda now?" asked Nathan.

"About 760 per square kilometer," I said, "now that the refugees have returned."

"So, pretty much the same as before. Have you read Jared Diamond's new book, *Guns, Germs, and Steel*? He believes what happened in Rwanda illustrates Malthus's worst-case scenario. In a place where farming depends on handheld hoes and machetes, there's never enough surplus to support fewer farmers, so land is an essential resource just for staying alive. Consequently, when human population growth outruns the growth of food production . . . boom!"

He had seen the news. In a renewed assault, Laurent Kabila and his allied forces were sweeping across Zaire to oust Mobutu from power in Kinshasa. Worried that Africa's bloody chaos would once again upstage the gorillas' moment, I asked, "Would you like to see our plan?" and handed him a proposal.

He leafed through it while listening to me explain how we intended to tackle the threats to the gorillas and guarantee their survival in a goddamn war zone. "There's been conflict in the Congo for nearly a century. And the effort to save gorillas goes back nearly as far. We're used to conservation in conflict. A good deal of experience has gone into preparing this plan," I added. "We think it's got legs and we're hoping you'll put it in front of Mr. Gates."

"Cool," he said, putting the document to one side. We talked some more about this, that, and the other. I hardly needed encouragement to wander off on an irrelevant tangent. We kept each other entertained for about twenty minutes, and at the end of it, Nathan said, "OK. Here's what I can offer you. Your proposal's not there yet, but I'll help you fine-tune it, and when it's ready I'll take it to Bill with my endorsement."

As I left Building 9, I punched the air. "YES!"

I then met Richard Bangs, a whitewater river guide, founder of Mountain Travel Sobek and cofounder and editor at large at Expedia, an online travel agency. Over coffee in the Microsoft cafeteria, the travel guru told me about a dinner he had had with Bill Gates, who'd just returned from seeing mountain gorillas. "He was pessimistic about their prospects," said Richard, "aware of the political problems in the region and the enormous population pressures, and he thought the trend was not good. And at the end of a long conversation that spiraled through dessert, Bill bet me one hundred dollars that within ten years the mountain gorillas would be extinct."

"Huh," I said. "Do you know how incongruous that sounds: world's richest man has a Benjamin riding on an endangered species' extinction? How badly do you think he wants to win?"

Later that day at SEATAC Airport, before catching my flight to San Francisco, I bought a copy of Arthur C. Clarke's new novel, *3001: The Final Odyssey.* I was thrilled to discover the story included Frank Poole getting rescued from his eternal tumbling through space, which had haunted me as a child, and gorillas—genetically enhanced apes doing the heavy lifting for anthropologists excavating at Olduvai Gorge, where the original monolith is discovered. I sent him an email: "Just finished 3001. It is a sublime novel! As a frequent visitor to Olduvai in my youth, I often wondered where the original Monolith might be buried. I'm in San Francisco, midway through a very successful (and fully funded) tour of the US Pacific coast on behalf of the gorillas. I have had meetings with Dr. Nathan Myhrvold (CTO, Microsoft), Jane Metcalfe (President, WIRED) and will meet David Roman (VP Global Branding, Apple) tomorrow and Michael Crichton on Friday. You should be getting some background material any day now."

"Glad you enjoyed 3001!" he wrote back. "Just enjoyed the tape you sent. But how do gorillas get so fat when they only seem to chew on the same stringy piece of stem, without even eating it? Good luck with your trip—regards to Michael—but better not mention me at Microsoft—I chose the winner for HAL's First Words at the U of Illinois Cyberspace. 'I have taken the liberty of removing all Windows 95 programs from my hard drive.'"

Having just appointed Michael Crichton patron of the fund, along with Arthur, Douglas, and Sigourney, I felt a face-to-face meeting with the bestselling author was apt while I was in L.A. But he said he was too busy to meet me. I sent a barrage of emails asking him to reconsider, promised I wouldn't take up much of his time. He wrote back: "Greg, you're being an asshole. And if you continue in this way, I will cease to be a patron of your organization."

I got a similar response from David Gilmour after I pressed him to spare a guitar for our charity when I heard he was donating his entire guitar collection to Shelter, a charity. He called me a hustler. No sweat off my back. Asshole, hustler, ballbuster. I don't apologize. It was all for an important cause.

In a desperate dance of defiance, while Laurent Kabila and his army advanced toward Kinshasa, leaving a trail of massacres in their wake, I advanced down the Pacific Coast of the United States, trying to drum up support from the titans of tech. It was as though a stray bullet from the Congo conflict had hit my campaign in the side and it was staggering on regardless, trying to give the gorillas their best chance yet to survive while slowly bleeding to death. In May 1997, Mobutu fled Kinshasa and the "libérateurs" entered the capital without much resistance. The next day, Kabila declared himself president and renamed the country the Democratic Republic of the Congo.

Douglas was becoming jaded too. In an online chat, when asked how he thought the world should react to what was going on in central Africa, he said, "I have no idea. I was talking today to a friend of mine who runs the Dian Fossey Gorilla Fund UK about the plight of the gorillas in the area, which particularly concerns me, and it seems to me that over the period of time that I have been interested in these kinds of issues that virtually anything that anyone tries to do from outside has wildly different effects than those one intends and I must say that I now feel terribly pessimistic about coming up with new and better ideas about how to help."

"Don't get me started on Gates," said John Perry Barlow (JPB). It was nine o'clock at night and we were in Jupiter Room at the Sky Blue Hotel in Kisoro, "a 50-bucks-a-night concrete blockhouse with the rooms named after planets," JPB described it in an article he would later publish in *WIRED* magazine. Journalist, Wyoming cattle rancher, lyricist for the Grateful Dead, and cognitive dissident, JPB had joined tech entrepreneurs Eckart Wintzen and Jonathan Bulkeley and me on my first ever "Voyage to Virunga." Sitting on lumpy mattresses under a naked bulb, we were sharing a joint that Eckart had smuggled in from Holland in his shaving kit. Our room was located next to a latrine, and a urine-infused funk hung in the chilly mountain air that the cannabis smoke went some way to masking. "Bill lives in a world of his own," continued JPB, "breathing nothing but his own fumes. You'll be lucky if he even acknowledges your appeal."

"But he's met gorillas in the wild," I said, pausing to hold in a lungful of weed smoke, "like you guys will do tomorrow, you know." I exhaled and then said, "How could he possibly turn us down after an experience like that?"

"Because he's a mercenary."

"When will you be ready to approach him?" asked Eckart. "You need to strike while the iron is hot."

"All our ducks are in a row," I replied, passing him the joint. "We've settled on a $35 million endowment fund, which will bear interest of around $2 million a year—enough to fund a multidisciplinary conservation program . . . forever. It is a one-time investment, made on behalf of humanity, to save the greatest of our global heritage—the gentlest of the great apes—and preserve our link with a million generations past. Business guru Ian Charles Stewart is helping us hammer out the dints in the business plan."

"Ian's a good guy," said Eckart.

"I'm surrounded by good guys," I said. "You hear what Eckart did for us?" I asked JPB. "Gave us $50,000 for the sole purpose of preparing a winning bid to Gates."

"That has got to be the most enlightened donation of all time," said JPB.

"But it makes sense, yah?" said Eckart. "And you've used it well."

"I'm glad you think so," I smiled. "It paid for Mike Backes to travel around the world in eight days, interviewing Nathan Myhrvold, Richard Dawkins, Arthur C. Clarke, and Douglas Adams about why it's so important that we save the endangered mountain gorillas. Mike's currently editing a short film that we're calling *Time to Act*, with music by Pink Floyd. It's part of the dazzling package that I will soon give Nathan so he may present it to Bill."

"Really?" asked JPB. "You got the Floyd to donate music?"

"Yeah, 'Marooned' from their album *The Division Bell*. They licensed it to us for our video, 'for up to ten thousand copies or ten years, whichever comes first,' the contract said."

"Don't fuck this up, Greg," said Eckart.

"I won't," I said, taking a hit on the joint.

"Listen to Eckart," said JPB. "The man's amazingly prescient when it comes to money. And he's got a Midas touch. Even the ventures he dabbles in become runaway successes."

"Don't put that shit in your article!" cried Eckart. Like other successful Dutch people I'd met, Eckart Wintzen was somewhat uncomfortable with the trappings of wealth. It was a Calvinist thing. Still, he ran his company, Ex'tent, in a castle surrounded by a moat. He'd just retired as head of Origins, a company he bought for ten guilders and then thirty years later sold to Phillips for $1 billon. Now, according to a recent article in *WIRED*, he was looking to change the basis of the world economy, eliminate global unemployment, and save the environment. JPB took a hit of grass and assured Eckart he wouldn't mention him in his piece.

"The vibe here is so different," said JPB. "People we see along the road smile and wave. I see them waving even from the distant fields, genuinely glad to see us. Imagine average Americans smiling and waving at a carload of passing Africans."

Pie-eyed and relaxed in our pungent Jovian digs, we coughed and laughed about this and that. And all the while JPB wrote. During the entire nine hours that it took us to reach gorilla country by road from Kampala the day before, JPB's PowerBook remained open on his lap as he banged out his piece for *WIRED*. "I'm on my way to see gorillas. It's not clear whether the trek will really relate to my main mission, but I'm persuaded that there is a role for the Net in figuring out how to deal with the international and interagency information flows—information that is critical to the survival of the 600 or so remaining mountain gorillas. Also, on this junket would be Jonathan Bulkeley of America Online UK, who is part of an effort to get continuous data on the gorillas online. . . . Jonathan plans to report from the rain forest to a special gorilla section on AOL using the satphone, to which he has finally been able to connect his PC."

Douglas Adams had originally said he would join us too, but as he prepared for the launch of his digital game, *Starship Titanic*, work and family commitments got in the way. I was disappointed. But then he had already met mountain gorillas in Zaire and was already our most devoted patron. My idea for Voyage to Virunga, or V2V, was to put powerful people in front of gorillas so that thereafter word of the cause would circulate in powerful circles. We also wanted to explore how we might take visitors to meet mountain gorillas via the Internet: a virtual trek. Only two of the ten habituated groups were accessible to tourists then so the concept of a virtual gorilla tour made sense. It was certainly one way to expose the conservation threats to a global audience without ecological impact. I planned to host a series of V2Vs over the next two years to introduce influential supporters to the difficulties we were facing in the Virungas, while at the same time develop a platform for virtual gorilla trekking.

Early the next morning, before sunup, we set out to find the Nyakagezi group in Mgahinga National Park. Hours later, after crawling on our hands and knees through a bamboo forest, we came upon the gorillas in a clearing. JPB had a ripped sleeve and was bleeding from a couple of places, and his palms were burning from a giant stinging nettle he'd tried to grasp along the way, but he couldn't contain his excitement about meeting Bugingo the silverback: "Now they come closer and peer at my PowerBook. I am pretty sure this is the first time a wild mountain gorilla has ever seen a computer." (Well, no, actually—that was five years earlier in Rwanda, thanks to Dieter, Mtwali, and me.)

Soon after leaving the gorillas, Jonathan Bulkeley took the opportunity to download the pictures he had taken to his computer. He then opened the sat phone and emailed thirty-minute-old digital pictures to AOL to upload into the online area. Within minutes a gorilla photo was online. He then posted a report and conducted a live chat over a satellite phone and answered questions from AOL subscribers. One wrote, "I just read Jonathan's report, with my 2 kids. I got the kids to close their eyes and imagine they were there with the Gorillas, and this led to them doing some drawings and writing some great poems about endangered species." Now that *was* a world first.

Six months later, Koko the gorilla would also do a live AOL chat, into which I tuned, writing to Douglas about it afterward: "Did you catch Koko the gorilla doing her AOL auditorium last night? Unbelievable! 20,000 people logged on to this momentous cyber-event to learn Koko wants 'food and smokes' for her birthday (Smokes is the name of her kitten). Has anyone thought of studying the kitten? Dr. Francine Patterson secures $7 million plus in annual donations for her foundation but eschews gorilla conservation in the wild."

John Perry Barlow wrote a twelve-thousand-word piece, "Africa Rising," that was published in the January 1998 edition of *WIRED*. I was extremely proud to have an account of my maiden Voyage to Virunga published in such a reputable rag. Even if Kevin Kelly edited out all of JPB's references to the Dian Fossey Gorilla Fund, the article helped galvanize the tech industry and turn them on to the cause. We were becoming practiced at the subtle art of precision PR.

Our endowment proposal now had three weighty endorsements: World Bank resident representative in Rwanda Mr. R. Venkateswaran, professor of primatology at UC Davis Alexander (Sandy) Harcourt, and paleoanthropologist Richard Leakey. On that basis, I reengaged Nathan Myhrvold. We discussed arranging a meeting in Redmond between Bill and the three independent specialists endorsing our approach, at which Bill could cross-examine them about his doubts about our proposal. Nathan also said that Bill would likely want to see an initial donation from another donor before he would seriously consider donating to our $35 million endowment.

So I began to broaden the field, research other wealthy names, find out who knew whom and where their philanthropic interests lay. Rock stars and movie stars lacked the level of disposable income that was necessary to fit the bill. Seattle and Silicon Valley were much better bets. Tech was run by baby boomers who were raised on the Whole Earth Catalog and predisposed to dig environmental causes. Gorillas appealed to them. I appealed to them.

I flew into the West Coast wired for the times. I had a Palm Pilot, which I "hot-synced" with my laptop, a portable modem, and a tri-band mobile phone that worked on either side of the Atlantic and in Africa. Thanks to a donated account from MyDocsOnline, the fund's most important files were stored online: annual reports, strategic plans, funding proposals. With a tap of my Palm Pilot stylus, I could send whatever was stored there to anyone with an email address. I could be reached anywhere and was ready for anything. But success leads to excess. I began to feel entitled. I turned appreciation into expectation, traded my chinos in for 501s, and grew my hair long. I lacked humility. If I'd been less cocky about our successes, we might have had more. Instead, I saw myself as a rock-star fundraiser and began to make this about me. Gorillas may have given me a backstage pass to the world and access to powerful people whose time was more valuable than money, but it was my charm, ready pitch, and faith in Africa that sealed the deal.

In February I hand delivered our appeal package to Nathan in Redmond, Washington. It contained Mike Backes's film *Time to Act*, a high-res copy of the radar image of the gorilla habitat acquired by the space shuttle *Endeavour*, and an elegantly bound, fifty-page business plan clearly explaining how $35 million would guarantee the survival of the endangered mountain gorilla forever.

Next stop: Monterey, California. Kai Krause, inventor of Kai's Power Tools and founder of MetaCreations, had invited me to attend the annual Technology, Engineering and Design (TED) conference at the Monterey Conference Center. Tickets were highly sought after, and TED had sold out months before, but Kai assured me he could get me in. Richard Brandt, the charismatic editor of *Upside* magazine, met me at the Monterey airport, and we drove into town in his sports car convertible.

"Anybody who's anybody attends this gig," said Richard, his long ginger hair flowing in the wind. "If Kai's successful in getting you in, you'll have a host of potential big-gift donors to pitch to. I'd be surprised if Richard Saul Wurman lets you in without a pass, though."

"He's the guy who founded TED, right?"

"Right. And he is also one uncompromising SOB."

"So how did you get a ticket?" I asked.

"I have a press pass."

He dropped me off at my hotel. We arranged to meet at the conference if I ever made it in. I dropped my stuff in my room and set out walking. The Monterey town center was dominated by the conference center, a modern, state-of-the-art building with glass walls and skylights. In its spacious forecourt, a dozen or so concept cars were parked at odd angles and gleaming in the California sunshine. General Motors had sent them down from Detroit. It was as though I had stumbled onto the set of a sci-fi film.

Kai Krause was hard to miss as he stood waiting for me. The German software guru looked like a hippie Nietzsche. The entrance was manned by a force of TED officials checking names and handing out laminated passes threaded with color-coded necklaces. "I was unable to get you a pass," sighed Kai, "but if you meet me at the side door, I can sneak you in."

What the fuck? Was I really going to gate crash a $2,000-a-head gig? But how else would I get inside? I found the side door. Kai opened it and smuggled me in. Soon I was walking tall down the corridors of power. And just as soon, Richard Wurman was on to us. Our shenanigans had not slipped past him. I was the only person not wearing a pass. Still, he didn't go so far as to throw me out. Cheekily, I even posed for a group photo with twelve hundred other delegates, including Billy Graham and Jane Goodall.

Don't ask me how, but during one of the breaks, I managed to get Mike Backes's film *Time to Act* shown in a simulcast room, after David Tate's film about the *Pathfinder* mission to Mars. I reckon it had an audience of around a hundred. Many more saw it in the background as they talked excitedly over coffees about the third culture, the coming convergence, the digerati in the petri dish. The film received some positive reviews from Stewart McBride, Joe Khirallah, Jerrold Spiegel, and *WIRED* cofounder Louis Rossetto. Jane Metcalfe, the other *WIRED* founder and Louis's wife, was also in the room, trying to keep young Orson from barfing. Stewart McBride offered to host a fundraiser for the fund in New York City in May at his company, United Digital Artists, and said he would ask Douglas Adams to be guest of honor. I managed to talk for five minutes to Oracle founder Larry Ellison. My pithy pitch, endowment proposal, and video were warmly received by him and he nodded approvingly. After all, he was already on the board of DFGF International. (Oops!) Who cares? The titans of tech were taking notice of our cause, hearing about our endowment appeal. It seemed the gorillas would have their day.

That evening, Richard Brandt invited me to join him at the Billionaire's Dinner at Cibo, a restaurant in town. He said all the big names in finance, business, philanthropy, and science would be there. As John Brockman, the host of the dinner and the founder of *Edge*, an online magazine, described it, "For one night, the richest people in the world come face-to-face with the most intelligent individuals in history."

Jillian should have been there with me. Together, we would have worked the room more thoroughly, maybe even come away with a few donations. I was one of thirty people there, in the eye of the tech storm, hanging out with a cabal of brilliant minds, the so-called digerati who had achieved so many great successes in new media, and I didn't even raise a dime. Nathan was there too. I spoke to him about Gates. We had been unable to bring together the meeting in Redmond that he had envisaged, but Bill was nevertheless considering our proposal as we spoke, and a decision would be imminent.

Guess who else was there, checking out the ladies? Jeffery Epstein, then head of the Wexner Foundation. We weren't introduced, but if we had been, I'd have recognized a fellow high-functioning narcissist.

After the dinner, I stood outside Cibo and tried to hail a cab. Next to me stood Jeff Bezos, who was trying to do the same. I struck up a conversation with him and tried valiantly to pitch the gorillas. "My wife handles all our charitable donations," he said dismissively.

"Does your wife like wildlife?" I asked.

"She likes jazz."

My nerve and swagger in the corridors of power and ivory towers of tech was because I knew we were doing such exceptional work in the field. Jillian and Luiz Fabbri were designing a durable and effective gorilla conservation program. The idea was that if the people living adjacent to the gorillas gained some benefit from the gorillas' protection, they would become the front line of their conservation. Many African wildlife parks at the time were distributing a portion of their gate fees to communities, thereby incentivizing them to respect the park, but the locals had no stake in it. They were excluded from decision-making.

Our strategy was different. We showed the local communities the consequences that encroachment into protected areas would have on their own livelihoods. In Rwanda, honey collection was a problem. Local honey collectors would tramp into the forest and use bundles of burning sticks to smoke out the bees from wild beehives before collecting the honey. Occasionally fires started, with dire consequences for the gorillas and the bees. So we brought in wooden hives and partnered with a Rwandan beekeeping NGO to teach modern beekeeping to the locals. They soon saw the wisdom of setting up hives outside the forest and letting just the bees venture inside. The result was more honey, so we then teamed up with the honey marketing board to find a market for the surplus.

In time, we would set up resource centers in the three mountain gorilla range states: Rwanda, Uganda, and Congo. The centers were an evolution of our concept to build a state-of-the-art conservation center on the edge of the park, which proved too impractical. The resource centers would act as information nodes where visitors could find out more about the mountain gorillas. The centers would also provide a focus for the dozen grassroots organizations that we were now funding as part of our field program. These organizations were variously involved in microcredit, water provision, beekeeping, and education in art, farming, and conservation.

Jillian and Luiz formed FONCE, a network of local conservationists. FONCE was a new, grassroots force for conservation. Wildlife authorities were represented. Their rangers were among the bravest conservationists in the world, staying at their posts no matter what crisis was hurled at them. One of the most active members of FONCE was Magasin Equatorial des Arts (MEA), which was based around a core group of graduates of the Gisenyi School of Art in Rwanda. The fund provided tools and materials so they could begin producing original artworks for exhibition. As a result, embassies and hotels in the capital began showing their work. We also gave them a permanent workshop next to our Ruhengeri resource center. Jean-Marie Matabuzi, the head of MEA, who was a talented artist, explained that they had "started helping street children traumatized by the genocide make sense of their experiences by using art as a means of expression." Who else in wildlife conservation was doing this? At that time, no one.

———————

After four months of arm-twisting by Nathan, Bill Gates finally asked his father, who was then director of his foundation, to look into the gorilla donation in more detail. Hence, I began corresponding with Bill Gates's dad, who was also called Bill Gates. His main area of concern was the gorilla range state governments. "What can you tell us about the geography and politics? What countries are involved? What action is necessary on those countries' parts to affect your program? What is going on that indicates, one way or the other, that they will cooperate?"

After consulting my gorilla gurus, I sent Bill's dad a comprehensive response to his questions and then pressed him for a face-to-face meeting. We received an email from Suzanne Cluett at the foundation saying, "Mr. Gates has asked that I respond to your request for a meeting in Seattle. We would be pleased to meet with you." Finally, a breakthrough.

Jillian joined me on this trip. We planned to drive California State Route 1, through Big Sur, and then rendezvous with Douglas Adams in Santa Barbara. First stop, the lobby of the Edgewater, at 9:00 AM on August 12, for our meeting with the William H. Gates Foundation.

Bill Gates Sr. was a towering man in his midsixties. He wore blue check shirtsleeves and chinos. There was a calmness about him that his son had apparently not inherited. Suzanne Cluett was a not-for-profit veteran who had hands-on experience in the developing world. She asked most of the questions. We sat on soft chairs beneath a balustrade. The lobby had a large stone fireplace and floor-to-ceiling windows overlooking Elliott Bay. With his eyes closed, Bill listened intently to our presentation. Jillian and I gave the pitch of our lives, in spite of a hotel cleaner pushing a vacuum cleaner across the balustrade above us with a deafening whine.

"We'll consider it," said Bill at the conclusion of our ninety-minute meeting. He shook Jillian's hand and then mine. "We'll let you know as soon as possible."

After they left, we high-fived each other and paced back and forth across the lobby in a state of utter excitement. "We did it! We pitched the richest guy in the world. Well, his dad."

"I could have strangled that cleaning lady," fumed Jillian.

11

WTF?

Timing is a fickle friend. It swings both ways. On the same day as our meeting with Bill Gates Sr. at the Edgewater, a Congolese army major broadcast the following message from a radio station in eastern Congo: "People must bring a machete, a spear, an arrow, a hoe, spades, rakes, nails, truncheons, electric irons, barbed wire, stones, and the like, in order, dear listeners, to kill the Rwandan Tutsis." All hell had broken loose, again. The Second Congo War, a.k.a. the Great War of Africa, had begun. It was to become the deadliest war in modern African history, directly involving eight African nations and twenty-five armed groups. Some five million people are said to have lost their lives as a result.

We couldn't have picked a worse time to appeal to the world's richest man. Throughout the month of August, American news broadcasts showed images of the grisly massacres in the Congo. Who would invest in such a place? And war wasn't the only factor working against us. The US Justice Department had just summoned Bill Gates III to the *United States v. Microsoft Corp.* antitrust trial. In video footage of the deposition that he gave to the Justice Department on August 28, he is clearly under duress, rocking back and forth in his chair. Not the best frame of mind in which to consider saving mountain gorillas.

Jillian and I were nevertheless full of reckless optimism as we drove south on California State Route 1 in our rented convertible. We had become blasé about jungle militias disrupting our gorilla-saving work. It came with the territory. Besides, what could we do about it? Passing through Santa Cruz and Monterey, we joined an official National Scenic Byway, which routes through Big Sur, between Carmel and San Luis Obispo. The sixty-year-old road was as beautiful as it was precarious and, in some places, in dire need of repair. For 116 kilometers, with gravity-defying feats of engineering, it hugged the cliffs of Big Sur. The landscape was breathtaking—Patty Hearst country. I prefer to think of it as Henry Miller country. He wrote about it in *Big Sur and the Oranges of Hieronymus Bosch*. It was the first wilderness that either of us had visited in the United States. The road weaved through a multitude of coastal parks. We saw tree trunks the size of houses and waterfalls pouring out of cliff-top forests onto the beaches below. We took note of the park infrastructure and signage and struck up conversations with the rangers, who were naturally intrigued by our cause and the people involved. Part of our modus operandi was to make other park rangers we met in the world aware of our brave environmental warriors in Virunga who were protecting the world's few remaining mountain gorillas against impossible odds.

We stopped for lunch at Nepenthe, a cliff-topping restaurant with sweeping views. I had an Ambrosiaburger, and Jillian had the roast chicken with sage stuffing. The restaurant opened in 1949 and was once a favorite haunt of the Beat generation. It is owned and operated by the same family today. From our table on the patio we could see the flanks of the Santa Lucia Range leading to the ocean and miles and miles of blue Pacific fading into a ravaging fog. We stayed the night at Plaskett Creek near the highway. There were no phones, no TV, no influences from the outside world, no Congo war to worry about. Quiet simplicity. The wilderness embraced us. Magical.

Americans love live music. In every town, no matter how small, that we visited on our way down the coast of California, a live band was playing in a bar. In San Luis Obispo, we stayed at a crossroads motel—nothing special. Built in the 1960s, the motel had an enormous cafeteria made of chrome and Formica. But the floors were carpeted, which led us to believe this was considered a swanky joint. We were the only ones in there when we ordered our dinner—apart from an old White guy playing an electric piano on an otherwise empty stage. He was pretty good, played a few jazz standards. More remarkable was the change in atmosphere as, for every new song he played, he was joined by an additional band member who'd walk onstage, pick up an instrument, and accompany the old guy, until a dozen musicians were up there, including a horn section, blasting out big band favorites to a cafeteria that was now full of revelers.

The next day we visited Hearst Castle in San Simeon, a palatial pile on a hill that was built by William Randolph Hearst, Patty Hearst's granddaddy. It was a mecca for decadence during the golden age of Hollywood in the 1920s. Charlie Chaplin, Cary Grant, the Marx Brothers, Greta Garbo, Buster Keaton, Winston Churchill, Jean Harlow, and Clark Gable all partied there. In 1958, four years after Patty was born, the Hearst Corporation donated the castle, its gardens, and many of its contents to the state of California. It was turned into a museum. Orson Welles's seminal movie *Citizen Kane* was loosely based on the life of William Randolph, who tried to have the movie banned. In it, Charles Foster Kane's palace Xanadu is said to contain "paintings, pictures, statues, the very stones of many another palace—a collection of everything so big it can never be cataloged or appraised; enough for ten museums; the loot of the world."

Welles had nailed it. Hearst Castle was the mac and cheese of architecture, a hodgepodge of styles from a mix of old-world countries, carelessly thrown together in an impossible mishmash of periods. Nothing matched. Jillian bought a copy of the recipe book that was used for the lavish parties they threw at the castle for Hollywood's crème de la crème. "I don't believe it," she said. "Every recipe calls for a tin of Campbell's cream of mushroom soup." No self-respecting European aristo would ever set foot in such an abomination. (Well, except Churchill.)

My wife and I were not highborn. *Au contraire*! But we were snobs, especially when it came to aesthetics. Our loathing may have been swayed by the fact that we never got a dime out of the Hearst Foundation, but we both agreed Hearst Castle was gauche. The previous year, my wife and I had stayed at Villa Cetinale, a seventeenth-century baroque villa in Tuscany that was the epitome of sophistication. We'd been invited by Claire Ward and her partner Lord Lambton. Christabel Holland and Lambton's son, Baron Durham, were summering there too. The baron claimed he'd driven down from London in his Porsche in just eleven hours. Only possible if he'd managed to maintain an average speed of eighty miles an hour through France. I doubt the *gendarmerie nationale* would have let him get away with that kind of impudence.

As guests of the owners, we spent the night in a four-poster bed in one of the villa's thirteen lavish bedrooms. It was by far the most opulent bed we'd ever slept in. The room was decorated in seventeenth-century fabrics, tapestries, and paintings, and had a secret door that led through a labyrinth of service corridors in between the walls. The villa was built in 1680 by Cardinal Flavio Chigi for Pope Alexander VII, who was born Fabio Chigi. Joseph Forsyth, an English traveler, noted in 1800: "Cetinale . . . owes its rise and celebrity to the remorse of an amorous cardinal who to appease the ghost of a murdered rival transformed a gloomy oak plantation into a penitential retreat, and acted there, all the austerities of an Egyptian hermit." The villa stayed in the Chigi family until 1978, when Claire Ward and Lord Lambton bought it for a mere £90,000.

Because of her unyielding support, we had just made Claire a patron of the fund. She knew the cause well and was an ardent champion of wildlife. Her daughter, actress Rachel Ward, was married to Bryan Brown, who played Bob Campbell in *Gorillas in the Mist*. "In the 1950s," Claire told us, "when I was in my twenties, I embarked on a flying boat tour of East Africa that took me to Lake Kivu at the foot of the Virungas. The safari was facilitated by my great uncle, Evelyn Baring, 1st Baron Howick of Glendale, who was then governor of Kenya—the last governor."

Lord Lambton was an affable man: "Please call me Tony." He wore an off-white linen suit and bow tie and had a blue handkerchief tucked into his jacket pocket and pair of black spectacles perched atop his prominent nose. Over lunch in the villa garden, he told us amusing anecdotes from his time in Parliament. He'd once been part of a delegation that traveled to Cuba after the revolution. "I knew my room was being bugged," he said, "so I sat there and read poetry to the eavesdroppers all night: Yeats, as I recall."

Jillian sat next to him, basking in his gentrified glow, and listening intently to his stories while lighting her cigarettes off his cigar. She knew his backstory. In 1973 Lord Lambton's liaisons with call girls were revealed in the *News of the World*. He'd been secretly photographed by a prostitute's husband, who then sold the photos to Fleet Street. A subsequent police search of Lambton's home found a small amount of cannabis. (Word!) After the scandal, he resigned from government, separated from his wife, and bought Villa Cetinale in Tuscany, where he lived happily ever after with Claire. They never married.

As a big-gift fundraiser, I feel it is worth noting the different giving styles of wealthy Americans and wealthy Britons. Claire Ward was one of two major donors we had endeared to the fund from the British upper classes. The other was Sir Kenneth Kleinwort, 3rd Baronet and head of Dresdner Kleinwort Bank. Sir Kenneth was the first big-gift donor with whom I tried to build a relationship. The fund was just getting started when he called and asked to meet me at my office. He was soft spoken and lionhearted. He had served for many years on the main council of WWF and devoted much of his time to conservation issues. He gave me a cheque for £30,000.

Sadly, a month after our meeting, at the age of fifty-nine, Sir Kenneth died of heart failure. Thereafter his widow, Madeleine, Lady Kleinwort, took up the baton and continued to fund us. She became our first patron. And when we needed to secure funding for our new regional coordinator for development, Madeleine stepped up and paid his salary for three years. The Ernest Kleinwort Charitable Trust became the fund's foremost benefactor.

Toffs can also be quite tight-assed. I visited Lord Forbes in Aberdeenshire one winter. He picked me up from the airport in his Land Rover. I expected the foremost Laird of Scotland to speak with a deep burr but he sounded like an eccentric Etonian. "We're very proud to have a nesting pair of osprey at Balforbes," he said as we drove over the snow-laded countryside of his vast estate. "There's the tree where they roost."

We drove for another forty-five minutes before reaching Castle Forbes. "Oh no, we don't live there," he said. "That's where our American cousins stay when they visit." Farther down the road, we pulled up outside a nondescript, prefab 1950s bungalow. "This is where we live."

Nigel and Rosemary Forbes were superb hosts. However, I wished I'd brought a thicker sweater as they were reluctant to turn up the heating. I stayed a couple of nights. They hosted a dinner for me and invited a local conservationist and a Texan oil magnate, Anne Savage, who later donated a five-figure sum. And when my weekend at Balforbes was over and I was about to return to London, his lordship handed me a cheque for £120.

The English aristocracy will go all around the houses to avoid any discussion of money—noblesse oblige—whereas Americans are predisposed to make big gifts. I've walked into offices in the United States where the checkbook was already on the desk, ready to be cut. They knew why I was there and quickly got to the point. Time is money. Of course, neither of these trends applies to middle-income givers on either side of the Atlantic who donate a higher proportion of their income to charity than the wealthy do. Meanwhile, at the time that we were working their turf, philanthropy had yet to take hold among the tech titans. They were too preoccupied with code and product to worry about good causes. And who can blame them? That's their business.

Some potential benefactors were more forthcoming than others. Jillian and I had begun our road trip at the Apple headquarters in Cupertino. "Hello, (again)" proclaimed a giant blue inflatable computer wobbling in a warm wind blowing across the leafy grounds. Steve Jobs was once again CEO of Apple, and the company was rolling out its very first iMac. Whether excited by the promise of a brighter future or the free beer, Apple staffers seemed to have gotten their mojo back. The atmosphere was electric. Jillian and I had come to discuss a donation of Macs with Kanwal Sharma, who ran AppleMasters, a group of influential Mac users who helped promote the brand globally. Kanwal gave us no prior warning that our visit would coincide with a major product launch at Apple. "Come," he said, "I'll introduce you to my boss."

Standing next to the inflatable iMac, dressed in a black T-shirt and jeans, Steve Jobs calmly drank beer from a plastic cup. Naturally, as soon as we were introduced, we pitched him. He was inattentive and punctuated each of our points with a dismissive "Cool," like how other people say, "Fuck off." I saw straightaway that our passion for the big fellas had no traction with Jobs. That's how it goes. No matter how wealthy they may be, you cannot make people give.

On the other hand, Apple's senior vice president of hardware engineering, Jon Rubinstein, was interested in what we had to say, and asked about trekking gorillas. I told him about V2V, our virtual gorilla treks, and the work we were doing with his technology in the field.

Next to Rubinstein stood Jonathan Ive, the company's thirty-one-year-old British designer. The iMac was his baby—the first in a range of stunningly innovative products he would design for Apple over the coming decade, including the iPod, iPhone, and iPad. He was wearing a blue silk shirt identical in color to the iMac.

"How did you manage to find a shirt exactly the same color as your computer?" asked Jillian.

"Other way around," laughed Ives. "I bought the shirt on Bondi Beach a few years back, and then used it as the color swatch for iMac's translucent shell. I call it Bondi Blue."

"Cool!" I said.

We ended our road trip at Walt Disney Animation Studios in Burbank, where we met Kevin Lima and Chris Buck, directors of the new animated film *Tarzan*. They gave us a tour of the "set": a hive of animation cells connected by corridors decorated with large images of the story's main characters. Every frame of the movie was drawn in one of those cells by an animator working on an easel. The image was then scanned and, with massive rendering power, made to run in sequence. (*"Aah-eeh-ah-eeh-aaaaaah-eeh-ah-eeh-aaaaah!"* cried Tarzan.)

Buck and Lima told us the team had researched exhaustively to prepare for animating gorillas: attended lectures on primates, made trips to zoos, witnessed a gorilla dissection to learn about its musculature, even visited Bwindi Impenetrable Forest in Uganda to observe how mountain gorillas behave in the wild, and to gather inspiration for the setting. The movie's breathtaking sweeping backgrounds evoked the real thing, which required a rendering technique known as Deep Canvas, software that keeps track of brushstrokes applied in 3D space. We asked them if the gorillas could be the beneficiary of *Tarzan's* premiere. They agreed to consider it, but in the end, Disney gave the premiere to the Los Angeles Zoo. For all that benefited the well-being of gorillas in the wild, they may as well have given it to the Akeley Hall of African Mammals in New York City.

We spent a night in Santa Barbara. Douglas Adams, who had relocated there to oversee Disney's script rewrites for its movie production of *The Hitchhiker's Guide to the Galaxy*, invited us to attend a dinner in *our* honor at Emilio's, a bistro on the Santa Barbara waterfront. A hero's welcome awaited us in the restaurant at the end of our journey. Seated at a large table were Kai Krause, Savannah Brentnall, Jody Boyman, Berkeley Breathed, and Douglas Adams. Mike Backes arrived late in his gold Porsche 928 that he'd driven down from L.A. Over a lavish vegetarian meal, Jillian and I regaled our friends with tales of our Pacific Coast journey, how we'd sealed the deal on the Gates appeal, and had pitched some of the most influential people in tech.

"Timing is everything," I said. "I mean, to have shown up on the day they launched the iMac. It didn't take much to get them to agree to a further donation of Apple gear."

Douglas, who was befuddled by a magic trick involving a cork that Mike had just shown him, looked up at me and beamed proudly. "How many AppleMasters do you have now?"

"Eight," I said.

"That must constitute an orchard," he quipped.

———

A week later, in London, I received a letter from Bill Gates Sr. informing us that the foundation would *not* support our effort at this time. Really? Not? It continues to be a knot in my old brain. How could they? Our proposal was sound—still is. They knew the yearslong effort we had put into it, the great and the good who we'd rallied to get behind it. Gates had even visited gorillas in the wild and called them one of the natural wonders of the world. I guess he really wanted to win that hundred-dollar bet with Richard Bangs. The political uncertainty of the region combined with the "multiplicity of the agencies working in this area" were the reasons he gave. I never figured out what he meant by "multiplicity of the agencies." I suspect there may have been foul play behind the scenes. I wouldn't put it past DFGF International to have sabotaged our bid by bad-mouthing me to Gates, despite the setback this would cause for the gorillas. But I had no proof of that.

With heavy heart I conveyed the sad news to a stone-faced gathering of our field staff in London. Mt. T. manager Vital Katembo and regional coordinator Luiz Fabbri had flown in for three days of strategy meetings. "We did our utmost," I sniffed. "We gave this damn appeal its best possible chance of success. It couldn't have helped that civil war broke out in Congo just as Bill Gates was deliberating, but this is the very nature of the beast and the reason why a privately funded endowment is the only way to ensure that mountain gorillas survive."

Determined to make a silk purse out of a sow's ear, I browsed the *Forbes* list of the world's five hundred richest people on the web, researched the wealthiest of them, and gleaned as many names and addresses as I could find before sending my prospects an appeal for the beleaguered Congo rangers. It was a cold mailing that I hoped would engender a new crop of prospects. I also sent a reply to Bill Sr.: "Thank you for your letter of August 26th. As you can imagine, we were surprised and dismayed by your rejection to our proposal for an endowment to save the endangered mountain gorillas. . . . I am somewhat baffled by your reference to the multiplicity of the agencies working in this area. Could you please clarify how this situation might be improved?" No clarification was ever made.

It was late afternoon on the final day of our strategy meetings. My colleagues were preparing to fly back to Africa. We were drinking pints of lager at a long wooden table at Pembroke Castle in Primrose

Hill. No one was saying much. It was a dark day for the gorillas. Just then a gleaming blue Porsche 911 pulled up outside, engines roaring. A giant of a man emerged, unfolded himself onto the street, and then strode through the pub door. It was Douglas Adams. He had come to join us for a farewell drink.

We embraced. "Thank you for all your help in trying to make this work for the gorillas, mate," I said. I introduced him to my colleagues. For the next hour, as we quaffed pints of Abbot Ale, Douglas entertained them with anecdotes from his global travels while researching *Last Chance to See*.

Congo was of particular interest to Vital. Evident by his hysterics, he had read the story of the obfuscating border official. "If we ever get a UN High Commission for Great Apes," Vital said to Douglas, "you'll be general secretary." We talked about the Mount Tshiaberimu project, for which Michael Crichton's two-year funding had just come to an end. Vital had identified a gorilla group of seven gorillas with two infants. It was the first close encounter with these remote, shy, and rare gorillas in over ten years, and they were now being monitored daily.

"Photos are on their way from central Congo," I said. "The board has asked us to make big PR of this."

Douglas wore his heart on his sleeve, and when an idea struck him, he could become quite animated about it. He would often call me up at the office to relate some new notion he had about gorillas. One time he asked me what I thought of the aquatic ape theory, the idea that our ancestors were more inclined to wade in water than other great apes. I told him I thought it was a distraction from the real issues facing endangered gorillas. That was me, a one-topic dilettante who only felt confident discussing subjects I'd previously researched. The fund was debating changing its name to better reflect the work we were doing, and I asked for his advice.

His response was unequivocal: "I really think it's a bad idea! I think that organizations sometimes change their names out of a kind of restlessness, but it's not a good use of time and resources. The name Dian Fossey is well known and recognized and also gives a distinctive label to DFGF. Change it, and a lot of people who aren't necessarily paying day-to-day attention will simply see yet another apparent gorilla charity and think, 'Oh God, another one, I can't keep up.' And if they do realize that it's the same organization, then a change of name often rings alarm bells that something's not right somewhere. Like Windscale changing to Sellafield. When the WWF changed their name from the World Wildlife Fund to the World Wide Fund for Nature, at a cost of £250,000, I was so outraged I stopped giving them any donations—that wasn't what I thought I was funding. A name is merely a label—you don't change the thing by changing its name. A lot of people know, recognize, and respect the organization you've been instrumental in building up which has a name they're familiar with. Don't jeopardize that goodwill!"

———

"Greg, Birken Productions is on line two," said Rose, looking back at me from her desk in the adjoining office, "calling from L.A." It took me a second before I recalled recently seeing the name "Birken" on a letterhead.

"Holy shit!" I picked up my desk phone and punched the line.

"This is Irmelin DiCaprio," said the caller, "Leonardo's mother. I believe my son sent you a check for $25,000. The problem is, he wrote it against his personal account, which is not tax-deductible. Would you mind tearing it up, and we'll send you a new one, this time from his foundation?"

"I wish I could," I sighed, "except that I've already banked it."

"In that case, may we send you a form to fill out for tax purposes?" Leonardo DiCaprio's donation was in response to my cold appeal for Congo's rangers. The actor had just established the Leonardo

DiCaprio Foundation. We also received $10,000 from Herbert A. Allen, president and CEO of Allen & Co, the largest private bank in America. My revenge mailing had paid off.

But processing donations from the United States wasn't so straight-forward. The US government did not consider gifts to foreign charities to be tax-deductible, so to process those gifts we channeled them through the American Fund for Charities, a 501(c)(3) as it's known in the trade. Philanthropists with foundations, however, cut their checks from an already taxed sum, as was the case with Herbert Allen, who then invited me to meet him in New York City.

I wasted no time. Within a month, I was in his office on the fourth floor of the Coca-Cola Building on Fifth Avenue. On a bourbon-soaked bender the night before, I had been advised by my buddy Robert to travel to my meeting the next morning by subway, otherwise known as the poor man's helicopter. A torrential downpour turned Grand Central Terminal into a waterfall. Nevertheless, I arrived ten minutes early for my 8:00 AM meeting.

Herbert invited me to enter straightaway. In a wood-paneled room with a leather couch where his hound dog Holler slept, Herbert served up cappuccinos, then asked, "How did you find me? Am I on some list?" Turns out he'd been to meet gorillas a number of times, once while Dian Fossey was still alive. It was better he didn't know about my arbitrary selection process, that I simply lifted his name from the *Forbes* 500. I told him about V2V and asked if he wished to visit the gorillas again. He said he'd consider it if he could bring a sidearm. He then wrote me a check for $30,000. "I won't hand over my address book," he said as I was about to leave. "But I'll recommend you to my friends."

I'd also arranged to meet Arne Glimcher at the Pace Gallery. I wanted to ask him about the possibility of rereleasing *Gorillas in the Mist*, which he had produced. I told Sigourney Weaver about the meeting, but she had a scheduling conflict, so it would be just Arne and me. My buddy Robert, who was putting me up in his apartment in Lower Manhattan, drove me to this meeting in his sky-blue Lincoln Continental convertible with white upholstery. He said he would wait for me.

"What if there's no available parking?" I asked.

"That's OK," said Robert. "I'll just drive around the block. New Yorkers love this car."

Arne Glimcher was welcoming and friendly. We met in his office upstairs in the Pace Gallery. Since he had become a power player in Manhattan's art scene, Hollywood had become a distant memory. "I looked into it," he sighed. "And on paper, the movie failed to make a profit."

"Really?" I laughed. "That's surprising given its popularity among our constituents."

"Yeah, and it's also not true. It's an accountancy trick that all the studio executives play. In its first year, the movie did so poorly at the box office that it was projected to go into the red. From then on, studio execs began billing their various trips to Europe and China, and wherever else they saw fit to travel on behalf the movie business, against *Gorillas in the Mist*'s budget. Sadly, this means it's highly unlikely Universal Studios will consider rereleasing it. I'm sorry. I wish I had better news."

That was it. Our meeting had lasted just nine minutes. I was about say goodbye when Arne's assistant buzzed his intercom: "Ah, Sigourney Weaver is here to join the meeting."

The long-legged movie star walked straight up to me, planted a kiss squarely on my lips, and then turned to Arne and said, "This man gets everything done he sets out to do."

Our meeting was back on. We talked for twenty more minutes. Sigourney cajoled Arne into agreeing to show a print of the movie at the Ziegfeld Theatre. For the first time, she also allowed me to take a photo of her without insisting on having her hair done. In the end,

DFGF International would be the sole beneficiary of the Ziegfeld Theatre screening. So what? The gorillas won the day and that's all that fucking matters.

Robert then drove me down Broadway to the Singer Building. In a spacious loft office, I met Dana Giacchetto, moneyman to the stars. Leonardo DiCaprio had asked Dana to organize a gorilla safari for him and his entourage. Dana was dressed in a beige linen Prada suit and seated in a leather swivel chair that he wheeled around the room as he spoke. "Two years ago, we went to Havana," he said. "And last year I was with Leo in Thailand, on the set of *The Beach*. That was a blast. We're thinking around fifty people this time. Let's see who's said they're interested, Tobey Maguire, Cameron Diaz, Billy Corgan, Whoopi Goldberg . . ."

"Whoa," I said, scratching my head. "Fifty people, did you say? That's way too many."

"Get Leo on the phone in L.A.," snapped Dana. Leo got on the phone. "Tell him what you just told me."

"Hi, Leonardo," I said. It was my first time speaking with the actor. "Really excited about you and your friends coming to meet the big fellas. I was just telling Dana here one or two things in preparation of your safari. And I explained that, uh, fifty people would be kinda difficult to fit in, because the maximum number allowed to visit any one gorilla group at any one time is eight, you see. I'd suggest no more than fifteen people. Otherwise, the logistics could be quite a nightmare."

"That's cool," said Leonardo. "We can limit it to fifteen. I'll tell my mom."

"Great. I'll organize the permits." I then briefed him on what to expect while tracking gorillas in the wild, the distance to be kept, the number of people permitted at any one time, the length of time to stay with them, and not being allowed to see any if you've got a cough.

Mike Backes advised me to play Leonardo DiCaprio "like a Stradivarius." I understood what he meant. Getting the Hollywood star involved was a triumph. But he surrounded himself with professional people who were hypervigilant about his image. Ken Sunshine, his "image consultant," was responsible for steering the actor away from any controversy. So it was no surprise that when rumors about Dana Giacchetto's financial impropriety began to circulate after a damning piece was published in *Vanity Fair*, Birken Productions airbrushed him out of the picture, despite his close friendship with Leonardo. As a consequence, I was left with fifteen nonrefundable trekking permits for Leonardo's safari.

At least he was still on board. In an online web chat celebrating Earth Day, when asked which endangered animal he was most concerned about, he said, "Mountain gorillas. Supposedly, now the poaching of mountain gorillas is worse than ever and they are actually starting to use them for food, for nearby warring armies. If you want to help, contact the Dian Fossey Gorilla Fund."

The Dian Fossey Gorilla Fund works internationally to save the mountain gorillas from extinction and ensure local people genuinely benefit from their unique natural heritage.
—Headline banner on DFGF Europe's website

In cyberspace, gorillas were way ahead of the competition. Apple Computer was sponsoring us with donated equipment, while Douglas's company, The Digital Village, was managing our website—www.dianfossey.org—and CTO Richard Harris was advising us on appropriate technologies for our virtual Africa office. Jillian had designed the website and Storm Thorgerson was creating a series of exclusive screen savers—or "Gorilla Savers"—to help launch it. It had four sections: the "Gorilla Story," "Online Adoption," "Latest News," and "Fun Stuff." And it was dynamic. The "650" in "There are fewer than 650 mountain gorillas left in the world" was animated. There were quotes from Douglas Adams ("Mountain gorillas are almost the closest relatives we have and they will die if we don't help them."), Arthur C. Clarke ("Protect these harmless gentle cousins"), and Leonardo DiCaprio ("We CAN make a difference"). It had simplicity of both form and function and was a beautiful work of art.

Apple News interviewed Jillian and me in San Francisco:

> "When we started this," Greg Cummings laughs, "we said to each other, 'What we need is an all-singing, all-dancing, gorilla-loving culture.'" . . . "With iTools," Miller explains, "you can go in and grab the documents you need at your convenience. It gives the staff much more freedom. Even though we work in four countries, it seems like we're working together on a network in an office." . . . "These projects thrive on regular reports, and we've always aimed at providing a direct connection between the donors and the projects," Miller says. But because of the problems of getting information, she adds, it's been difficult to maintain communication with supporters.
>
> "This is where Apple technology can really help," Cummings says. "A few weeks ago, I sent an email through my wireless modem on the PowerBook while I was sitting at the foot of the volcanoes in Uganda. I spoke to my communications consultant in London from within the park, not 20 minutes after sitting with the gorillas. We can do miracles with our Apple technology. . . . The possibilities are endless."

It was precision PR. We got the message to the people who most needed to hear it and galvanized Douglas's efforts to maintain Apple's sponsorship.

The web was where it was at. We were accustomed to online events. Hence, while searching for new fundraising ideas, Douglas suggested "an online celebrity car boot sale." He would invite his friends to donate some eclectic junk, and we'd auction it online for the gorillas, getting eBay to feature it and waive their fee. Turned out to be a bloody good idea. We were gifted a cornucopia of incredible items: Richard Dawkins's complete works, every one of them signed. A large, illustrated copy of *The Hitchhiker's Guide to the Galaxy*, also signed. Bob Campbell's original prints from the walls of Dian Fossey's cabin at Karisoke. David Attenborough's limited-edition copy of *Life on Earth*. One of the most beautiful gifts was a multicolored Senegalese vest that Youssou N'Dour had given to Peter Gabriel when they toured together, which Peter kindly donated to the fund. But the item that fetched the highest price at auction was Sir Paul McCartney's signed artist proof from one of his original artworks, *Pintos in the Sky with Desert Puppy*, which sold for £5,000. Sir Paul and his wife Linda were so chuffed about this that they asked assistant Shelagh Jones to write to me and explore how they could further help the cause. I suggested that Paul host a benefit lunch for the gorillas and invite the titans of tech. He agreed! Our endowment appeal was back on.

As Shelagh Jones gave me a tour of Sir Paul's office, MPL Communications at 1 Soho Square, I was buzzing. *The Beatles built this*, I thought. (Well, not technically, because the Beatles famously did not own their music.) On the second floor was a stately dining room where Sir Paul kept his "magic" piano from the Sgt. Pepper's era, which was painted in a lavish psychedelic design.

"He wrote 'Getting Better,' 'Sgt Pepper's Lonely Hearts Club Band,' and 'Fixing a Hole' on that magic piano," said Shelagh. "He's suggested doing a sing-along after gorilla fundraising lunch."

A private sing-along with Paul McCartney, I thought, my eyes widening. *This is going to be massive.* I was thrilled, too, by the prospect of meeting him and Linda in person, as by then they had made several donations to the fund.

Shelagh informed me, however, that Sir Paul found it hard to retain complex information for longer than a day. "So, if you want him to do your bidding with the billionaires," she smiled, "it's best we postpone meeting him until the day before the lunch." Not patron material, then.

I wrote to everyone with whom I'd previously been in contact among tech's eight-hundred-pound gorillas, inviting them to attend an exclusive lunch with a former Beatle to talk about saving a species. Steve Jobs and Larry Ellison responded positively. Paul Allen prevaricated. Then Shelagh called with even better news, which I immediately relayed to Douglas: "I am sure you'll be pleased to learn that, in addition to Paul McCartney, Ringo Starr has also agreed to join the luncheon—*half the Beatles*—and we've set the date for Wednesday, 16 June 1999."

Douglas naturally assumed that he would also attend the lunch. But I had the great displeasure of informing him otherwise: "A handful of very worthy candidates have suggested, with good reason, that their participation at the Beatles Lunch would advance the Fund's appeal to prospective donors. However, after discussions last week with Shelagh Jones, we have decided it is best if Jillian and I are the sole representatives of the gorillas at this event. With Ringo involved, it's also more important we get the balance right: Paul and Ringo to charm, Jillian and I to consolidate. As much as this may come as a disappointment, please understand that we have but one chance to make our pitch and believe this plan gives us the best opportunity."

I can't believe I fucking wrote that and sent it to him. After all he'd done for us?

He wrote back: "As I mentioned on the phone, absolutely no worries on my part. However, if I earn a few billion dollars in the next three months, I will insist."

Over the next three months, Steve Jobs and Larry Ellison dropped out of the event due to conflicting schedules, but Paul Allen confirmed that he was coming—not least because they weren't. As the Microsoft cofounder was reportedly worth $30 billion at the time, we felt confident that he would make a handsome donation to our endowment. But we hadn't banked on Ringo. With just six days to go before the event, Shelagh Jones called again. "Before he agrees to participate, Ringo wants to know how much Paul Allen's going to give."

What?

In desperation, I sent off emails to all my patrons. Douglas worked frantically behind the scenes and kept providing me with sound advice: "We're not going to get something out of Paul Allen with leverage. . . . Shouldn't try and force anyone into an uncomfortable position. Peter Gabriel is terribly sympathetic—when asked if he can help, however, a sort of hunted look comes over him." Mike Backes replied with, "What? *The Beatles are the door prize?*"

Nathan Myhrvold sent a more considered response: "I am not sure what to say. One fairly obvious point is to double and triple check that Paul McCartney isn't going to flake on you at the last minute for the same reason. That would be a disaster. . . . You can't very well demand the donation up front if that isn't what Paul [Allen] is expecting. Even broaching the topic could be very off-putting . . . don't be presumptive. What if Paul is thinking of donating say $5 million? This would be a very generous gift by any absolute standard, even if it is less than you want. . . . The mix-up with Ringo is very awkward, and very odd. If lunch with the Beatles was a $100,000 a plate fund raising luncheon, then it is proper to make it prepaid. But this isn't that sort of thing—you don't typically have a $30 million a plate fundraising luncheon. At this level of philanthropy it would be odd to ask, 'and if you make the donation you get lunch with the Beatles.' . . . If you show your film, and make a presentation on the overall program, you might not need to literally ask. But, then again, you may well have to. . . . I am not sure what else to say other than good luck!"

My hand was forced; I wrote to Paul Allen explaining that a hiccup had occurred: "Sir Paul and Ringo are keen to meet you but have asked that there be a confirmation of a donation first. I know this is very unconventional and certainly not what you were led to believe would transpire at this luncheon. My only hope is that you understand our predicament and agree to proffer an idea of what you would like to donate. Subsequently, the lunch will go ahead as planned and we can launch our $35 million endowment for the endangered mountain gorillas. Generations will thank you for it."

Allen replied by simply saying, "What?" In the end Paul McCartney did flake, got behind Ringo's mystifying last-minute demand, laying waste to all our plans. I can just hear Richard Starkey, in his Thomas-the-Tank-Engine Scouse drone, saying, "The Beatles were never about money, Paul. We were always about love. . . . All you need is love."

I felt hung out to dry. It was a significant blow to my ego, and an embarrassment. But I guess I needed that. I sat under a tree on a park bench at the top of Primrose Hill. The air bristled with the freshness of spring. A strong wind blew, rustling through the newborn leaves. Mother Nature's soothing hush tones were not enough to keep me from sobbing, however. "Nobody ever hears me," I wept, paraphrasing the Beatles. "Or the sound I appear to make." Seeing the mock-up animal habitats in the Regent's Park zoo below me, I wondered, *Is this all the future holds for the gorillas: incarceration for our pleasure? Damn you all to hell!*

To comfort myself, I reached over the top of my head with my right arm to touch the left side of my face, like a gorilla might do, and wiped the tears away. No question, I'd let the big fellas down. Handing in my resignation would have been the honorable thing to do, but I stayed on.

Imagine where the gorillas would be today if our endowment appeal had been successful, the standard of innovation in conservation we would be applying in the field. We'd likely have gorilla cams in the forest monitoring their movements, thermal cameras to trigger auto-mated alerts for rangers when suspected poachers cross into the park, real-time gorilla trekking in their habitats using virtual reality, haptic devices feeling the path of least resistance, a high-tech gorilla con-servation center featuring an exhibit of silverback holograms, and an all-singing, all-dancing, gorilla-loving culture. Most important, we'd have peace of mind. Oh man, it still makes me weep to think about how it all fell through in the end. It should have worked!

12

OUR DNA

After the fallout from the Beatles nonlunch, I wrote to Douglas Adams and tried to put a positive spin on things:

> Dear Douglas, obviously we've repudiated Dian Fossey's fear that gorillas would be both discovered and extinct in the same century. Unless a Virunga volcano erupts, we should be clear of that infamy. But we're still a long way from saving them.
>
> Still, thanks to your good guidance and generosity of vision, we have taken the plight of the mountain gorillas to some of the richest people in the world—Bill Gates, Paul Allen, Michael Dell. It's been a heady journey, Douglas, but worth every effort even if we're not there yet. I hope your move to Santa Barbara is a success for you and your family but let's not let the distance between us restrict the regular inspiration you have given us in the London office.
>
> The Fund is making some fundamental changes in its strategy plan this year, despite not yet securing our endowment. Because we are finally raising the kinds of funds necessary to conduct some long-term planning in a war-torn central Africa. Next year, we aim to move our Africa HQ from Kigali, Rwanda to Kampala, Uganda which will bring down

our operating costs. We will also find it easier to operate in an English-speaking country. When I first wrote to you in 1994, we were a small organization, raising £250,000 a year to fund a stop-and-go Karisoke research center. Now, thanks to you and others, we're £1 million organization.

Miraculously, the gorillas have survived this decade of war in central Africa better than we feared and will probably continue to be relatively ok. We have not secured our endowment yet but I believe we are close.

In response, Douglas relayed a note he'd received from David Gilmour suggesting we approach Disney. "Their PR machine could make that one run and run," wrote the Pink Floyd guitarist. "If the bloody Beatles can't afford it maybe Walt can." Sadly, the Magic Kingdom was out of reach, even after Michael Hawley had given me the keys with contacts at the company's highest level. "Hands off Disney," I was told by Terry Maple, president of DFGF International's board. The US charity was now based in Atlanta, Georgia. Terry, director of Zoo Atlanta and boss of zoo bosses, was a fleshy man who threw his ample weight around. As instructed by him, I handed my Disney contacts over to our sister charity, where they withered and died on the vine. Now nobody had access to the Magic Kingdom. That's because, whether in sales or fundraising, clients don't like being handed off to someone else. People do business with people they like. Remember that.

At the turn of the millennium, we received another letter from Bill Sr.: "It is a pleasure to inform you that the Bill and Melinda Gates Foundation has approved a grant of $10,000 to The Dian Fossey Gorilla Fund. This grant is made in response to your request dated December 13, 1999. A check in the amount of $10,000 is enclosed. If an announcement is to be made of this award, we feel that it should come from The Dian Fossey Gorilla Fund at whatever time and in whatever form you consider to be most appropriate. However, we would like to have the opportunity to comment in advance on the proposed release."

"That's approximately one ten-millionth of his net worth," said Douglas. "Good going, Bill." To mark a new century for mountain gorillas, the world's richest man had made a five-figure donation on the promise the fund would put his name on a plaque in the Virungas that would honor his patronage. Somehow, as much as I tried, I never did manage to get that darn plaque made. Boomlay, boomlay, boomlay, boom.

Even after moving to Santa Barbara, Douglas remained active as a patron and did not give up on trying to find a donor for our $35 million endowment. "Do you know anything about Wendy McCaw?" he wrote. "I didn't until I read a piece about her in today's *LA Times*. She's the billionaire ex-wife of Craig McCaw, she's very quiet and publicity shy; she's an environmentalist and she lives in Santa Barbara. . . . Maybe I should try to reach her." He planned to do an interview for her newspaper in which he would emphasize his support for wildlife conservation—in the hope that she would read it and it would strike a chord.

I wrote to Douglas in the autumn with a new proposal: "I wanted to discuss Kanwal's idea of an Apple Masterclass in Rwanda with you. He suggested this as a way Apple could get involved in our effort to train project partners in web design and construction. He is keen to get in touch with the right people at Macromedia and Adobe before I get to SF and has asked me to draft a paper. We would like to get some AppleMasters involved to add the PR element and I wondered if you would consider taking part. I envisage 4–5 days in Kisoro, Uganda, sometime in the spring next year. What do you reckon?"

Douglas was keen: "That sounds a terrific idea and—schedule allowing—I'd certainly be up for it. (Incidentally, was this idea discussed before or after the recent plummet in Apple's stock price? I think that budgets are being hit hard)." He also suggested, as another opportunity to revive the endowment appeal, that we get an iBook out to the Virungas and onto a gorilla's lap so we could take the photo that finally intrigues Steve Jobs. (Again, we'd already done that.) I was thrilled by the prospect of finally taking Douglas, our most stalwart patron, to see our projects and meet field staff. I had six months to prepare for my next Voyage to Virunga.

With the endowment campaign now on the back burner, the division of labor that my wife and I had agreed on three years earlier—her in Africa, building a sound conservation program, and me in Europe and America, raising the money to fund it—left me twiddling my thumbs. I was restless, raring to get my teeth into a new campaign.

A fortnight before I was meant to fly out to California, I met Douglas in the lobby of One Aldwych in London. I had not seen him in months. The American lifestyle had taken its toll, and he attempted to disguise the extra pounds with two-tone attire: white shirt and black trousers. His hair was white and closely cropped. He looked every bit the new media guru and blended in faultlessly with the plush surroundings. "How can I help you this time, Greg?" he smiled.

"Coltan," I said, "an entirely new threat to the gorillas. The mining of it in eastern Congo is decimating the eastern lowland population. We had no idea what Coltan meant at first until I circulated an email about it through my tech network and none other than Gordon Moore, the inventor of the microchip, wrote back to say he thought it was probably short for 'columbite tantalite,' an ore. Apparently, it's processed into tantalum, which is indispensable to computers. I mean, there's no point in pointing a finger at the slaughter when we're buying up the proceeds."

"So now tech's the villain," smiled Douglas. "Interesting." He leaned back, crossed his imposing limbs, and gazed up at a pair of azalea bushes hanging above his head. "You need a really constructive solution. Talk to Nokia, they're the industry leaders in mobile phones.

And see if you can't get an article into *WIRED* about it. Ask John Perry Barlow to pen something."

"Did I mention that DiCaprio's agreed to lead our campaign?"

"Has he now," said Douglas without a hint of jealousy.

"Yeah, the other day I got a call from Ken Sunshine, his image consultant, in response to an email I sent. He wanted to know if I was certain about putting the movie star's photograph on the cover of a mining magazine. I assured him I was. How else are we going to get through to these people? I'm also writing an appeal letter to all the companies involved."

"Don't appeal," said Douglas. "Write your letter to inform, ask them to take the initiative. And make sure you send me a copy of the draft before you circulate it."

Two weeks later, I was at an event in Haight-Ashbury, San Francisco. John Perry Barlow was there along with a few other journalists. I asked Douglas to join us, but he declined. No matter, we were scheduled to meet up later that week in L.A. to discuss our forthcoming trip to Rwanda. I told the gathered digerati everything I knew about coltan and the threat it posed to the eastern lowland gorillas in Kahuzi Biega National Park in Congo. They promised to do their best to get the story out. But tech was hiding in its shell. The industry was not used to wearing the black hat. I had a hard time getting through to them with this campaign. Go figure.

Later, while riding in the back seat of a Yellow Cab returning me to my hotel, I opened up my Palm Pilot, attached my modem and phone, and then checked my emails. There was one from Kai Krause: "While working out at a gym in Santa Barbara, Douglas's heart stopped beating today and he died instantly."

Noooooooo! I read it again and again. The news was too grim to bear. I read the email again as if a third time would reveal my erroneous interpretation of it. No, this could not be. Not Douglas. He was only forty-nine. In addition to being my friend and mentor, he was the gorillas' best damn hope. He had moved mountains for them, exhaustlessly invested his time and imagination into saving them. I felt numb, adrift, like a parrot without a perch. I cried and cried and cried until my tear ducts ran dry and my face was just a moist crimson mush.

Five days later, I was at Mike Backes's house in Sherman Oaks when we learned that Douglas's funeral was going to be held that afternoon in Santa Barbara. "Let's go," said Mike.

"But we weren't invited," I said.

"So what, let's drive up there anyway."

"We won't make it in time. It will take us an hour and a half to drive to Santa Barbara. The service starts in half an hour."

"We'll take the Porsche," said Mike. We made it to the chapel in forty-five minutes. An organist was playing the Beatles song "Hey Jude" as we crept in. We stood at the back. In front of the altar lay Douglas's wooden coffin. How did they find a tree tall enough? Afterward, Jody Boyman and Berkeley Breathed held a reception at their house. I met a few of Douglas's friends and relatives including his brother James, sister Jane, and mother Janet, who was the opposite in character to her famous son. She chain-smoked. I also met Terry Jones from *Monty Python's Flying Circus*. He was listening to Ron Cobb recount how he had bought a farm in Australia from the fortune he'd earned from the one point he had on the movie *E.T.*, which he was supposed to direct until Steven Spielberg came along.

"I imagine you're persona non grata in Oz," I said to Terry Jones.

"Why's that?" he asked.

"Because of the sketch about Aussie wine that you did," I said. I then quoted a line: "Real emetic fans will also go for a 'Hobart Muddy,' and a prize-winning 'Cuiver Reserve Chateau Bottled Nuit San Wogga Wogga,' which has a bouquet like an aborigine's armpit."

He cut me off: "That was Eric's sketch. Not mine."

Fancy quoting Python to a Python. I was a real jerk sometimes.

Richard Dawkins wrote an obituary for Douglas in the *Guardian*: "Science has lost a friend, literature has lost a luminary, the mountain gorilla and the black rhino have lost a gallant defender. . . . Apple Computer has lost its most eloquent apologist. And I have lost an irreplaceable intellectual companion and one of the kindest and funniest men I ever met."

After I returned to the UK, Jillian and I drove to Oxford to pay the professor a visit. It was a clear, fresh spring day. The sun was shining. Richard's wife, the Honorable Sarah Jill "Lalla" Ward, an actress who played Princess Astra in the TV show *Doctor Who*, joined us for lunch in the garden. We told Richard that his obituary had given us a real boost. He and I shared an affinity to Kenya, where he was born. Jillian was a staunch follower of his atheist views. After our visit, he published a short piece about it in the *Times*:

> A visit from two representatives of the Dian Fossey Gorilla Fund. They want me to step into Douglas Adams's shoes as Patron, and of course I am delighted and honoured to accept. I give them a computer for use in the field (there could be no more appropriate gift in Douglas's memory). It is a sad day for them. They've just had an appeal for money turned down by the Gates Foundation. They are more philosophical and understanding than I would have been. They wouldn't wish me to say it, but a tsunami of dollars is being thrown into medical research whose effect will be to increase the already 6 billion strong population of *Homo sapiens*. Couldn't a small ripple of dollars be spared for *Gorilla gorilla* whose population is now only a few thousand and dwindling catastrophically? Perhaps the thinking is that the gorilla is already a lost cause. But suppose a small relict population of Australopithecus (Lucy) were suddenly discovered in the Ethiopian highlands. Wouldn't the Gates

Foundation move heaven and earth to stop these priceless walking archives of hominid history going extinct? Right then. Gorillas are your walking archives. The only difference is that the ancestor we share with them is a little older, and we haven't only just discovered them, we've known about them all along. Over to you, Bill.

When our invitations to the memorial service at St. Martin-in-the-Fields arrived—"Douglas Noel Adams, 1952–2001"—I noticed for the first time that his initials were DNA. At the church door, ushers collected donations for rhinos and gorillas. Everybody who came to bid him a final farewell was in awe of Douglas's take on life, the universe, and everything. The tributes were glowing. I noticed Richard Dawkins sang along with the hymns. David Gilmour played "Wish You Were Here," solo, on an acoustic guitar, causing tears to flow from the gallery like rain in a rain forest.

Following the service, a group of friends walked through Leicester Square together—Stephen Fry, Hugh Laurie, Margot Buchanan, Peter Gabriel, Richard Harris, Sophie Austin, Robbie Stamp, Richard Dawkins, Geoff Carr, Jillian Miller, and I (David Gilmour and his wife Polly took a limo)—to attend his wake at the Groucho Club in Soho. Once there, Jillian and I worked the room; Douglas would have wanted us to. I chatted to Peter Gabriel, another AppleMaster whom DNA had recruited to the cause. It was our first time meeting, though I'd been a fan of his music since high school. Sad that Douglas had to die before we would meet. "You're not going to like what I've been up to," said Peter in a soft, raspy, posh voice.

"Why is that?" I asked.

"I've had a bonobo in my studio playing keyboards."

"You're kidding me," I laughed.

"No, it's true. The bonobo speaks sign language and has an extensive vocabulary. So we asked her to come to my studio and play the piano. We had to bribe her with Jell-O, but she played pretty well."

"Can't wait to hear what that sounds like," I said.

"What do you think about gorillas communicating with each other using video conferencing?" asked Peter. "Putting monitors in their habitat to see if they make contact with each other."

"It could be done," I said. "The equipment would have to be ruggedized to withstand a hell of a beating." I then told him about the Media Lab's idea for a hologram of a silverback. Storm joined us. He had designed album covers for three of Peter's solo albums and a couple for Genesis, too. I had been trying to persuade him to design the fund's annual report for us.

"If I do design it," said Storm with an air of contempt, "there'll be no gorillas in it."

"No gorillas," I laughed.

"Maybe a hand print or two, but that's all."

"Why? I don't get it."

"For the sad fact that there are far too few left in the wild," said Storm. David Gilmour stepped in and said, "Go on, Storm, design his annual report."

Everyone had a poignant story to share about Douglas. He had touched so many lives. My favorite memory is from when he and I were walking along a Santa Barbara sidewalk, after our dinner at Emilio's, toward Mike's Porsche 928, as Mike had offered to give us all a lift. I told Douglas how, over the past eight months, I had transcribed handwritten journals that I kept while traveling through Southeast Asia and the Horn of Africa, to the tune of 250,000 words.

"Bloody hell!" roared Douglas. "That's more than I've written in my entire career."

While I was writing this chapter, Douglas's former assistant, Sophie Austin, marked the anniversary of his passing with a post on Facebook to which I added a comment: "I'm currently writing about how we worked together to raise a once-and-for-all-fund to save the gorillas in perpetuity. We failed but what a ride! Reliving it is almost as thrilling." Douglas's brother, James, replied to my comment, "Remember him telling me about that, boy was he excited." It made me smile.

Douglas still makes his presence felt, even decades after he's gone. Welcome back, old friend. I've missed you. Your plan to save the gorillas is no less compelling now than it was then. For today's tech titans, $35 million is chump change. Surely one will read this and step up with the cash. "A bargain at the price!" says Douglas.

13

IN TOO DEEP

IT WAS TEN o'clock at night. The forest seethed with ceaseless nocturnal calls: crickets, frogs, and the occasional chimpanzee pant-hoot. There was another sound, unusual for that time of night. It was coming from two different locations in a densely jungled ridge that rose from the boundary of Bwindi Impenetrable National Park on the opposite side of the valley from where we were situated. In the flickering light of a hurricane lamp, Jillian and I sat silently together on the veranda of "Weaver," a luxury tent with wooden flooring, sipping iced Amarula and Makers's Mark, respectively, and listening intently to the darkness. Again we heard the sound in the forested ridge opposite. To the untrained ear, it sounded like the panicked flapping of a giant bird, but we knew it to be two silverbacks one-upping each other with chest beats. The somnambulant silverbacks continued their aggravated exchange for an hour. What could have gotten them up at such a time when mountain gorillas are usually tucked up and asleep in their night nests?

It was our first time in Bwindi. We were staying in Gorilla Forest Camp, a Sanctuary Retreat, a high-end brand of lodges owned by Abercrombie & Kent. In his capacity as A&K's European director and our chairman, David Rogers had arranged for us to stay at the lodge for free because he believed our talents for turning Africa's morbid episodes into PR gold might just help restore the lodge's reputation. A year had passed since a group of tourists on their way to see gorillas, and their guides, were attacked by rebels here. They were assaulted, taken hostage, and then force-marched toward the Congo border. A Ugandan ranger, Paul Ross Wagaba, was burned alive. Eight of the victims were beaten to death. A handwritten note by the rebel leader stated the massacre was intended to send a message to the United States and other countries to abstain from supporting the new Rwandan government. Gorilla tourism ceased. Two of the victims, Susan Miller and Robert Haubner—employees of Intel, a computer chip giant where he was worldwide director of customer support and she was a senior trade show manager—stayed in Weaver the night before they were murdered. Tonight, an armed guard was hidden in the vegetation that surrounded our tent. We didn't see him or hear him, but we knew he was there.

Jillian and I fought. She remonstrated with me about my status in the fund and for letting my ego get in the way of my decisions. We exchanged insults. I'm sure the silverbacks could hear us. The argument ended with cold shoulders. Our bed was large but the night was interminable. I lay awake in the dark and wondered if our marriage would last. A close working relationship was essential to the day-to-day running of the fund, and it prevented us from letting our marital problems get in the way of our jobs. Consequently, our emotions got suppressed, buried deep down inside. And like a callus, it built up and built up until it turned ugly. Something had to break.

The next morning, as we gathered for breakfast in the lodge restaurant—eggs, bacon, fruit, and toast—Jillian asked Vince Smith, our regional director, if he had heard the commotion in the jungle the night before. "How could I," he laughed, "when I was sleeping in the radio room? All I heard were the calisthenics of cockroaches and the occasional blast of static from the radio."

Vince had been appointed to the position after we terminated Luiz Fabbri's contract. We changed "coordinator" to "director" and dropped "development" to reflect the broader range of projects we now had in the field and the greater responsibility of our field coordinator's position. He was traveling with Jillian and me as a part of his job's induction, and to review the fifteen projects we were currently funding in the region. Of French and British mixed descent, Vince was bilingual and understood Francophone sensitivities in Africa, which made him ideal for the position. He also retained a healthy dose of English wit and cynicism. And he and I shared a similar sense of humor.

"Have you seen *Tarzan*?" I asked while looking at the forest and thinking those animators really nailed the look and feel of Bwindi, I mean for a cartoon. "The Disney animation?"

"Let me tell you about *Tarzan*," said Vince. "When I was in charge of Sweetwaters in Kenya, a couple of Disney animators working on the production came and stayed on the reserve. I was taking care of an orphaned infant chimpanzee named Sophie at that time who was about the same age as my son, Oliver. Sophie and Ollie were inseparable. She taught him how to climb out of his crib and to bypass the child-safe systems we'd installed in our home. The two toddler primates caused all sorts of havoc. Anyway, their behavior at my house didn't go unnoticed by the animators, who asked if they could model their infant *Tarzan* on my son. So some of the scenes in that movie are actual reenactments of Sophie and Ollie's apish antics in our house."

"Well, you'll be happy to know the *Tarzan* premiere went to L.A. Zoo's gorilla enclosure."

"The bastards!" cried Vince.

Unlike Luiz Fabbri, who was an odd egg who always seemed out of his element, Vince was an everyman with a down-to-earth style that our field staff found easy to relate to. He nurtured a strong rapport with our resource center and Mt. T. managers and had regular face-to-face meetings with them in Goma, Ruhengeri, and Kisoro. Vince was creative and regularly found ways to keep his colleagues entertained. A surprising camaraderie developed between him and me.

For my third Voyage to Virunga, I was joined by Dan Richter and his son, Will. Arthur C. Clarke had recommended that he get in touch with me, and on short notice we arranged a trip to Uganda and Rwanda. Today Dan is a mountaineer who has climbed over five hundred peaks and instructs for the Sierra Club, but he has lived many lives. Dan was a mime artist when Stanley Kubrick hired him to choreograph the tribe of ape-men in the "Dawn of Man" sequence in *2001: A Space Odyssey* and then cast him to play Moonwatcher, their leader who throws the bone that turns into an orbiting satellite—a cut some film critics consider the greatest in movie history. Then Dan was John Lennon and Yoko Ono's personal assistant, a job he held for four madcap years. "I was the guy with ten grand in one pocket and an ounce of heroin in the other," he told me. When he and his son joined my V2V, Dan was a recovering addict who had just undergone surgery to have most of one lung removed. I, of course, was a huge fan of John Lennon as well as the movie *2001* and anything to do with it. Dan had lots of stories to tell, like when Stanley Kubrick found out he was a heroin addict and, instead of trying to get him help or, worse, fire him from the set, the moviemaker sat down and asked Dan to tell him all about heroin addiction.

The three of us took a small plane from Entebbe and flew over half the length of Uganda, landing briefly at the foot of the Mountains of the Moon. The countryside was rich and green and almost every inch of it was cultivated. Edward, our driver and guide, met us at Kisoro airfield in a rented Land Cruiser 4x4 and drove us into town. We were the only guests staying at the Travellers Guest House, an old colonial-style one-story hotel where Dian Fossey used to have her mail delivered. We stayed for a week.

On our first day, Dan insisted we climb Mount Sabyinyo, where the borders of Rwanda, Uganda, and Congo meet. The name means "old man's teeth." "Devil's teeth," I grumbled, as we climbed up its 3,669 meters. Despite his recent surgery, Dan was raring to get up that mountain. He showed me how to tie my bootlaces for climbing: loose on the way up and tight on the way down. "Otherwise, you end up crushing your toenails," he said.

The old man's teeth were shrouded in fog when we reached the summit. We could barely see a thing, so we guessed where the apex of the three African nations was located and danced around it in the mist like man apes. I had a great time with Dan and Will.

We trekked Nyakagezi group in Mgahinga National Park. I was happy to see Bugingo the silverback again. He was massive. Reaching out as if to touch an invisible monolith, Dan reenacted a scene from *2001* for the benefit of my camera. Bugingo folded his arms and seemed unimpressed. The next day we crossed into Rwanda. Edward, our driver, was a keen birder who stopped for every new species he saw. Dan, too, was a budding ornithologist; he'd brought along a monocular to view them. Progress was slow. At the wildlife veterinary center in Ruhengeri, the actor brandished a gorilla's femur, again for my camera.

Our Land Cruiser had two sunroofs that popped open, and Will and I spent most of our time with our heads through the roof, wind in our hair, and causing havoc in the villages that we passed as children ran after us crying, "*Mzungu! Mzungu!*" Will had never experienced such joyful hysteria. "We're the Beatles," he laughed.

"Fuck the Beatles!" I said.

One night at the Travellers Guest House, I screened a video for them on my PowerBook. The three of us sat in the empty dining room, ordered ESB beers and watched *Imagine*, a 1972 documentary about the making of John Lennon's seminal album of the same name. Dan Richter is in it: he features prominently in a heartwarming scene where a homeless guy from California shows up, believing John's been writing lyrics about him after which John, though sympathetic, sets him straight. Will Richter had never seen the film before. "You sure were a sharp dresser, Dad."

"So how do we get Arthur up here to see gorillas?" asked Dan.

"It's not impossible," I said. "Once he's in Kigali, we can take him in a wheelchair-accessible 4x4 to the park's edge."

"But Arthur's probably beyond flying commercial for all the connections he'd have to make to reach Kigali."

"OK. So we borrow a billionaire's private jet to fly him in from Colombo."

"Then what? How does he get up the mountain?"

"We carry him in a litter. Well, not us. The porters do. They took Ruth Keesling up that way the last time she visited the gorillas. It's no big deal. The people who live in these mountains are strong and sturdy. It may seem archaic, unjust, and a throwback to colonial times, but they sure don't mind. Money's hard to come by. And porters can earn more in tips on a morning carrying things up a mountain than the average person earns in a month."

"OK," smiled Dan. "And the billionaire's jet?"

"I'm working on that."

As we traveled from Kisoro to Gisenyi—one end of the Virunga massif to the other—driving south on a road that ran parallel to the volcanoes, we saw *génocidaires* working in a field. They were clearly identifiable by their all-pink outfits. At the end of the genocide, the new government cited more than 130,000 alleged génocidaires. The main perpetrators were tried at the tribunal in Arusha, Tanzania. But the vast number of the accused who remained made it highly improbable they would all be convicted. Rwanda would eventually try them through its traditional court system known as *gacaca*. Gacaca courts were installed to establish truth about what happened, accelerate legal proceedings, eradicate the culture of impunity, and reconcile Rwandans. Until that time, the accused were permitted to live in their own communities but were required to show up for work duties every day and to wear pink at all times.

Situated just across the border from Goma, Gisenyi is a sleepy town on the shores of Lake Kivu. At the time, the border was closed, so after strolling to the frontier and putting a toe in the Democratic Republic of the Congo, Will, Dan, and I spent the rest of the day in Rwanda, relaxing at the lakeside Ubumwe Hotel. Vince Smith drove down from Kigali to join us. From where we sat in the garden we could see the Bralirwa Brewery, uniquely powered by the methane in Lake Kivu. Only Vince and I were drinking its products. "Vince used to run Sweetwaters," I said to the others, "a private game reserve in Kenya owned by a rich Arab arms dealer. And he raised a chimp in his home alongside his own son."

Dan, having just seen the chimpanzees at Gombe Stream National Park where Jane Goodall conducted her long-term study, was intrigued. "How did you become involved in the fund?" he asked.

"I'd been popping into the London office off and on for a couple of years to see if there were any job opportunities," he said as he poured himself another glass of Mützig beer.

"We knew Vince was perfectly qualified to run our field program," I said, refilling my glass as well, "but we already had a guy in the post, Luiz Fabbri. By then we felt that Luiz had been in the post long enough, however, so we decided not to renew his contract. Vince stepped into his shoes. He doesn't stir shit the same way Luiz did. Vince goes with the flow. And he understands and relates to Africans better than any other *mzungu* I know."

"Gosh. You flatter me," laughed Vince, adjusting his collar. "Let me tell you, Dan. Greg here's the one who really deserves the accolades. He's a bloody good boss and truly passionate about the gorillas. You've probably noticed he's at ease with anybody at any level, which makes him a bloody good networker too. And he's always great company." We looked at each other and smiled deviously. We already had stories that we would take to our graves.

"So, tell me about the kind of things you do as regional director," said Dan.

"Well," said Vince, launching into presentation mode, "the fund now supports some twenty projects in Rwanda, Uganda, and Congo that I oversee, each of which addresses one or more of the human encroachment issues affecting the mountain gorillas' habitat. We're building water cisterns in Rwandese schools around the park and each twenty-five-cubic-meter cistern will provide at least five hundred families with an alternative and easier source of water than the Virunga mountain streams. Batwa Pygmies in eastern Congo—evicted from their forest land by conservationists—now have better health care and sanitation, schooling, agriculture, and income-generating activities such as pottery production, all of which contribute to more sustainable and legitimate alternatives to hunting duiker in the forest for bushmeat. Our partners include a honey-marketing association, a group of civil engineers, an alliance of artists, a microcredit bank, a wildlife veterinarian center, a radio station, a top national football club, just to name a few. And they all share our commitment to preserving mountain gorillas within their native habitat. In essence we are backing the mountain gorillas' best bet: a fast-growing environmental movement emerging directly from the communities which formerly put pressure on their habitat."

"We're beginning to see the dawn of a conservation culture, Dan," I added.

Dan was determined to help. When he returned to the United States, he went on a hunt for gorilla bones in the American Museum of Natural History, found a sizable femur in the attic from one of the mountain gorillas that Carl Akeley had brought back in 1921, then cast a replica of it in resin and sent it to me in London. Then, to get them to autograph the bone, Dan and I sent emails to as many of the man apes who acted in the "Dawn of Man" sequence in *2001* as we could find. Arthur, too, added his name. We intended to auction off the bone to raise money for the gorillas.

At a black-tie reception at the Playboy Mansion "with a bunch of stars and science guys" to honor Arthur C. Clarke, Dan spoke about and showed them the bone. In the group photo of the gathering, Dan and Morgan Freeman stand out as the only ones who ignored the dress code and wore regular suits and ties. Also, Dan is holding the bone. Tom Hanks was a big fan of the movie *2001*, and he told Dan that he used to practice throwing a stick in his backyard when he was a kid. I followed up with a letter to Hanks's agent, but nothing ever came of it. We never did sell that bone. It remained on a shelf in the London office until the man ape autographs faded.

A new print of *2001* was screened at the National Film Theatre in London. Arthur C. Clarke flew in from Sri Lanka for the occasion, and from his wheelchair he introduced the film to a full house. Later, Jillian, Storm Thorgerson, and I visited Arthur in his suite at Brown's Hotel. Arthur was lying in bed under the covers. We gathered at the foot of his bed. Storm asked if he would consider writing the foreword to a new book he was writing about "black objects." Arthur agreed. With humor, he then reached up to an imaginary monolith. Made my day.

Soon after that, I received a crushing letter from Lady Kleinwort: "The news is not good . . . EKCT decided at their Board Meeting last week not to continue supporting DFGF. . . . Important as it doubtlessly is to run small business initiatives in Rwanda in order to create alternative sources of livelihood for resident communities—and essential it is to provide environmental education, we should like our giving to be more directly involved in gorilla conservation itself. . . . Business ventures and education do not come under our Conservation heading. Indeed, trustees voiced misgivings as to whether DFGF itself should be treading down that path. Sadly, for all the above reasons I feel I must stand down from my patronhood . . . I cannot lend my name to any cause without the full backing of the organization I represent."

Jillian and I were devastated. EKCT's support was worth £50,000 a year. Plus, we hadn't lost a patron before. Reading between the lines, her reasons seemed to be echoing the growing number of critics we found ourselves up against for our Afrocentric, economic-based approach to wildlife conservation. We were proud of this approach. The Dian Fossey Gorilla Fund Europe was now very much a people-to-people organization. "We enable people in Britain and other developed countries to help people in Africa to protect, understand and benefit from their gorilla neighbors," wrote Jillian in *Digit News*.

Until recently, saving Africa's wildlife was largely the domain of White Africans and well-meaning foreigners. Few Black conservationists ever got a look-in on protecting their own wildlife. Thankfully, that is now changing. However, back then, our approach was considered highly unorthodox. Our work was not entirely dismissed. We won the International Award for Outstanding Work in Conservation at the BBC Animal Awards. Jillian was immensely proud of this accolade and advertised it in every subsequent issue of *Digit News*. We felt it was high time Big Wildlife begin including local stakeholder ownership.

DFGF International was gunning for us too. They didn't understand what Jillian was trying to do in the communities next to the gorilla habitats. "I didn't join this organization to save people," grumbled Judge Musgrave. And they were fed up with me fundraising on their turf. Their CEO, Clare Richardson, who was an Americanized Brit with more attitude than status, became a real thorn in my side. Her boss, Terry Maple, asked my boss, David Rogers, to fire me. David refused, saying he'd take "a hotheaded maverick over an anodyne academic any day."

I was spending a lot of time in Africa without my wife. Vince and I traveled many miles together driving between projects in the fund's Mitsubishi Pajero, groovy music blaring the whole time. Much to Jillian's annoyance, he and I had become quite chummy, which she felt got in the way of the proper lines of communication. Whatever. Vince turned me on to hip-hop and showed me that, along with reggae, it was key to grasping the psyche of young Black people.

With the help of Vince's Afrocentric view, I began to see the continent with new eyes. When I grew up in Kenya, Nigeria, and Tanzania, our family may not have lived in a walled compound as other expats did, but neither did we live among the Africans. Our immediate neighbors in our little suburb in Dar es Salaam were expats. And when I returned to Africa as an NGO man I never had time to immerse myself too deeply in the culture. Now, however, lubricated with local beer, intoxicated by the smell of African sweat, and emboldened by Tupac's rhymes, I crossed a Rubicon, one I'd previously resisted crossing, into the heart of Africa. Vince showed me the way.

Our revelries were legendary. DJs in the clubs would announce our arrival: "Gorillas in the house!" Status did not go unnoticed by the young women who frequent clubs. And their attention was flattering to a man approaching middle age. No one got hurt. Out of sight, out of mind.

Around this time, an incident occurred that changed the course of DFGF Europe. Ute Eilenberger had just become the new veterinarian at the Veterinary Centre in Rwanda, whose costs were supported in part by our donors. Local vet Antoine "Tony" Mudakikwa, who was the first Rwandan vet to treat gorillas, told *Digit News*, "It is good for me to be working the forest so well. Ute is an academic who also knows the practical side of working with animals in the wild." Tony was a heartthrob—good looking, fit, and a former football star. Eilenberger, an attractive and gregarious German woman, caught his eye. But Tony was already dating Karisoke director Dr. Liz Williamson, a British woman employed by DFGF International. One night in Ruhengeri, the town nearest to Volcanoes National Park in Rwanda, a few conservationists had gathered for a party, including Liz, Ute, and Tony. Taking exception to Ute flirting with her crush, Tony, Liz grabbed a full bottle of red wine and smashed it over Ute's head. There was blood and wine everywhere. Police were called to the scene, and a crime report was filed. "Next time I'll kill her," said Liz defiantly.

Ute, the apparent victim, immediately lost her job at the Vet Centre. Liz, the apparent perp, stayed on as Karisoke director for another year. The whole affair got brushed under the carpet. Seems International's board had no qualms about one of their staff attempting to kill a colleague. To us at DFGF Europe, the incident demonstrated that, at the very core, International was morally corrupt. I met Ute five years later, in Kampala, and she told me that because of her injuries she still had trouble sleeping and suffered terrible headaches. Our trustees were appalled when they heard what happened, and they decided to distance Europe from International. Thereafter we ceased funding both Karisoke and the vets. We were on our own now.

Soon after that, Robert Lewis, a lawyer in California, contacted me saying he had some personal effects of Dian Fossey's that might be of value to the fund. He was Kitty Price's lawyer. Kitty was Dian's mother. Before Dian was murdered, she bequeathed all of her estate to the Digit Fund to pay for antipoaching patrols, but she left her will unsigned. So, with Robert Lewis's counsel, Kitty challenged it in court, stating the document "was simply a draft of her purported will and not a will at all." A New York State Supreme Court justice threw out the will and awarded the entire estate to Kitty: about $4.9 million in royalties from Dian Fossey's book and movie.

Kitty Price claimed she was working on a project to preserve the work that her daughter had done for the mountain gorillas in Rwanda. But she did nothing of the sort, and by the time of her own death, most of Dian's estate had been whittled away. Robert told me Kitty Price, in her dementia, saw elephants in her kitchen and cried out for Dian. Perhaps in his old age he had time to reflect on his role in all of this, because when we met at his home in Redwood Shores, he seemed profoundly contrite about it. He gave me a stack of letters Dian had written to her mother while at Karisoke, right up until just before she died in 1985. Included were some photos she had enclosed. Robert Lewis knew that when DFGF International got wind of this, they would be furious, but he had observed them over the years, all their infighting and backstabbing and conniving, and had concluded that the DFGF Europe was a far more worthy beneficiary.

In the basement of our London office, I began archiving the material. With painstaking attention to detail, each item was scanned and cataloged. Using optical character recognition, I then transformed her words into clean text. It was a labor of love that brought me closer to our founder. Written in a more congenial voice than her normal writing style, Dian's letters to her mother were a treasure trove of insights into her life and the gorillas ("Tell no one, or they'll lock you up as well as me, but I sing show tunes to them: 'Cool Clear Water' and 'Oklahoma.' And they love it.").

No doubt, Dian would have been appalled to learn of the schism that had grown between the US and UK charities, both of which she had set up after Digit was killed, and were raising money in her name. And while she may not have liked the conservation methodology we were deploying in communities adjacent to her beloved mountain gorillas, even Dian understood that "the gorillas' destiny lies in the hands of those who share their communal inheritance."

14

CAMPAIGN FOR GORILLA-FRIENDLY TECHNOLOGY

These shy apes and their Afro-montane habitat form a unique part of our Planet's bio-diversity. But more than that, they are almost literarily our cousins. Anyone who can look into a gorilla's eyes without feeling a sense of kinship, is to me less human than the gorilla itself.

Yet if we do not act quickly, these gentle creatures could become victims of our progress. Ironically, the ubiquitous computer chip, which has transformed human culture is now threatening theirs. (Yes, I use the word "culture" deliberately: recent studies have confirmed what many have long suspected—that the great apes do have a culture, only quantitatively different from our own.)

A vital component of the microchip is tantalum, and this is now found in the same area of the Congo as the gorillas, so both mining and warfare are combining to destroy their environment. It is perhaps appropriate that I am using my computer—which doubtless contains a few micrograms of tantalum—to draw attention to this new threat to our endangered relatives.

—Sir Arthur C. Clarke

AN ONLINE CHAT was scheduled for September 27, 2001: Sir Arthur C. Clarke and Leonardo DiCaprio would answer questions from the public on Yahoo.com to raise awareness of the coltan crisis. To coach our oldest and youngest patrons, respectively, on the facts and figures as they prepared to go online, Jillian flew to Colombo, Sri Lanka, and I flew to Hollywood, California.

We scheduled our chat for 9:00 PM PST—9:30 AM Colombo time—a reasonable time for Arthur, who was eighty-three and on the other side of the world from Leonardo. Jillian was at his house on Barnes Place. I was at Leonardo's company, Birken Productions, on Sunset and Vine. Leonardo's parents were there, too, though in separate rooms due to an estrangement. To prep himself for the chat, the young movie star anxiously bounced between them, seeking advice. George DiCaprio explained to him, in no uncertain terms, how important a figure Arthur C. Clarke had been to spaceflight in the twentieth century. And Irmelin encouraged him to speak from his heart.

A moderator from Yahoo.com managed the online chat, choosing which questions from the public our patrons would be asked to answer:

> **bwindsor99:** Leonardo, as an environmentalist, what made you focus on the endangered gorillas as opposed to any other endangered species?
>
> **leo_dicaprio_chat:** It's a complicated question. Partly because they're so closely linked to us: virtually our cousins. Animals on the verge of extinction . . . one of the saddest things in the world to have them wiped off the earth. It's affected me since I was a young boy. In no way do we want to make light of the situation in America by talking about gorilla conservation. We discussed postponing the chat, but . . . this is a desperate situation. These gorillas are being killed off at an alarmed rate. Every day, they get closer to extinction. Experts say these

gorillas are THE most endangered mammals on Earth! Thank you everyone for being here and trying to give some attention to the subject, especially with all the other situations going on around the world.

lizzielovesleo: Will stopping the use of cell phones be effective in helping stop the mining of Coltan?

leo_dicaprio_chat: Stopping the use of cell phones would be more harmful to the Gorillas. We have to find a way to work with the people who are involved in mining tantalum so Gorillas can actually benefit from having this material in their back yard.

leo_dicaprio_chat: . . . To lose these animals would be an insane tragedy.

sir_arthur_clarke_chat: If one day any superior alien comes to earth, we may be judged by the way we've treated the other inhabitants of our planet.

Josh2282: Do you see an American government role in this cause?

sir_arthur_clarke_chat: Obviously governments have to play some role, but private individuals will start it, and then convince their governments. It all starts with the individual.

leo_dicaprio_chat: Absolutely. More active in all walks of the environmental struggle, from Global warming to endangered species. As an economic superpower, we could make some dramatic changes. I want to really thank everyone for being a part of this chat. It means American citizens are focused on these kinds of issues. It shows that you know it's important.

sir_arthur_clarke_chat: I'm very glad to have joined you for this, and I hope the work we're doing will make the world a better place for human beings and all life forms.

When it was over, I inquired about a cab to take me back to my hotel. "I'll drive you," said Leonardo.

"I really wasn't expecting *you* to drive me," I smiled.

"I want to drive you." We took the elevator down to an underground parking garage and found his silver Mercedes SL500 convertible. I climbed into the passenger side. He bummed a cigarette from me and was about to light it when he spotted his mother, Irmelin, getting into her car. "Hang on," he said. "I better wait until she's gone before I light this. She thinks I've quit."

The night was warm. With the top down and under a starry California sky, we drove along West Sunset. I brushed my hair from my face and looked around. The sidewalks were eerily empty. At first, I thought it may have been a 9/11 thing, which had happened two weeks earlier, but Leonardo assured me it was just La-La Land going to bed early. The movie business was up at daybreak to take advantage of its sublime light. That being so, me driving through Hollywood in a silver convertible chauffeured by a screen idol went largely unnoticed. I watched our reflection bounce off the glass fronts of hotels and shop fronts on the Sunset Strip, the SL500's smooth silver flow coat blending the reflected colors of the city's neon lights into a mesmerizing psychedelic blur. We passed Chateau Marmont, a landmark for a lost generation where comedian John Belushi overdosed, Led Zeppelin's drummer John Bonham drove a Harley through the lobby, and Jim Morrison went wild on the roof. The Doors singer claimed that his time spent at the hotel used up "eight of my nine lives."

Dana Giacchetto, money manager to the stars and Leonardo's erstwhile best buddy, once boasted that he was part owner of the venerable star hangout. It was a barefaced lie from which he later backpedaled. Leonardo's close association with Dana had resulted in some unfavorable press. *Vanity Fair* published an article, Leveraging the Stars, that pulverized his reputation: "Being with Dana the last half of '98 and most of '99, you were at the center of power. If you wanted to get Leonardo DiCaprio in a movie, you'd have to go through Dana. If you wanted to talk to Leo, call Dana's house—he lived there. All those people—Tobey Maguire, Q-Tip, Alanis—stayed there." So, with Ken Sunshine's guidance, Leonardo was now trying to shake his bad-boy image and become more respectable. I told him that we still had fifteen gorilla permits on ice, waiting for when he was ready to voyage to Virunga.

"I still want to go," he said. "My mom has the antimalarial medicine still stored in her freezer."

We talked about many things. I told him my first-ever journalistic assignment for my university paper was to interview Jim Carroll (whom Leonardo portrayed in *The Basketball Diaries*) at the premiere of the film *Poetry in Motion* in Toronto. "He was suitably gritty, eloquent, and vague," I said.

Leonardo told me that when he was a kid he got punched in the arm by an orangutan at Michael Jackson's Neverland Ranch. "Made me so happy," he laughed. Clearly, his love for the environment ran deep, even though his lavish lifestyle left a sizable carbon footprint. And controversy had surrounded the making of his last film, *The Beach*, due to the filmmakers' bulldozing and landscaping a natural beach on Ko Phi Phi Le to make it more "paradise-like."

Leonardo was full of contradictions typical of a twentysomething dilettante star. He was smoking a cigarette when he told me he thought cities were a cancerous growth on the planet. "Especially when you're in a plane about to land and you look down and see it all spread out like that. It looks like cancer." He also said he'd always wanted to go to Madagascar.

"I went to boarding school there," I said.

"Really?" smiled Leonardo. "That must've been mind-blowing."

"It was," I replied. "I'd be happy to take you there and show you around if you like."

"OK," he said as we turned onto Santa Monica Boulevard. He then took a deep breath, hesitated for a moment, and said, "I'm thinking of giving up acting and becoming an environmentalist."

"Interesting idea," I smiled. "But don't you think, as a famous actor, you're much better placed to benefit the cause? What about doing an environmental film?"

"I'd love to do an environmental film. It's a hard subject to take on, though. I considered doing one about Chico Mendes, but the script was too depressing. It's a very morbid story, considering how sad the outcome was and what's in store for us in the future. But I would absolutely be enthusiastic as long as it was well made and hit all the important issues. So far, I haven't seen a real environmental film since *Gorillas in the Mist*."

As we drove down Santa Monica, I felt like I was hanging with a buddy. "You know, it's unusual to find such commitment in someone so young. I mean, you took on this campaign, agreed to lead it alongside Arthur, to be a spokesperson. It's really commendable."

"Thanks. I intend to do this for as long as I live. It's a lifelong commitment, a lifelong pursuit. And I'm sure there are many more out there like us who take this as serious as we do."

After he dropped me off, I strode into the lobby of the Radisson Beverly Pavilion, wide-eyed and slack-jawed, and said to the two receptionists on duty, "Did you see who was driving that convertible? Leonardo Di-fucking-Caprio!"

I took my PowerBook up to the rooftop of the hotel and sat poolside in the dark. I logged on to my cell phone and checked the web to see if our online chat had generated any press. There were a few dribs and drabs but nothing like we'd hoped for. Not surprising, considering how badly timed our event was—just after 9/11, when the world's press was still wholly taken up by that grisly geopolitical story ("That's the end of our freedoms," wrote JPB). But we'd scheduled the event months in advance, a prerequisite when trying to pin down an industry player like DiCaprio. Consequently, we missed another great opportunity for the gorillas.

In retrospect, I think I was beginning to lose the plot because of my self-image, behaving less like a fundraising professional and more like a star-fucker, which the Urban Dictionary defines as "a person who obsessively seeks out personal interaction with celebrities." It certainly looked that way. But I told myself that as long as the gorillas benefited from my frequent star-fucks with the rich and famous, it was all worthwhile. And lots of fun.

As 2001 drew to a close, the fund began to prepare for an auspicious anniversary in the gorilla calendar. The year 2002 marked 100 years since Captain Robert von Beringe "discovered" the mountain gorilla. (The quotation marks acknowledge that while 1902 may have been the year the species first became known to science thanks to a trigger-happy German captain, Africans who lived near them had known of the mountain gorillas' existence for eons.) Choosing to mark the occasion with a big bash, we booked the Royal Opera House in Covent Garden for what we hoped would be a star-studded gala fundraising event. Our event committee included Peter Brightman, one of the top world-class professionals in the entertainment industry; Giles Martin, music producer and son of the Beatles producer, George Martin; Nickolas Grace, an actor best known for his role as the flamboyant aesthete Anthony Blanche in *Brideshead Revisited*; and Michael Kamen, a composer, conductor, and musician who had worked with Pink Floyd.

Committee chairman Savage later described his role on the committee: "In the middle of all this I was asked to be the chairman for this magnificent event. Something that caught me by surprise. I am used to chairing meetings, but the people involved were true heavyweights in their respective fields. Almost intimidating. I figured that since we have a prestige venue, we can get any artist that happens to be in town. I was wrong and naive. I called my mates at Sony, Warner Bros, and every contact worth remembering. But with no luck. The artists that did agree or gave an initial nod were all mates of Michael Kamen, our musical director."

Celebrating the mountain gorilla centenary with a star-studded evening in Covent Garden would be an occasion for Jillian and me to tell our wildlife conservation story to the world. We discussed our roles at the gala and agreed we would give a joint speech and take turns recalling to the audience the amazing milestones we'd passed during our decade as a husband-and-wife codirector team saving endangered mountain gorillas. We would demonstrate our solidarity, love, and the value of working together.

"We said we'd only do this for ten years, Jillie," I sighed. "But I'm having too good a time to jump off this crazy merry-go-round now."

On Thursday, January 17, 2002, Mount Nyiragongo erupted, ejecting a large cloud of smoke and ash high into the sky and spewing lava down three sides of the volcano. Thankfully, the prevailing winds blew its noxious gases away from the mountain gorilla's habitat. The eruption occurred after an earthquake opened up fissures in the southern flank of the volcano. The world's largest lava lake then drained in a matter of hours, releasing slick, runny lava that flowed at sixty kilometers per hour. One river of lava swept straight across the airport, through the center of Goma, and into Lake Kivu, effectively bisecting the city and cutting off two passenger planes parked at the end of the runway (where they would remain until construction crews blasted through the rock two years later). The lava piled up in layers two meters high in Goma and created a new kilometer-wide delta in

Lake Kivu. Mercifully, because of ample warnings from the resident vulcanologist, not many lives were lost. The biggest death toll occurred after the lava reached a large gasoline storage tank that was being looted at the time. It blew up, tragically claiming fifty lives.

Our staff were fine, but the eruption took out our Goma resource center. Vince, who had been due to arrive the day of the eruption but got delayed in Kigali, said he found both our office and his hotel in Goma buried in lava. "The two places I was meant to be conducting business," he sighed. And on the street where our office had been, what had once been the first floor was now the ground floor. We lost all our equipment, though our insurers would eventually pay out. Some future archaeologist will scratch her head in wonder when she finds the iMac Richard Dawkins donated buried in rock. What could it mean?

The next day I circulated an email appealing for disaster relief and raised $75,000 over the weekend—most of which came from Leonardo. On Monday, Jillian arrived in Goma to distribute the aid to those who most needed it. She said the ground was still steaming in many places. Within days, she and Vince had relocated the resource center to a building out of the line of fire from any future volcanic lava flows, and we were back in the gorilla business.

Meanwhile, the event in Covent Garden was coming together nicely. Musical director Michael Kamen, a highly sought-after music arranger, had spun gold from his Rolodex, booking the Opera Babes, Alessandro Safina, chart-topping solo artist Bryan Adams, and Queen guitarist Brian May to perform for free. Meanwhile, Nickolas Grace recruited fellow thespians Rula Lenska, Alan Bates, Eileen Atkins, Sinéad Cusak, Jeremy Irons, and Terence Stamp to read excerpts from Dian Fossey's letters to Kitty Price. Michael Palin would perform his own ecological comedy sketch. And to open the show, Peter Elliott would amble down the aisles in an animatronic gorilla suit after which Rwandese Ituri dancers would take to the stage.

I invited Leonardo to take part in our gala, but he said that that was the weekend of his birthday, which he planned to celebrate skiing with his buddies in Aspen. He suggested that we film him meeting Koko the gorilla in Woodside, California, instead. He would record a message to the camera that we could project onstage before the concert began. (That old chestnut.) So I made all the arrangements with the Gorilla Foundation and Dr. Penny Patterson, who was Koko's minder, and three days before Leonardo was scheduled to come face-to-face with the world-famous signing gorilla, I flew out to Los Angeles to meet Irmelin DiCaprio and Darlene Malott, who were college besties and together ran Birken Productions, to make arrangements for the film crew to join us in Woodside.

"Oh, I thought you were taking care of that," said Irmelin.

"Really? You're asking *me* to find a film crew for your son, the Hollywood star?"

"That's correct. I'm sure you'll find someone willing to do it for free. I've also got a tote bag full of merchandise here that you can give to Koko as gifts from Leonardo: a *Titanic* hand towel, a couple of *Titanic* baseball hats, some *Titanic* T-shirts, a *Titanic* washcloth . . ."

"I'm sure Koko will be thrilled," I said, then left in a panic. Where was I going to find a film crew at such short notice? Before boarding my flight to San Francisco, I sent out an SOS to my gorilla peeps. As planned, Jillian flew in from London and met me at SFO and we drove through the city and across the Bay Bridge to Berkeley, where Eckart Wintzen had lent us his home for our stay—a stunning three-story townhouse nestled in the hills behind the university. Woody Harrelson had been the previous guest, and he'd left his stash of weed in the freezer. Having read my SOS, Eckart called from Amsterdam and suggested I contact his friend Peter Laanen, who ran Ex'pression College for Digital Arts, an exclusive media school in nearby Emeryville in which Eckart was a major investor. "And feel free to smoke Woody's weed," he added.

The next day, after we explained our predicament to Peter Laanen, he called Chris Dugan, the manager of Ex'pression's equipment department who was also an engineer for the band Green Day. Chris described the call. "I get this phone call while I'm browsing in a video store," he said, using his thumb and pinky to symbolize a phone. "'Are you available to go to Woodside tomorrow and film Leonardo DiCaprio meeting Koko the gorilla?' 'Get out of here,' I said, and hung up. So then he calls me again, says, 'No, Chris, it's for real and a good cause. The gorillas need you.' So I say, 'Yeah, sure, why not. Count me in. What time?' I still didn't believe him."

The day began at Alice's Restaurant, a bikers' joint at the crossroads of Skyline Boulevard and La Honda Road, where we'd arranged to meet Leonardo. Tucked away in a rural part of Woodside amid thousands of redwood trees, the large wooden building and its wide decking was a sublime place to pass the time on such a glorious day. "A little slice of bliss among the redwoods" claimed the restaurant's website. Sitting at a large wooden table outside, Jillian, Chris, a Gorilla Foundation staffer, and I clocked every fancy car that drove through the crossroads, wondering if that might be the one containing our movie star.

We should have known he'd pull up in a black stretch limousine. I went to the parking lot to meet him. The back window whirred down and an instantly recognizable goateed face peered up at me and smiled. Stepping out of the limo, he stretched and yawned as if awakening from a deep sleep. He was wearing jeans and a blue T-shirt and a blue baseball cap and was taller than the archetype actors who are often goaded into the profession by short-person syndrome. We ordered coffee cake and made small talk. The needles of the redwoods sang in the wind while Arlo Guthrie's eponymous song played over the restaurant's PA. We briefed Leonardo on what to expect when he met Koko. He'd read up a lot about her and was intrigued. Indeed,

Koko had watched some of Leonardo's movies, so she knew who he was too. Apparently, she was very excited to meet him.

"I'm stoked," he said. "To come face-to-face with a real gorilla who I can also communicate with." He seemed genuinely thrilled, but his mood changed when he looked inside Irmelin's tote bag of goodies that he was supposed to give to Koko: "What am I, *Titanic* Boy?"

We then set off for our rare encounter—Leonardo in his limo and us in our rental. But the limo driver didn't follow us. He turned the wrong way and was heading back down the mountain. Without any means of contacting Leonardo, we took off in hot pursuit, recklessly racing around hairpin turns to try and catch up with him. Jillian attempted to call Irmelin to get her to call him on his personal cell phone. But the reception in the forest was patchy. With each perilous turn, I felt our PR coup slipping farther away. Eventually Jillian got through and Irmelin then managed to reach her son, who then got his limo driver to turn around and follow us up the hill in the right direction. Phew! Close call, *Titanic* Boy.

Koko's Place was a reserve on a ridge in the Santa Cruz Mountains, surrounded by redwood forest. Run by the Gorilla Foundation and animal psychologist Dr. Francine "Penny" Patterson, the nonprofit had relocated there with Koko after the female western lowland gorilla had learned sign language and Penny completed her study of great ape communication. Koko could sign one thousand words and understand two thousand spoken English words. The jury was still out as to whether she was merely "flailing around producing signs at random," as one linguist put it, or genuinely trying to say something. When I first met her, she blew in my face, using her breath as a kind of olfactory sonar. The rebound told her about me. "You smoke," she signed. Penny translated. "Smoking bad." Then, noticing a dental implant, Koko called me "Upper fake tooth."

Leonardo handed over his mom's *Titanic* gift bag, and in return, received a Koko gift bag full of Koko books, videos, stickers, and a T-shirt. Chris then set up his gear and filmed them relaying the specifics of what Leonardo would expect to encounter. Chris would not be allowed to sit with Leonardo and Koko and film. The Gorilla Foundation had a strict policy of allowing only its own videographer, Ron, to film Koko's encounters with celebrities. Ron had set up a Betacam to record everything that went on between Leonardo and Koko.

"Hat? No hat?" asked Leonardo before going in to meet the gorilla in her playhouse.

Meanwhile, Jillian, Chris, and I waited outside. Chris intended to put the camera in front of Leonardo the moment he stepped out of there and capture his initial impressions. We waited for about two hours. What were the two world-famous primates up to in there? When Leonardo finally emerged, he was visibly elated, if not a bit shaken. Chris grabbed his camera, hit record, and asked the question, "How was it?"

"I was her bitch!" gasped Leonardo. "The whole time Koko kept trying to lift my shirt so she could tweak my nipples. She was obsessed!" Still, the actor was clearly in awe of Koko and seemed to have made a profound connection with her. "It was like talking to an alien life form."

Chris then filmed Leonardo and Penny discussing gorilla behavior and Koko's extraordinary talents. And on our way out, we stopped just outside of Koko's habitat and waved goodbye. She seemed sad to see Leonardo leave. The feeling was mutual. We walked a little farther up the road to conduct an interview with Leonardo. He had written a few things down, based on information we had provided him, but mostly he ad-libbed, speaking from the heart, which was highly unusual for the stagestruck actor who usually preferred a script to improvising.

Chris Dugan, in an interview he later gave for Ex'pression College for Digital Arts, described the scene: "We set up in a very quiet, woodsy area next to a hiking trail. There was just enough light shining down through the trees and the birds chirping in the distance made for a perfect nature setting. Greg and Jillian conducted the questioning. Leonardo began with a short speech about how thankful he was to everyone who was able to make it to the event and how unfortunate it was that he couldn't be there in person. Then he added how this cause was so dear to him. Those words seemed very heartfelt and I got a sense of how important the Dian Fossey Gorilla Fund is to him. . . . The whole interview lasted about twenty minutes before Leonardo had to leave to catch a plane. All in all, I got some great footage. I've spent some time editing it all together and sending copies to England and Los Angeles so everyone has had a chance to see the progress. With just a few more small changes we should have a very informative, yet touching interview with Leonardo DiCaprio about a very important cause."

Leonardo was an exception to the rule that celebrities are happier endorsing a cause than they are funding it. He stepped up on both fronts. He knew the value of his image, but he also put his money where his mouth was. He regularly sent us five-figure donations in response to my appeals. However, he wasn't always so reliable. In August 2002, at a press conference for Global Green USA, the US affiliate of Green Cross International, Leonardo lambasted President George W. Bush for not attending the forthcoming Earth Summit in South Africa. The UN had recently launched the Great Apes Survival Partnership (GRASP) and had invited Leonardo to speak on its behalf in South Africa.

Jillian and I were not happy about GRASP's underhandedness, bypassing the fund, a member of GRASP, to get to our patron. And I'm always dubious about an "umbrella organization" that suddenly opens up above my head right after I make it rain. We needn't have worried. In the end, citing contractual obligations, Leonardo bailed and was a no-show at the Earth Summit. Huh. That didn't quite sit quite right with me either. Was this guy for real?

———————

More than two thousand people celebrated the hundredth anniversary of the scientific discovery of the mountain gorillas at the Royal Opera House on November 10, taking the fund to new heights and focusing world attention on the plight of the gorillas. We took in £130,000 at the box office and raised £21,000 on the night. And it was also a damn good show. All the performances were first-rate. Plus, the point of the evening was never far from people's minds. With touching candor, Dame Eileen read a letter Dian had written to her mother after the death of Dian's favorite gorilla, Digit. In contrast, Michael Palin's "Save the Plankton" sketch was hilarious: "An international organization, which I run from my flat—or my mum's, when I'm out." Joe Strummer and his band the Mescaleros shook the 150-year-old venue with a twenty-minute set to end the first half, including stomping renditions of "Rudy Can't Fail" and "White Riot."

Though billed as the first-ever rock concert at the Royal Opera House, the show also had some operatic moments, with the Opera Babes' adaptation of Delibes's *Lakmé* and Alessandro Safina performing "Band of Brothers" for the first time publicly with its composer and the man who brought the whole evening together, Michael Kamen, and the London Metropolitan Orchestra. But the highlight of the evening was Bryan Adams's closing "unplugged" set in which he was joined by a special guest, Queen guitarist Brian May. With hits like Adams's "Run to You" and Queen's "Crazy Little Thing Called Love," they literally rocked the house. Brian May told the audience he'd searched Queen's catalog for songs "which might speak for this all-important cause," before starting a tender version of "Is This the World We Created . . . ?" with slow-motion film of gorillas in the background.

"The Dian Fossey Gorilla Fund is a small organization with a huge reputation," one long-standing supporter said to me at the after-show party in the Vilar Floral Hall. The success of this massive undertaking in the center of London could only have enhanced that reputation yet further and given the gorillas a better chance for survival.

It was Monday, November 11, 2002—Leonardo DiCaprio's birthday—and I was sitting in my office in Primrose Hill after the staff had all gone home, still buzzing from the success of our gala the night before. Outside the sky was overcast, autumn twilight adumbrated the office, and gorilla faces on posters, maps of Africa, and stuffed toys hanging from the fittings all faded to black. I was remembering the high points (there were no low points) of our night at the opera. We had the run of backstage at Covent Garden, which had recently undergone a multimillion-pound upgrade and was gleaming with all modern conveniences. Remnants of the original Georgian brick building remained, which is where Jillian's and my dressing room was located. How thrilling!

As planned, before a packed house, dressed in our finest, we gave a joint speech onstage, talked about all we'd achieved in ten years. It was, hands down, the high point of my fundraising career. Chatting with Joe Strummer, he told me about a blues band that he jammed with in New Orleans that was authentically masochistic. Sadly, just two weeks after our event, Joe died of a heart attack.

I was still buzzing when the phone rang. It was Ken Sunshine in Los Angeles calling on a conference call with Irmelin and Darlene at Birken Productions. He was hopping mad: "Who gave you the permission to release that clip to *Entertainment Tonight* of Koko kissing Leonardo?"

"I'm sorry, Ken, but you seem to have gotten the wrong end of the stick," I said. "Irmelin, Darlene, back me up here. Last Friday, two days before the concert, I sent the clip to Birken with the proviso that if I hadn't heard anything back from you guys beforehand, it would go out on Reuters on Sunday at 11:00 PM, after the concert was over. Having not heard back from you, I assumed you were happy with it."

"Well, you assumed wrong," snapped Ken. It seemed that Leonardo, while celebrating his birthday with his compadres in Aspen, turned on the TV set to see *ET* running the clip with the headline LOOK WHO LEO's LIP-LOCKED WITH NOW!, and after his amigos saw him kissing a gorilla they razzed him mercilessly. "You'll never work with Leonardo again!" added Sunshine, flooring me.

"Really? That seems a bit extreme."

Sunshine's response was too disrespectful and so full of expletives that I dare not repeat it. He gave me a dressing down that I did not deserve and turned my joy into dread.

"Excuse me," I interrupted, "but I'm an officer of a charity. You don't need to speak to me in that way." Darlene and Irmelin remained silent throughout the call. I was gutted.

I never spoke to Leonardo again. In the end our campaign proved too complex, if not for him then for his people, who felt vulnerable and awkward. I didn't fit their romantic ideal of an ecosavior, and after the fallout from Dana and *The Beach*, none of DiCaprio's people really knew what to do.

I missed Douglas. He wouldn't have flaked so easily when the stakes were so high.

15

DIGGING IN THE DIRT

IN THE 1940s the US government used a consignment of twelve hundred tons of uranium from the Shinkolobwe mine in the Belgian Congo to develop Little Boy, the atomic bomb that was dropped on Hiroshima. Shinkolobwe mine is a freak of nature. It contains a tremendously rich lode of uranium pitchblende. Nothing like it has ever been found elsewhere. Thanks to its exploitation, Belgium had zero debt after World War II. All the spoils went to Belgium—the Congolese got nothing. To add insult to injury, when Congo gained independence in 1960, the Belgians sealed the Shinkolobwe mine with concrete. Since then, various terrorist groups, along with Iran and North Korea, have tried to get their hands on it. How do we get this shit so wrong?

Congo is cursed by its mineral wealth. To this day, an immense economic, social, and physical gap exists between those who mine the resources in deepest darkest Africa and those who turn them into advanced technological components in the industrial world. A hundred years ago, in the Congo Free State, because the people were threatened by King Leopold with avulsed limbs if they failed to do so, poor Congolese men and women tapped rubber trees to harvest latex, which then got shipped to Europe and America, where it was converted into rubber tires—an essential component of motorized transportation.

In 2001, in the Democratic Republic of the Congo, because alluvial columbite-tantalite was so plentiful and selling on the black market for eighty dollars a gram, poor Congolese men and women began digging by hand to mine coltan, as they called it, an ore that then got shipped to Europe and America and China, where it was converted into tantalum—an essential component for electronics.

See a pattern here? What also fits a pattern is that following the inevitable international outcry against these injustices, every one of the associated economic channels, be it Congolese rubber or coltan, gets shut down. And the Congolese stay poor.

––––––––––

The outcry over coltan was deafening. Nokia and Motorola issued a complete ban on Congolese coltan to ensure that their suppliers stop using ore mined illegally in Congo. The world's largest maker of tantalum capacitors, KEMET in the United States, asked its suppliers to certify that ore did not come from Congo or bordering countries, including Uganda and Rwanda. Cabot Corporation, another US company and the world's second-largest processor of tantalum powder, announced that it would not buy any ore from the Congo. The UN wanted an all-out embargo on all coltan from the Congo, Burundi, and Uganda until those nations were thoroughly investigated. Unsurprisingly, this met with stiff resistance from trade groups that claimed that legitimate traders would be hurt by such draconian actions.

Jillian and I knew nothing about mining when the crisis reared its ugly head. We were soon on an incredibly steep learning curve. Each day I assimilated stacks of research on a complex and unfamiliar industry. My brain hurt. But I had to get on top of this. I learned that in every other place on Earth where it is found, columbite-tantalite ore is mined by big mining companies. Australia provides 60 percent of the world's supply. But as much as 35 percent comes from Congo, where the ore is mined by poor artisanal miners who literally dig for it with their bare hands.

While others called for an outright ban of tantalum from Congo, my codirector and I knew this would only drive control of the trade into dodgier hands. And in a region as poor as this, notwithstanding those who were getting rich and financing a war from the mineral, the rise in the price of tantalum was having a profoundly positive effect on the local economy. Few opportunities to earn a living of any kind, let alone a good one, were available in eastern Congo. We believed we would alienate our target communities if we joined calls for an outright ban. Instead, we decided to work with local groups, industry leaders, and conflict resolution specialists to determine a win-win solution that would both save gorillas and improve conditions and economic returns for the Congolese.

Following the late Douglas Adams's advice, I sent an open letter to the tech and mining industries, drawing their attention to the unfolding environmental crisis. It raised the alarm. Four months into the campaign, we were so convinced of the value and viability of our gorilla-friendly technology campaign that we wrote to specific individuals in tantalum processing companies. Peter Kählert, chairman of the executive board of H. C. Starck, the largest tantalum processing company in the world, liked our positive, open-minded approach. He wrote back: "While the world's environment monitoring bodies are calling for an outright ban of tantalum from central Africa, the Dian Fossey Gorilla Fund understands that, if successful, a ban will be devastating to a region that has known so little prosperity. 'Coltan fever' is the most positive economic trend to come along in many decades and we cannot afford, if we hope to achieve anything for gorillas, to get in the way of its exploitation. Gorillas and tantalum are among

Congo's most valuable natural resources. . . . Why should one rule out the other? Why can't tantalum in the midst of gorillas be seen as a worthwhile opportunity to provide added value to an otherwise ruinous source of such a rare mineral?" Our approach, while controversial, won industry support and that was key to our success. Don't shoot the piano player.

In August, we traveled to Goslar, a historic town in Lower Saxony, Germany, to meet Peter and his colleagues at H. C. Starck and its parent company, Bayer Pharmaceuticals. It was my first time in Germany. Extended forests dominated the landscape. Immediately to the south, the Harz range rose above the historic town of Goslar to Rammelsberg mountain. Iron ore mining had been common in the region since Roman times, and when the Rammelsberg mine closed in 1988 it had been working continuously for over one thousand years. No doubt, then, we'd come to the right place to learn about mining. Peter Kählert put us up in a medieval castle owned by the company. Our room had meter-thick walls. I couldn't get over the TV shows: so much soft porn during regular viewing hours. The beer was fantastic. The mining company executives were very supportive of our principle of trading in ethically sourced coltan.

We drew up an action plan that included Starck sending an expert to Congo. I then received a letter from a Chinese firm, Ningxia Non-Ferrous Metals, expressing deep concern for the situation and stating that the company could be interested in investment that would contribute to the regulation of the coltan mining industry in Congo. Even Herbert A. Allen gave me some useful advice and warned of potential pitfalls in forming a Congolese coltan cooperative. We were only too aware of the risks involved in seeking to establish a venture such as this in a war-ravaged country like Congo, but we believed that this was by far outweighed by the inevitable result of failure to engage with the issue. And besides, I had my teeth into a new campaign.

We needed some heavyweight advisers. None of the usual tree-hugging gang qualified. Mining was a whole new ball of wax. We hired Kevin D'Souza, a British artisanal mining consultant with Wardell Armstrong, to undertake a scoping mission in and around Kahuzi Biega National Park in Congo. Being of Goan descent, he blended in better than either Jillian and I would have, and knew a lot more about the subject matter. If anyone could untie this Gordian knot, it was Kevin, who was an international authority on small-scale mining. He was prepared to go where others feared to tread.

"There were soldiers everywhere," Kevin said in an interview that he gave to the BBC after his mission, "and most of the park is a no-go zone for foreign visitors because of the threats from militia groups. I wasn't frightened, but I was apprehensive at times—especially when we were stranded for at least an hour in rebel-held territory. Luckily we didn't attract attention. The park is now largely in the hands of military groups and its fragile ecosystem is being destroyed. As well as the rainforest disappearing, both the elephant and gorilla populations are being decimated by poachers. There were originally 8,000 gorillas in the park, but it's believed 90 per cent of those have been killed and only two of the 250 elephants remain."

We also sought to identify an experienced professional body that could advise the fund on how to proceed setting up the multiparty dialogue that was essential to establishing a Congolese coltan-mining cooperative. Addressing the political situation in and around Kahuzi Biega required diplomacy, tact, and credibility. My research led me to Glenda Caine, director of the Independent Projects Trust (IPT) in Durban, South Africa. IPT had an excellent reputation in the field of conflict resolution. Called in after the end of apartheid to help integrate Black South Africans into the KwaZulu-Natal provincial police force, they knew their stuff. And they were Africa based, which made a difference.

In August, after Jillian and I met with them in London and briefed them on our campaign, we hired them. IPT then completed a literature review, concluding: "What is apparent from all the literature is that while there are numerous concerned individuals and organizations, only a concerted multiagency approach has any chance of success. This would support the [fund's] proposal for a well-designed and focused gathering of key stakeholders to define a coordinated response to the current crisis."

Having a new crusade on my hands helped put me back on track after losing Leonardo DiCaprio as a patron. I was shattered. It seemed I'd lost my touch. He never did revoke his patronship, and in July 2003 his foundation paid for all the airfares of the Congolese delegates, some of whom were involved in coltan mining, to attend the launch of the Durban Process in South Africa. He stepped up and made one final gift to the fund when it really counted. Kudos!

DIGGING A GRAVE FOR KING KONG? is the title of an article published in the *Economist* (July 31, 2003) about our meeting in KwaZulu-Natal: "With people still killing each other in horrific numbers in eastern Congo, why worry about the destruction of a national park and its few hundred gorillas? Because, according to the Dian Fossey Gorilla Fund, one is closely tied to the other." To have such a venerable and respectable paper send a journalist to cover our meeting, and then see our charity mentioned in it, filled me with tremendous pride. My dad turned me on to the *Economist*, and I had read it almost weekly for ten years by then. It's still my go-to global news rag.

We chose to hold the meeting in a remote location so that the delegates from less developed nations would not get distracted by Durban's bustling waterfront restaurants and gleaming shopping malls, stacked to the rafters with shiny consumer goods. Tala Private Game Reserve, a wildlife sanctuary in the hills of a farming community near Durban, was an ideal spot. Roaming across a mix of acacia thornveld, open grassland, and sensitive wetland were herds of kudu, hippo, giraffe, rhino, and the rare sable antelope—most of them farmed wildlife.

Our campaign for gorilla-friendly technology had generated a lot of heat among some conservationists who wanted an all-out embargo on coltan from Congo, and many tried to sabotage our meeting in South Africa, advising our invited delegates, including the Congo minister for environment, not to attend. But the Congolese warmly welcomed the Durban Process—they considered it a more realistic way to facilitate solutions and dialogue around the issues of coltan mining in Kahuzi Biega and to address the impact those activities were having on the eastern lowland gorilla population.

Upon arrival we were all given black fleeces and beanies embroidered with the Durban Process logo, which I had designed to combine both its English and French name. The first night, as we gathered around a blazing fire for a traditional South African braai, everyone wore their branded DP gear, which served to put us on the same level. I met Mr. Olive of Olive Enterprises. He was a coltan trader in Bukavu, perhaps the most profitable trader in the region. Congo's deputy minister of mines, Victor Kasongo, showed up late by taxi after flying in from Johannesburg, where he had meetings with De Beers, the diamond company. Changing from his expensive Armani suit and tie into his fleece and beanie, his stature was instantly lowered to match ours. Trinto Mugangu was there. Vince, too. H. C. Starck, the German tantalum manufacturer, sent two delegates. Around the fire we all began to get to know each other better and focus on coltan.

The most surprising delegate to show up was Solomon Balike, sent by General Padiri, the leader of the Mai-Mai rebels who were responsible for controlling the mining of coltan in the "Red Zone," a section of the park that no outsiders had visited until we sent in Kevin, our intrepid consultant. Solomon was interviewed on camera by M-Net, a South African broadcaster, and, when asked how he felt about eating bushmeat, he said, "We had tears in our eyes as we ate the gorillas and chimpanzees. They are our brothers."

On the first day, IPT divided the thirty delegates into five groups of six people. Mix rather than match was the strategy. We all had to get along—Mai-Mai rebels and government ministers, CBOs and mining associations, local businesses and national and international NGOs. We sat face-to-face and quickly got down to the brass tacks of clearly identifying the problem and then solving it. Over three days we explored solutions that might at the same time improve conditions for the miners and guarantee the integrity of the park. H. C. Starck pledged to establish a training program for a collective of artisanal miners and teach them environmentally sound management of small-scale mines. A new Congolese NGO was established: the Comité de Suivi du Processus de Durban, whose mission was to implement our recommendations. A list of initiatives and actions was drawn up and we voted for the four most effective ones. It looked so straightforward on paper.

The *Economist* concluded: "Indeed, some people think that the coltan traders could make the gorillas an asset. Bill Gates and several other hi-tech tycoons are keen gorilla spotters. They might arrange for payment of a premium on coltan from well-run Congolese mining sites (outside the park), and could then exploit the sort of consumer sentiment that drove the 'blood on their handsets' campaign to sell 'gorilla-safe' gadgets, rather as supermarkets sell 'dolphin-safe' tuna. If this happened, everybody would have an interest in making the park secure. King Kong could yet avoid being buried." Back to Bill again. He could still come through.

––––––––––––

The air was cool and fragrant with wild sage as we climbed out of our game-viewing vehicles at the conclusion of a thrilling tour of Tala

Reserve, where we spotted a pair of male giraffes that mated for life. "They've got some neck," said Jillian. Up-lighted pathways lined with fiery aloes led us into La Tala Restaurant for our final dinner at the reserve. Twilight came up and we watched through large windows as the savanna light's hues of beige and yellow softened into purple and mauve. The thatched-roof restaurant had a stone fireplace that was blazing. And a beautifully aged tree stood in the center of the room, elegantly draped in fairy lights. The Durban Process logo was projected on a screen next to a photo of a silverback holding its chin in its hands, like a bored delegate. The slide then switched to our recommendations: (a) disseminate Congo's new mining code, which strictly forbids mining in protected areas; (b) strengthen ICCN's monitoring capacity of the park; (c) provide incentives to move from a war economy to a peace economy through a microcredit scheme; and (d) initiate a pilot project combining agricultural and artisanal mining activities to provide sustainable income-generating activities for the miners.

It may not have looked like much, but it had taken us twenty-eight months to achieve this breakthrough. Jillian and I proudly filled our plates to overflowing at the succulent buffet spread and then sat down with Kevin D'Souza and Henri Maire, who were already tucking into their nosh. Kevin and Henri came from a world far different than ours, and we found working with them to be refreshing. Henri Maire was a Swiss mining adviser who'd been on the UN Security Council's Panel of Experts on the Illegal Exploitation of Natural Resources and Other Forms of Wealth of the Democratic Republic of the Congo. He took our campaign to the UN, World Bank, and to the highest authorities in the world. Together, our two mining advisers helped us find a cutting-edge solution to the coltan crisis, and in the process we got our feet into the nitty-gritty of mining.

"It's a tragedy," said Kevin D'Souza. "Destitute people feel they have no alternative but to dig for tantalum and then smuggle it out of the park." Kevin's head and heart were in the right place to look at the problem both rationally and compassionately. "On the flip side," he continued, "many in the development sector found it slightly insulting that in a country where millions are hungry and coltan is helping to feed some of them, a de facto embargo managed to gather momentum among high-tech companies apparently worried less about human beings than about the public-relations downside."

"So, when are we going to Kahuzi Biega, my friend?" I asked him.

"I'm scheduled to return in January," said Kevin.

"Excellent. May I join you?"

"Absolutely, mate," said Kevin.

Jillian glared at me. "Really?" she asked. "You know his schedule conflicts with mine."

"That's OK," I said. "I can manage on my own. I'll make sure everything runs smoothly, my love." I smiled. She frowned. I frowned. Her frown turned into a leer. I lowered my gaze.

"What's this I hear about a race you're planning to hold in London?" asked Kevin.

"The Great Gorilla Run," smiled Jillian. "A seven-kilometer fun run with a difference: all the runners will be dressed in gorilla costumes which they get to keep afterwards."

"Sounds like great fun. Which one of you thought up this brilliant fundraiser?"

"It wasn't me," I laughed. "Though I wish I *had* thought of it."

"Becky Guinea, our fundraising manager, dreamt it up about three months ago," said Jillian. "She believed the idea was crazy enough to catch on, and she was right. Within days of going online with the details, 250 people had registered."

"Fantastic," said Kevin. "Who supplies your gorilla suits?"

"We found a manufacturer in China who could ship us a thousand units. We've got them stacked up in our basement in Primrose Hill. Each runner who signs up for the fun run gets a gorilla suit and pledges to raise £500 in sponsorship. They then use their suits to raise money, clowning around in parks and on videos that they post online. It generates a kind of hysteria."

That night in our cabin, Jillian and I hollered expletives and tried to press each other's buttons. No doubt the other delegates heard us. We argued about work. Jillian saw the Durban Process as me muscling in on her territory. I argued that the Great Gorilla Run was her invading my territory. Our marriage was beginning to unravel. Still, we kept up appearances at work.

Chimanuka, an eastern lowland silverback gorilla, appeared to be scowling but it was just the shape of his mouth, perpetually turned down. As he kept watch over his group, his stoic expression remained unchanging. I was sitting about five meters downhill from him in Kahuzi Biega, with four Congolese members of the Durban Process. Kevin chose not to join us, having trekked gorillas on his last trip.

It was my first time seeing eastern lowland gorillas. At first glance, I found it hard to discern the difference, but they do have a little less fur and mass than their mountain cousins, and there's a patch of brown on their brows. Suddenly, Chimanuka stood all fours, stiffened his arms, raised his shoulders, and glared down at us as if to say, "I own you."

Proper gorilla etiquette demanded that we avert our eyes. I made a gorilla belch vocalization. *Mmwaah*. It was meant to calm the gorillas down, but its effect was better appreciated by us bald apes—it calmed us down. I was elated, as always, to be back communing with the big fellas. Different forest, different subspecies, but same effect. When I'm with them, I tap into the primal flux and reestablish the seven-million-year-old link that exists between us, which invigorates me to do my job. I didn't set out to be a gorilla man; I just wanted to get back to Africa. But whenever I spend time with them, I quickly fall under their spell. I slept well at night knowing that my nine-to-five was keeping a species alive.

Chimanuka survived the influx of coltan miners to his habitat largely because his group ranged in the southern section of the park, which was better protected by rangers. But the Durban Process had also helped. Our meeting at Tala got widespread coverage in the Congolese media. In September, more than three hundred representatives of small-scale miners and coltan traders met in Bukavu. Some had come from Kahuzi Biega. "We are now with the environmentalists," they said, "and will no longer buy coltan mined within our national parks." Essentially, they told the miners that coltan from within the park no longer had any value, and encouraged by the recent reunification of Congo and the return of relative peace to the region, the miners had apparently already left the park in droves. As a result, DFGF Europe was flavor of the month. A Congolese musician even wrote a rumba about the fund called "Wale Wale" and name-checked Jillian and me in the song. It didn't get more all-singing-and-dancing than that.

My codirector and I joined Henri Maire on a flight from Goma to Kinshasa. Vaulting over the Congo jungle took all of three hours flying time, which gave us a sense of its vastness. From above you could see the deforestation that extended out from every jungle track like a cancer.

It was our first time visiting Congo's capital, Kinshasa. The wildlife authority sent a fixer to help us through N'djili International Airport—a welcome and wholly necessary service. There is no other airport in the world quite as chaotic as N'djili. At least five different officials inspected our passports. The police were running more than one extortion racket at a time. If we paid in dollars, we received our change in local money. And straight out the gate, the traffic was atrocious. It took forever to drive in from the airport. On the way we passed through Masina, where I was told local craftsmen can turn anything into anything. "They will turn your Toyota Corolla into a Mercedes-Benz, if you like," said our fixer. "And they can forge most passports."

The city was a sprawling, steaming clutter of buildings and monuments from different decades spread out across a wide bend in the Congo River. As many as eight million people lived there then. In some ways it was more like a European city than other colonial centerpieces I had visited, such as the way it was spread out across such a large area and adorned with plenty of green spaces, had a commuter train service, and a communication tower fixed atop every building. In other ways it seemed like a long-forgotten fixer-upper town—some dusting, a lick of paint here and there, a couple of things put back on their hinges, and it could be as good as new. The water supply and electricity ran out on most days. And the economy was largely based on buying goods, however small, and selling them, slightly marked up, a little way down the road. Kinshasa gave me a new definition for the word "ramshackle." Traffic jams were a boon to street vendors. We passed a toilet shop, no bigger than a newsstand, next to a banana, papaya, and mango stall. And as we wobbled over the cracks and holes of a downtown street, I watched a man navigate his way around half a dozen black-water potholes while carrying a satellite dish on his head.

The Memling was an oasis from the urban mayhem, a clean, medium-sized, air-conditioned hotel with well-trained staff, modern rooms, good food, and wireless Internet. The buffet breakfast was the best in Africa. A pot of fresh, strong, real coffee was already on the table. There was a choice of fresh and flaky bread, fruit chunks and butter kept cold, honey in little honey jars, juice that tasted like it came from a fruit, cold meats and sizzling bacon, and eggs however you wanted them. And the hotel was located in the center of the city, which made walking to meetings a pleasure. Across the street was an air-conditioned delicatessen where they sold fresh cheeses flown in from France, and where I could buy Wild Turkey bourbon.

The fund's Kinshasa resource center was also downtown. Sebu Mugangu, Trinto's brother, managed it. To get online, he had strung a coaxial cable all the way down the street from a nearby Internet café and up two floors of his building. At least we *knew* he was Trinto's brother. Africans were always switching their names around and adding new ones to keep foreigners fooled. And if one family member got a plumb job, suddenly siblings started turning up with jobs in the same organization. Such was the case with Vital Katembo, project manager at Mt. T. Only when we met his older brother in Kinshasa did we learn that Henry Cirhuza, who ran our Goma resource center, was also his brother. Their apparently different "surnames" were simply nicknames they had been given as kids; Cirhuza the sound sleeper and Katembo the elephant.

The Congo River was inaccessible. With one or two exceptions, every access route was guarded by police, and official permission was required to proceed to the banks of the river, which made meeting Olivier Kamitatu at his house on the river all the more pleasurable. Olivier was a class act, a bona fide member of the Congolese elite, which showed in his dress sense and stoic manner. He was the main reason we had come to Kinshasa. As speaker of the National Assembly, he was the highest-ranking official to get involved in the Durban Process. Along with Jillian, Henri, and me, Vital Katembo also attended the meeting. He was a trained ecologist who spoke English, French, and half a dozen African languages. Vital possessed admirable strength of character, and always spoke his mind. He spoke in a singsong manner, as though his voice was about to drop.

As Vital brought Olivier up to speed on the progress we'd made with the Durban Process, I became transfixed by the flow of the Congo River at Malebo Pool, a vast, swirling eddy some five kilometers wide in places. Flat and featureless forested lands banked either side of the

immense waterway, which had a deadly calmness about it that belied
the rushing currents below its surface, warping around the bend in
the river at speed. "Spread out in the tranquil dignity of a waterway
leading to the uttermost ends of the earth," wrote Joseph Conrad
in *Heart of Darkness*. Its width and a lack of finances prevented it
from being bridged, but the continent's second-longest river after the
Nile has the power to provide all of sub-Saharan Africa's electricity
needs. By a cruel joke of nature, impassable cataracts blight the Congo
downstream, near its mouth—a series of thirty-two falls and rapids
that fall 270 meters over 350 kilometers. It's a hapless twist in the
great river's story that renders it useless as a link between seafaring
and riverine transportation. Imagine how much more developed the
country would be if the Congo River basin were accessible from the
Atlantic. Still, it was at least a source of arcane inspiration.

I thought about my own turbulent journey to this place. An overworked Robin Hood with a dozen years in the service of the mountain
gorillas, globe-trotting to and fro across the vast divides between rich
donors and poor beneficiaries, between Beverly Hills and Kisoro, the
Upper East Side and Goma, Belgravia and Ruhengeri. For all my
intercontinental vaulting, I had developed a kind of whiplash. I was
adrift on a river of madness, it felt like, with my wounded ego, twisted
psyche, and burnt-out career. And where would this obsolete boat end
up? Broken on the cataracts, I expect, within sight of the open sea.
Sweet Congo run softly till I end my song.

16

SAVE THE GORILLA

ONE FINE SUMMER day in 2003, our staffer Jo Carton was standing outside the office in Primrose Hill smoking a cigarette. Her good looks caught the attention of a passerby, who stopped to chat her up. The uniquely dressed man said he was concerned about the diminishing numbers of gorillas in the wild. He told her he loved music and said he wanted to do something that would tell the world about the gorillas' plight.

"What kind of music?" asked Jo.

"I like a bit of Adam Ant," said the stranger.

Jo was pleased. This was a perfect opportunity for her to recount that she'd recently been sent a tape by a supporter with a reworking of Adam Ant's hit single "Stand and Deliver," changing it to "Save the Gorilla" as a tribute to the mountain gorillas. Not only did Jo sing the song to the stranger but she also performed a little dance to illustrate it. "Do you know it?"

"I should do," said the man, "I wrote it. I *am* Adam Ant." The 1980s hitmaker then went away with the cassette and reworked the song to his own liking.

Over the summer, Adam grew more fascinated by the gorilla cause, and he became a frequent visitor to our office. He only lived a couple of streets away. Dressed flamboyantly—in blue polka-dot trousers, a black metallic T-shirt, and black homburg—he'd stand at the front by the door, smoking a cigarette, and say loudly, "Hey, Greg, are those fucking psycho poachers still massacring the gorillas? Bastards! They should have their balls cut off and fed to the fucking crocodiles." I'd then leap up from behind my desk, rush to the front, and smilingly escort him outside, insisting that, aside from all the expletives in the presence of the frail ears of our young staffers and volunteers, smoking wasn't permitted in the office. We became friends.

He invited me into his home, a large ground-floor flat in a Georgian house on Princess Road. The place was in disarray. He famously didn't drink or do drugs, and yet even in the absence of all that paraphernalia, this was clearly a rock star's pad. The wood-paneled studio was painted white, and shelves were stacked to the limit with books, LPs, and CDs. The walls were covered with random images, mostly of the pop star, that told the story of a dark and wonderful life. He showed me a demo of the Beatles' *Revolver* album that Paul McCartney had signed. "My mum used to clean his house," smiled Adam. On his mantel was an eclectic array of statuettes: Dandy Highwayman, pirates, hussars on horseback, and *Star Wars* figurines. And in and among all the clutter and toot-and-tat were two Ivor Novello Awards. In 1982 Adam and cowriter Marco Pirroni won Songwriter of the Year and Best Selling "A" Side for "Stand and Deliver." That song topped the charts for fifteen weeks and made Adam the most successful British artist of that time.

Scattered around the flat were important documents in need of filing, including bank statements from three different banks. "I don't know how much money I have," said Adam, tossing a statement aside. He had no professional staff. His agent, manager, and PR consultant had all abandoned him—no one was looking after his career as a singer-songwriter. However much it had faded, he still had a loyal fan base. For me, to be working with a household name who had no "people" was a refreshing change.

He made me a cup of tea, and we sat at his dining table as he showed me the notebook where he had been reworking the lyrics to "Stand and Deliver." Soft-spoken with a cockney accent, he was thoughtful and articulate, yet tormented by demons. I could see it in his eyes.

"I've kept in the original lyric," he said. "'And even though you fool your soul / Your conscience will be mine, all mine,' but I've changed the chorus: 'Save the gorilla / Your money for their lives / Hug a gorilla / No bullet or a knife . . .'" We talked about gorillas: where they lived, what they ate, who was threatening their survival. He told me that he sometimes heard the chimpanzees in Regent's Park zoo at night. I said that might have been Peter Elliott, the ape actor, who lived one street over. Adam was intrigued. That night the police picked him up outside the zoo, where he had been remonstrating about poachers and gorilla baby buyers and howling at the apes.

He was terrified of getting nicked. Once while we were standing outside the office having a smoke, a police van drove past. "They're after me," cried Adam, bolting into our office.

"Don't be silly," I chuckled, but Adam hid in the basement.

The van screeched to a halt, did a quick U-turn, and then pulled up in front of the office. Two officers stepped out of the van and one of them asked, "Was that Stuart Goddard you were just talking to?"

"Who?" I asked.

"Adam Ant."

"Er . . ."

"Tell him not to worry, we're not after him. Just checking to see if he's OK." I went downstairs and relayed this to Adam. He grabbed hold of a donated magnum of champagne and marched up the stairs to confront the Old Bill. But before he could, I snatched the bottle away from him and insisted he talk to them nicely. He agreed.

"All right, Adam?" asked an officer.

In an instant, Adam's mood switched from antagonistic firebrand to wide-eyed child. "Yes, thank you, officer," he said sweetly. "I'm feeling peachy. Those are nice shoes you're wearing. You know you can always tell a London bobby, even in plain clothes, by his shoes."

We knew Adam was bipolar. Reports about disturbances involving the pop star were frequently on the front pages of the tabloids. He'd only just been discharged from the hospital when we met him. We weren't aware, however, that he wasn't taking his meds, as ordered by a magistrate. Consequently, that summer he would steadily ascend into full-blown mania. Channel 4 broadcast a documentary about him, *The Madness of Prince Charming*. "Mental illness depression is like having a fist smashed right in your skull," Adam says in the documentary. Behind the pride, courage, humor, and flair was a lost soul who was finding it hard to cope without fame.

But his mental illness was also a part of what drove his creativity. After a manic episode, he could bring a manic message back from the "far country" and engage his audience in its energy. Then came depression. Now the tabloids he had courted at the start of his meteoric career were turning on him. They shamelessly reveled in his downfall. They were ruthless. But Adam was his own worst enemy. Once, after some people in a pub laughed at him for the way he was dressed, he threw a car alternator through the pub's plate glass window. Two days later he was sectioned and committed to a psychiatric hospital. "There's only one thing worse than going to the workhouse," says Adam, "and that's going to the madhouse. You're at the bottom."

One Saturday afternoon in August, Adam called me at home. "I'm at the House of Boz, recording the songs. Come down!"

"Songs?" I said to Jillian. Boz Boorer, founder of the Polecats and Morrissey's lead guitarist, was barely a mile from our flat at his studio in West Hampstead. Boz was simultaneously at the controls and playing guitar, Adam played bass, and Adam's girlfriend Claire videoed the session. The pop star was jacked, on an episode. He insisted on recording every vocal track in one take before overdubbing a backing vocal, smoking all the while. As well as "Save the Gorilla," he sang "Jungle Rock" by Hank Mizell, "Stranded in the Jungle" by the New York Dolls, "Monkey Man" by Toots & the Maytals, and "Monkey Man" by the Rolling Stones—every one a one-take wonder. Obsessed with the idea of recording a song and releasing it the same week, Adam insisted we master and press the EP within days. It took us a month.

Claire's footage of Adam and Boz performing "Save the Gorilla" formed the basis of a five-minute video I edited on my laptop. We posted it on his fan site, adam-ant.net. *SPIN* magazine, in its January 2004 review of the video, wrote, "It's kind of poignant that Ant is wearing spectacles over his trademark eye makeup in the video. But this version, which substitutes ape sounds for the original's 'na deedly kwa kwa' vocal, tends to squander any goodwill at around the four-minute mark. Still, it's good to know he hasn't lost his way with a lyric: 'I don't know the next verse, because I haven't even writ it. Bollocks. Oh, shit. Poo.'"

Adam also signed up for the Great Gorilla Run (GGR). Thereafter, Jillian became his de facto PR agent, got him in tabloid newspapers, *London Tonight*, and the *Evening Standard*. Her and Adam's campaign proved spectacular in promoting the GGR and raising awareness of our cause. It also demonstrated the pop star's commitment to saving gorillas. Adam was amazing and, although tongue-tied at times, he never missed an opportunity to plug our charity.

Richard Bacon's interview with him on XFM radio is outrageous. They begin by rubbishing David Blaine, an American endurance artist and extreme performer who was at the time conducting an endurance stunt called "Above and Below," sealing himself inside a transparent plexiglass box suspended nine meters in the air next to the river Thames. The stunt had lasted weeks by then, during which Blaine had not eaten, only drunk water.

Londoners were cynical about the stunt, and Adam homed in on that sentiment. "David Blaine is going down," he says. "Adam and the Ants want David Blaine to eat . . . I bet you he's begging for a bacon sandwich. . . . And by the way Adam and the Ants are re-forming."

"Is this an exclusive?" asks Bacon.

"Yeah. Basically, we're re-forming if we can get Marco out of bed, because he's been eating pies. But if we can get him out of bed and he can lose weight . . ."

"Perhaps he could eat those pies in front of David Blaine," says Bacon. "Now I want to move on. On the 21st of September, Adam Ant is going to be running around the City of London dressed as a *gorilla!*"

"The idea is you pay a hundred quid for one of these." Adam passes a package to Bacon.

"What is that?" cries Bacon. "That's a gorilla outfit. *Is that for me?* I've just been handed a gorilla outfit by Adam Ant."

"Where does the race start, darling?" Adam asks Jillian, who's in the studio with him. "Jillian, where does it start?"

"The London Underwriters Building," says Jillian.

"Save the Gorilla" debuted on XFM. Thousands of Britons heard it, including Marco Pirroni, who must have already been seething after hearing Adam's comments about his weight. No doubt he was doubly pissed that Adam chose Boz to play guitar on the track.

Its broadcast generated a stir. Most people thought it was whack. But Adam's press coverage was doing wonders for the Great Gorilla Run. On the day of the race, the original Dandy Highwayman showed up in jeans, a black leather jacket, and a gray-and-black No Fear beanie. Posing for photographs with the other gorilla runners before the start, Adam with his very presence raised spirits and helped make it a great day, even if he didn't actually take part in the run in the end.

Hundreds of gorillas hooted and whooped as they brachiated across the Thames on Blackfriars Bridge. Londoners strolling along the riverbank that Sunday morning must have been mortified. Not since AD 43 when Claudius invaded Britain with war elephants had so many large charismatic mammals been seen in London. The route snaked back and forth across the Thames past world-famous London landmarks—Tower Bridge, the Tate Modern, and St. Paul's Cathedral. Adding to the pageantry, most of the runners wore themed costumes on top of their gorilla outfits: superheroes, ballerinas, pirates, Vikings. Some runners wielded giant inflatable bananas. Everyone was howling. A gorilla in a kilt played the bagpipes, another in chain mail carried the Cross of St. George, and one dressed as a clown completed the entire seven-kilometer course on roller skates. I saw a mother with a bikini over her gorilla suit pushing a pram with a baby inside who was wearing a tiny gorilla suit. I wore a straw hat and loud Hawaiian shirt over my outfit.

Not sure what I was. Tequila Baron Gorilla, perhaps? Every runner was given a unique number. Mine was 650, the number of mountain gorillas left in the wild. I was sweating buckets, my vision was hampered by lopsided eyeholes that shifted around, and my nipples were sore from rubbing against the latex breastplate. Barely halfway and I was already tapped out and seriously considering dropping out of this insane event. But as executive director of the benefiting charity, I had to finish. Also, £1,800 in sponsorship pledges were riding on me completing the course. A gorilla in my situation would likely take his responsibility more seriously. With the sound of my own breath thundering in my ears, I staggered on. A policewoman smiled and shook her head as I lurched past. "You're halfway, love," she said. "Go on! You can make it."

Running alongside dozens of other primates, I got into the mind of an ape. I was Caesar leading his apes into battle to build a better society for both apes and humans, except I was way behind the lead runners. The big fellas got a bad rap in *Planet of the Apes*, cast as brutes and members of an aggressive military, alongside conservative orangutan religious types and liberal chimpanzee experts. Wrong. Gorillas are much less violent than chimps, which conduct warfare. One way to illustrate the differences between them is to consider what each great ape species would do if they were handed a camera. An orangutan would use his amazing dexterity to take it apart without breaking anything. A chimpanzee would swing it around and around by its strap and then smash it against a tree. A gorilla would hold it carefully, sniff it, check out her image in the lens, and then nervously hand it back. And what would a bonobo do? Fuck it.

I wondered if I might be going mad. Not mad, just going through a transformation. A metamorphosis that began years ago was only manifesting itself now. I was becoming a gorilla man. In my thirteen years in this zany career, I had so often interacted with gorillas, gorillaphiles, people in gorilla suits, and the gorilla curious, that a kind of symbiosis had occurred. I even spoke their language. Not the belch vocalizations mimicked by researchers when they approach them in the wild but actual words. Onward, Upper Fake Tooth! Passing under the plexiglass box where the starving David Blaine was imprisoned, I joined those calling themselves the Primates of the Caribbean and threw bananas at him and beat my chest. It must have been amusing for him to watch. I crossed the line in just forty minutes. I was exhausted and elated. Kinda like how Leonardo felt after spending two hours with Koko. I should coco.

In addition to being a highly entertaining and photogenic carnival and utterly exhilarating to participate in, the event was an unqualified fundraising success, raising upward of £100,000. And the next day all the London papers had pictures of gorillas on their front pages. A Great Gorilla Run has been held every year since, raising millions for gorilla conservation.

From the ridiculous to the sublime. At the same time that she and Adam Ant were promoting the Great Gorilla Run, Jillian was putting together a scholarly project for the fund. She had been working with Palazzo Editions, a publisher of beautifully designed and illustrated works, to get Dian Fossey's letters into print. Bob Campbell stepped in and provided many of his own photographs that had never been published before, as well as some of his own personal letters from Dian. Ian Redmond, too, provided letters.

The project was particularly satisfying for us, having become involved in her charity after our founder had died, as it rounded a circle by closely connecting us to her origin story. I'm not sure who made the editorial choice to leave out most of the letters. "A unique and intimate portrait of an extraordinary woman . . . set in context by a compelling narrative," reads Camilla de la Bédoyère's blurb for *No One Loved Gorillas More: Dian Fossey: Letters from the Mist*, which the National Geographic Society would publish with a description of the UK fund on the cover, along with its web address: dianfossey.org. It was our first venture into publishing, and the book would be the ultimate undoing of DFGF Europe.

I bumped into Adam sitting outside a cafe on Regent's Park Road. He was wearing a Panama hat and gray silk scarf from Vietnam, and to illustrate his Romani roots, chunky silver rings of all shapes and sizes on his fingers. An attractive young woman was sitting with him. He invited me to join them. I sat for a moment.

Adam was proud of his association with the fund, and he let anyone who'd listen to him know it. "I've got a great idea, Greg," he said. "Why don't we do a Claymation? Boz and me get dropped into the jungle and we have to play music to save the gorillas."

Actually, it wasn't such a crazy idea when I thought about it. But who would fund it? I excused myself, saying I had to get back to work. I had begun walking up the road when Adam called out to me, "Greg! I love you," loud enough for all to hear. "I love you, Greg!" Made me smile.

Soon after that, Adam was again admitted into a psychiatric hospital. He called me and asked me to come visit him, said he had something to give me. I went down to the hospital and was led into a locked ward. Adam was sitting alone in a room surrounded by white-and-green medical trappings. Without his makeup and flamboyant garb, he looked fragile. "I wanted to give you this," he said softly. It was a chunky silver ring with the face of a screaming silverback carved into it. He said he'd bought it a couple of days before with me in mind at Camden Market. "A gift from my gypsy heart," he said. He then handed me a stack of mini Betacam cassettes—footage he'd shot over the summer.

Back at the office, we reviewed the footage. It was mostly of him walking around neighborhoods in London pointing out landmarks from his career: where the Sex Pistols opened for his band Bazooka Joe, where he opened for Madonna. He goes into Fortnum & Mason to use the posh department store's bathroom. And while he sits on the bog taking a dump, he carries on filming the whole time. The funniest clip is of him in a suite at the Groucho Club. As he pans across the surfaces of the suite's exquisite furniture on which large antique books are scattered, he gives a running commentary on the illustrations of hussars, and then we see someone lying in bed under the sheets: a man. "Hello," says Adam cheerfully. "What's this? A man in my bed? I'm not a shirt-lifter. I've never taken it up the jacksy before."

Adam was still in hospital when "Save the Gorilla" was scheduled to be released. The *Sun* gave the CD free exposure and generated a storm of publicity. Adam had not recorded any new material in over a decade. We were inundated with email inquiries and letters from his fans. The hype reached fever pitch.

Five days before it was due to be released, however, I was walking across Chalk Farm Bridge when I received a call from EMI: "Marco Pirroni refuses to allow the release of your CD."

"What?" I said, stopping in my tracks. "Why on earth would he do that?"

"As one of the cowriters of the original song, it's his right to do so. And as his publishers, it's our right to insist." Foiled again!

The next day BBC News website ran the headline EMI "BLOCKS" ADAM ANT CHARITY CD. The fund was out of pocket to the tune of £5,000. Some say we should not have embarked on this project in the first place, but neither Jillian nor I was inclined to turn down offers from celebrities to promote the cause. It was our job to keep that door wide open. What should we have said? "Sorry, Adam, but you're off your meds, and you could do yourself some harm by recording a benefit EP for the gorillas." Not our style.

A fan with the handle "Alex in NYC" posted his thoughts on adam-ant.net: "I don't think this is as tragic as some of you are asserting. Is it frankly bizarre? Hell yeah, but the cause is an established one. It's not like Adam is rallying for extradition to Narnia or making a plea for the heretofore unsung rights of magical fish. He obviously caught a late-night screening of 'Gorillas in the Mist' and sought to do his part." A fair assessment. And it was exciting working with Adam even if at times things got a little bizarre.

One evening I got a frantic call from Jillian, who had booked him on the *Richard & Judy* show. "The studio sent a limousine that's waiting outside his house, and Adam is loading all of his *Star Wars* figurines into it, insisting that he take them with him on the show. I told him, 'Adam, Richard and Judy are waiting. You're on at six o'clock. They're already talking about you, plugging your appearance. You can't let them down.'"

"No, I've changed my mind," said Adam. "I don't want to do that show."

"But you're booked: *Richard & Judy* at Channel 4 studios at six o'clock."

"I've got a better idea," said Adam. "Adam and the Ants versus Richard and Judy at the Pirate Castle at midnight." Such a natural showman.

I saw him once again after he came out of the hospital. This time he was on his meds. He didn't acknowledge me. It made me sad to walk away.

17

NO ONE LOVED GORILLAS MORE

WITH NEARLY TWO million people spread across 190 square kilometers of closely quartered dwellings made of cement, wattle, and corrugated iron, Kampala can feel like a sprawling urban jungle. Uniquely, however, Uganda's capital has a golf course in the middle of it. Rolling acres of grassy links shaded by large, wide spreading trees offer an oasis for the weary urbanite (so long as he or she is a member of the golf club).

Golf Course Apartments, as the name implied, faced the golf course. On the top floor of the foremost block was the fund's spacious two-bedroom apartment, which enjoyed panoramic views of central Kampala's lush greenery. The apartment complex featured two swimming pools, a gym, tennis courts, and a coffee shop that served espressos in the morning. The rent was high, but the fund was turning over millions at the time, so we could afford it and, besides, it came fully serviced.

Living there was a dream come true for me. Finally, I had an address in Africa. Of course, it wasn't mine personally and I never stayed longer than two weeks at a time, but I thought of it as my refuge on the Bright Continent. And when I awoke in the morning and realized I was there, my heart soared like a spiraling marabou stork.

Uganda suited me. Its climate was salubrious, its citizens spoke English, and marijuana grew wild. The herb was so prolific that the nation had earned the nickname Uganja. Best of all, the social scene was far more racially integrated in Kampala than in other African cities I knew. It lacked the crusty colonial legacy typical to places once run by Europeans. When the British arrived in the nineteenth century, while searching for the source of the Nile, they found not one but several kingdoms that had more or less agreed to a balance of power.

Britain liked what it saw, a society with inbuilt hierarchies and a laboring class, and it tried to convince its citizens to settle there and grow cotton for the empire. Hang the balance of power. The Foreign Office regarded Kenya, which was then overrun by warring Maasai tribes, as little more than a risky but necessary route from the coast to Uganda. To speed their settlers over dangerous badlands and onto the safety of a civilized hinterland, they therefore set out to build a railway from Mombasa to Kampala. The Lunatic Express, as it became known, was never completed. A railway station built at the line's exact halfway point is how Nairobi came to be, as it was then an uninhabited swamp. By the time the settlers reached it, however, they'd had enough of crossing the savage continent, so they settled in the Kenyan highlands instead. Accordingly, despite the risks, some fifty times more Britons settled in Kenya than in Uganda. This had a lasting effect on Uganda's colonial legacy. The locals didn't grow quite as weary of colonial rule as Kenyans or South Africans, and consequently were not as prejudiced against the *mzungu*.

Growing up, I heard "Mzungu! Mzungu!" wherever I went. I got called it more often than my own name. While it has come to refer to White people in general, literally translated from Kiswahili, *mzungu* means "someone who roams around" or "wanderer." The term was first used to describe nineteenth-century European explorers in Africa because they appeared to wander around aimlessly—if you can call a search, in the furtherance of science, for important rivers, lakes, and mountains aimless. *Zungu* or *zunguka* means "spinning around on the same spot," and *kizunguzungu* means "dizziness." Either way, I felt I'd truly earned the title. While lacking the hubris, godly purpose, and facial hair of a nineteenth-century explorer, I'd certainly spent enough time in the African bush to qualify. I'd suffered a few bouts of malaria as a result, though I was never quite *kizunguzungu*. Neither were my wanderings aimless. I still had a job to do.

It had been a busy twelve months. I traveled to Washington, DC, and New York City to try and drum up support for the Durban Process from the World Bank and the US Fish and Wildlife Service. Herbert Allen donated $30,000. Jillian and I toured East Africa's wildernesses, meeting as many innovators as we could, to glean the latest in community-based conservation.

Richard Leakey helped draw up our itinerary. The once-chairman of the Kenya Wildlife Service had since moved on, but he remained an active conservationist. His successor was David Western. We went to see him as well, at his house on the edge of Nairobi National Park. The two were known to have opposing views about wildlife conservation. Leakey favored electric fences and heavily armed rangers; Western favored fenceless parks and conservation through local communities. Both were equally valid approaches, we thought, as we bounced around the game parks meeting wildlife's future hopes.

It became clear that Africa's wildlife was wholly at the mercy of its exploding human population. The clock was ticking, but the more Africans who became conservation minded, the better the outcome for wildlife. We held a second Durban Process meeting at Tarangire Safari Lodge in Tanzania. Coincidently, the two lodges where our meetings were held—Tala and Tarangire—began with "Ta," the chemical symbol for tantalum, which was what it was all about.

I then took my friend Jon Simonson, who owned the Lodge, to Mount Tshiaberimu. The drive took half a day, and before crossing the Congo border, we spent the night at Mweya Safari Lodge in Queen Elizabeth National Park. I had stayed there when I was five. I clearly remember the view of the Mountains of the Moon. It's where my father decided that because of fighting in the Congo, it was too risky for us to continue on, that we should abandon our dream of seeing the elusive mountain gorillas and return home to Nairobi.

And just before Christmas, I got a call from Herbert Allen asking if I could join his friends Diane von Furstenberg and Barry Diller and their entourage on a gorilla trek in the Virungas on New Year's Day. I jumped at the chance, even if it meant abandoning my wife during the holidays.

It was Vince Smith who had first shown me around Kampala's dizzyingly decadent nightclubs. Thereafter I'd begun a crusade to convince Jillian and the board to move the fund's Africa headquarters from Kigali to Kampala. Vince had since resigned from the fund, after publishing *Sophie's Story*, a book about the chimp he raised, and we didn't see the need to replace him. Thereafter, our field projects would be managed by our resource center managers working at the conservation front line: Emmanuel Bugingo in Rwanda, Samuel Warike in Uganda, and Henry Cirhuza in Congo. Meanwhile, commuting between the UK and Uganda every month or so, Jillian and I would coordinate our field program through the Kampala office, which at the start of 2005 was staffed by one Ugandan accountant.

The office was a mere ten-minute walk from Golf Course Apartments—all downhill. And yet, on a morning when the clouds parted and the equatorial sun leaned on my sweat-beaded pate, it could be grueling, especially if I was nursing a hangover. That's when Patrice would come to my rescue in our fully air-conditioned, black-on-black Land Rover Discovery 4—a sleek, head-turning ride. The "Blackback," as he and I liked to call it, actually belonged to the Gorilla Safari Co., a company that Jillian and I owned jointly along with British investor Simon Lewis. The safari company and the fund shared the costs of keeping the Blackback on the road and employing Patrice Basha as its driver. It was a practical arrangement.

When he picked me up at Golf Course that night, Patrice wore a black T-shirt with a large multicolored marijuana leaf on it, black jeans, and a fresh pair of beige Timberlands—always a fresh pair. He had a pronounced forehead and was balding, and what remained of his hair was dreadlocked. He needed to wear glasses, but only ever took off his shades to wear them when it got dark. Our destination was Fat Boyz, a bar and grill that was also within walking distance of the flat, but arriving on foot at Kampala's hottest new joint didn't have the same cachet and dramatic impact as pulling up in the Blackback.

Darren Dooley, who owned Fat Boyz, made Patrice and me feel like a pair of high-rolling gangsters when we walked into his bar. He gave us the VIP treatment and always kept a parking space blocked off so we could park our fly ride directly in front of his bar. "To the window," he'd shout, quoting Lil Jon's hip-hop hit "Get Low."

"To the wall." I'd reply, matching his vigor while striding up to him with a jive limp.

"Till the sweat drop down my balls," he'd say, leaping down from the pool table.

"Till all these bitches crawl."

"Till all skeet skeet motherfucker," we'd shout together as we embraced. "Till all skeet-skeet, goddamn!"

Darren was African American, originally from Decatur, Illinois, but more recently from Atlanta, Georgia, where he'd met his Finnish wife, Tehri, during the 1996 Summer Olympics. In her capacity as an executive assistant to the resident representative of the European Union, she had taken Darren to a string of posts in far corners of the world. People thought he was crazy by the way he behaved, but one thing was for sure: you had to be on the ball to run a successful business in Uganda. Outside hung a large sign boasting, WARM BEER AND LOUSY FOOD. When questioned about this unorthodox marketing style, Darren smiled and said, "That way you'll never feel let down. I *know* my food's good." He was good looking, charming, and artful, and liked to think of himself as a self-made man. And he had a world-class hustle.

"Wassup, G-money?" cried Byron when he saw me. Byron Jameson, also African American, was from Long Beach, California, or "Strong Beach," as he called it. "Papi," as the girls called him, was having too much fun in Uganja. He was tall and old-school smooth. Whereas Darren wore cornrows, hip-hop colors, and funky brand-name threads, Byron always dressed in fine silk shirts and neatly pressed slacks. He charmed the hell out of regulars, like the host at a high-end nightclub. Food was a priority when Darren opened the place: slow-cooked meats in a Tex-Mex combination of sauces and vegetables. He'd even gone on local TV to promote his cuisine. The food was still reasonably good, but lately Fat Boyz had become little more than a beer machine that stayed open until dawn.

"Where you been, motherfucker?" asked Darren.

"On safari," I said. "Patrice and I just got back from a whirlwind road trip to Rwanda."

"Can I buy you a beer?"

"If you mean a cold, wet, fizzy, and refreshingly tasty alcoholic drink that's found in almost every place in the world with most of those qualities intact? Hell, yes! It's traditional at the end of a road journey."

I filled him in on the Diller–von Furstenberg safari, how they and their friends had flown in from Botswana on a Gulfstream 5 private jet. That Patrice and I had met their helicopter when it arrived in Gisenyi from Kigali. "We didn't have to do nothing but smile and look good beside the Blackback. Coca-Cola, on whose board both Diller and Herb Allen serve, organized the whole damn thing. The clients didn't even ride with us, which is just as well because the Blackback was where me and P. smoked weed." I told Darren that Diller and von Furstenberg were a polyamorous married couple whose entourage included Barry's friend Bryan Lourd, CEO of Creative Artists Agency; Brian Lourd's twelve-year-old daughter Billie, whose mother was Carrie Fisher; the shoe designer Christian Louboutin, and his boyfriend Henri, a Parisian landscape artist; and Hamilton South, an executive at Ralph Lauren. "Whose name sounds like a rough part of Ontario," I added. "And after they'd all registered at the Lake Kivu Serena Hotel, the receptionists said, 'Never before have so many men checked into so few rooms.'"

Darren laughed, then said, "Did any of them try anything funny with P-man here?"

"I'm not gay, motherfucker," cried Patrice, with typical African homophobia.

"Relax, P.," I said. "No, D., but I gotta tell you, I was surprised to find Rwanda so open to homosexuality. Damn, it's a progressive country. They know the value of the pink dollar and that lots of gay couples want to meet mountain gorillas and are willing to pay more to feel safe. Not like in Uganda where it's illegal and punishable by death. Fucking Bible-bashing morons. These were real cool people, more switched on to the local vibe than most first-time visitors to Africa."

"Oh, it's easy to get laid back about shit when you flying around in a G5," said Darren.

"Yeah, but get this, in the Okavango Delta, Diller tried to book level 6 accommodation for his entourage over Christmas and every one of the camps was fully occupied. So he asks the property owner to send a message to the party who were checked into them with an offer to buy them out. 'Fuck you, we're richer than you,' came the reply from the Saudi royal family."

"Sheeeeeet," said Darren, followed by a loud guffaw. "So that's how these rich bitches roll." He then ordered a round of tequilas from the bartender. "But now you and P. are back in KLA, right, and looking to get your swerve on again? Am I right, dog?"

"Damn straight, Dooley," I said, slapping him on the back. "Let's get this party started!"

"I'm down, like four flat tires," said Darren. "Let's do a bump."

"That's what *I'm* screaming about," said Byron.

It took me a while to tune in to how Darren and Byron related to each other. They'd say shit like "I was just lost in the sauce," or "Lie don't care who tell it," or, "If you're scared, then call the police," or "He needs checkup from the neck up." My favorite was, "I'm trying to hit you with this uptown shit, and you're hitting me with this downtown shit." But I had yet to decode what Darren meant by "Chuck-Wow and the Hareem Foundation, poppin' little Tiger Woods like pills." *Bump* was one of those vernacular words whose meaning was adrift, and it definitely needed context before you could be sure of what was being said. In this case it meant a line of coke.

"Sure," I replied.

On my way to the washroom, my phone rang. It was my wife and codirector calling from London. "What's up, Jillie?" I asked. "Trouble at mill?"

"You could say that," she said gravely. "A legal writ has just arrived at the office."

"Oh, Jesus Christ, no. From who?"

"DFGF International is suing us to give up use of the name 'Dian Fossey,'" she said.

"They can't do that," I cried. "Who the fuck do they think they are?"

"They've scheduled legal arbitration in Atlanta in September. We've got to be there. David Rogers has said he will come. I'm sending you a copy of the legal papers. They're also demanding that we give up the web address dianfossey.org."

"I'm calling Sigourney Weaver," I said. "She's a patron of both charities. Maybe I can get her to talk some sense into them."

I hung up from my wife and immediately called the movie star at her apartment on the Upper East Side of Manhattan. I explained what had happened. She told me she couldn't deal with it right now as she was about to take her daughter to the doctor.

"But you have to help us, Sigourney. They're suing us!"

"Yes, well, some people *need* to get sued," she said coldly. "Sorry, but I've got to go."

———

I couldn't believe DFGF International would stoop so low as to issue a legal writ against its sister charity in London. I knew they had it in for us, but this was nasty and utterly vindictive. Then I remembered the book, *No One Loved Gorillas More*, which the National Geographic Society was about to publish in the United States. The illustrated coffee-table book of Dian Fossey's letters contained the first new material from our founder since *Gorillas in the Mist*. But it had Europe's details on the dust cover, not International's, and our web address. International was tight with Nat Geo and must have gotten wind of the project before its publication date.

"Man, they must have been foaming at the mouth when they heard about it," I smiled.

"Motherfuckers are stuck on stupid," said Darren. "I mean, that shit ain't right."

"I now have reason to get fucked up," I said as I leaned over the glass coffee table in my apartment and snorted up a rail of cocaine— half in one nostril, half in the other. I then used my thumb and forefinger to twitch my nostrils as I inhaled sharply, to make sure every grain of the drug had gotten up into my nasal passage. "But don't worry, D.," I sniffed. "We gonna fight those motherfuckers.

We got just as much license, if not more, to use that name as they do. They're the ones who've brought her name into disrepute. I told you about that White bitch trying to kill that other Witch bitch in Rwanda over that Congolese dude, right?"

"Oh yeah, you told me that story."

"After all the effort we put into building the Dian Fossey brand, they think they can just snatch it away from under us, seize dianfossey.org. If those bastards think they can take credit for our good work, they got another fucking thing coming. Fucking litigious bastards!"

"Time to get lawyered up," said Byron.

"Too right! Our lawyers in London have already put us in touch with a copyright lawyer in New York who's going to represent us in Atlanta. Shit just got real, motherfuckers!"

"Chuck-Wow and the Hareem Foundation, poppin' little Tiger Woods like pills."

"The what . . . ?" I looked at Darren. He grinned and stared at me sideways like the way a goofy lizard looks at you before bolting. I turned to Byron. "Truth is, Jillian and I have done this job for two decades without anyone being there on the sidelines to cheer us on. It's just been us. It was about growing our own funk and then getting a buzz from that, know'm'sayin?"

"True dat," said Byron.

"Innovative ideas, successful methodology, and access to finance are what's required to get the job done in the goddamn African jungle. Everything else is just talk, right? We didn't just talk. We walked the fucking walk, know'm'sayin?!"

I didn't feel up to joining them at the Rock Bar. I needed to get my head straight. Soon it was just me alone in my flat. At Golf Course Apartments I felt like I was surrounded by ghosts. How could I not in such a place, where a conspiracy of silence existed between the dead and the living? Out on the edge of the golf course, in a valley that runs through it, the ghosts were pervasive. There Idi Amin

dumped the bodies of his torture victims—the ones he didn't leave
to float ashore on Lake Victoria—left them for storks to pick over.
The nation struggled hard to recover from Amin. Their recovery was
a thing of wonder. Now Kampala, or KLA as the locals called it, had
become the crossroads of Africa. Those who came were seduced and
came again or stayed. "To live and die in KLA," they said. Now, it
seemed, I too was being seduced.

———————

When in doubt, head to the hills. This time I flew. I adored Africa's
rugged landscapes. It's where I grew up. "A million miles of bloody
Africa," wrote Ernest Hemingway in *Green Hills of Africa.* For those
who'd seen it, his words were a term of endearment. A landscape so
vast and bold it was enough to absorb my deepest darkest sorrows, I
thought. It was the summer solstice and I was taking Geoff Carr to
meet the Mt. T. gorillas near the equator. It occurred to me, as our
twelve-seater prop plane descended into Butembo airport in Congo,
that the date and our destination would have been sufficient coordinates to rendezvous with an alien. We drove east in the fund's project
vehicle toward the Congo-Uganda border.

I was a swirling mass of fucking confusion. But as we neared our
destination, I became calmer. Gorillas would mend me. We drove in
from the west on a winding dirt road over a rolling plateau. "The
fund paid to grate these last six kilometers leading up to the park
boundary at Burusi," I told Geoff, "The locals were terribly grateful.
It certainly got us on the right track."

A montane forest covering an area of forty-eight square kilometers,
Tshiaberimu, or mountain of spirits, was all that remained of a forest
that was once ten times as large and straddled the Rift escarpment.
Mt. T. project manager Vital Katembo said gorillas were part of local
mythology, that children were warned by their parents not to play

outside after dark or they might be kidnapped by gorillas and never seen again. The fact that this mountain of spirits had legends and superstitions associated with it may be the only reason it had managed to remain intact—an island of thickly forested gorilla habitat surrounded by a sea of farmland.

It was normally a two-and-half-hour climb to Camp Kalibina at three thousand meters, the fund's project station. At times the incline seemed too steep to manage. Geoff, who stopped every five minutes to regain his composure, said it was the most arduous workout he'd ever endured. He was a large, hirsute man with uncommon knowledge of scientific research. So I stuck with him the whole way, if only for the conversation, even though I could now make it to Kalibina in an hour and forty-five minutes. Last time I arrived before the porters carrying the crates of beer and mattresses on their heads. It's all about understanding the trail. Once you know its shape it is easier to hike.

I told Geoff about a trip I'd recently taken with BBC director Marc Perkins and cameraman Fred Scott to a town called Walikale on the edge of the Congo jungle. "It was as far as I had ever traveled into Africa's interior," I said. "To get there we'd flown in from Goma on a Russian Antonov, more of a truck than a plane. We sat on sacks of potatoes the whole way. As we landed, the tips of the Antonov's wings clipped the dense foliage on either side of us. And the runway was the same road we'd later drive down: a paved segment no longer than thirty-five kilometers in the middle of nowhere. But when we tried to leave the next day, a group of militia stopped us and insisted on confiscating our footage. Reluctantly, Marc handed over the tapes. I was aghast but after our plane took off, Fred showed me the real videotapes. The ones they gave the soldiers were blanks. I thought, well played, maestros."

"Walikale sounds like the wild frontier," said Geoff.

"I'm planning to move there," I said. "Live out the rest of my days in deepest darkest."

"Really?"

"No." We continued climbing the impossible mountain in silence. "Give up the name 'Dian Fossey'?" I grumbled as I stomped breathlessly up the trail.

"Who are you cursing?" asked Geoff.

"Our sister charity in Atlanta," I said, choosing my words carefully because Geoff was a journalist and the science editor of the *Economist*. "They're a bunch of artless bastards who deserve to rot in hell." My hatred of them robbed me of all caution.

Geoff and I arrived at Kalibina after nightfall and then joined the others beside a campfire they had built. The fire was fueled by a bundle of old bamboo fanned out downwind of it. As the night progressed and we drank more beer, they pushed bamboo stalks progressively inward toward the flames.

"They should charge a $1,000 trekking fee to visit Mt. T.," I said, as I quaffed a Primus. "There are just too few of them and their habitat is just too damn fragile to ask anything less."

"Tell me about these gorillas," said Geoff.

"They're very special," I said. "A distinctive population that live only on this mountain. But the jury's still out on their taxonomic status. Based on their short body and facial hair, the gorillas on Mt. T. were thought to be a unique subspecies. Some say they're eastern lowland gorillas; others, mountain gorillas. They have markedly different body proportions, suggesting considerable population differences. But it may just be adaptive morphology."

"They were first described in 1927," said Vital, "as *Gorilla gorilla rex-pygmaeorum.*"

"But that name has since been scrapped," I said. "Clearly, there is still much research to be done. Nevertheless, these gorillas could be another distinct subspecies—another link in our evolution. We'll never know if we let them become extinct."

"How many are there?"

"Twenty-one," said Vital.

"Crikey, not many," said Geoff. "Remind me how long this project's been going?"

"The fund hired me in September 1996," replied Vital, "and we began immediately. We found only twelve when we conducted our first census . . ."

"With funding from Michael Crichton," I added, "whose initial twenty-five grand was invaluable 'pump-priming' support for this project. Others followed. Since then, the scale of the fund's involvement has escalated, like the road to the park boundary that we drove in on. The project's success is entirely down to Vital here," I said, slapping him on the back. "His delicate diplomacy, boundless energy, and insider knowledge of the region has won over the community."

"Progress has been made in community involvement," smiled Vital. "We've had fruitful discussions with community leaders. Together with the Congolese park rangers, we're redefining the limits of the park and reclaiming land which has been illegally cleared for farming."

"Tell him about the time you were chased off a farm by angry ladies armed with sticks."

We exchanged a few more stories but before it got too late, and with the aid of torches, we each found our bunks and literally hit the hay. Geoff got a real mattress, but the next morning, bemused by having to squat over the camp pit latrine, he asked, "Couldn't you've built a seat out of bamboo as well? My knees are knackered, mate."

"Yeah, but the view, mate . . . the view."

As a light rain fell, we set off on our gorilla trek. We tramped through the forest for an hour then found a small group of gorillas, so diminutive they appeared at first to be chimps. Silverback, mature female, adolescent female, and infant male. That's all there was to this group. Lusenge, the silverback, gave us the once over and then lost interest. The youngsters paid us their full attention. Mukokya, the adolescent female, was as much a source of amusement as she had been on previous encounters. She was more interested in the ranger than anything else, tugging at his clothing and looking him up and down. He tried to discourage her, but every time she retreated she was accosted by her younger brother, a third her size, who goaded her to return. She would apparently then pleasure herself, before charging back to grab the ranger by his trousers. To cap it off, she tried to follow us when we left, and it took a good deal of effort to discourage her. In all my years observing gorillas, I'd never seen anything quite like it.

After Geoff's encounter with the Mt. T. gorillas, we took a different trail back. I wanted him to see the spot where we hoped to build an exclusive lodge. "Last year, my old school chum, Jon Simonson, came up here," I said. "I invited him because I knew he knew a lot about lodges. So Jon flies out to Entebbe and me and Patrice pick him up. But the airline's lost his luggage so he has to wear the same jeans and T-shirt for the entire three days he's up here on Mt. T. Anyway, after tramping around the mountain and talking to the rangers, my friend identifies *this* spot as probably the best location on Mount Tshiaberimu to build a lodge. Whaddya think?"

The view was awesome. On such a clear day, we could see halfway across Uganda, the Rwenzoris to the north, and to the south, Virunga. And a thousand meters below, at the foot of an abrupt slope, lapped the waves of Lake Edward. I liked to view the farther horizon from higher up the ridge. I could see my career fading away from up there. I knew my tenure in the service of the gorillas was coming to an end. *But how will it end?* I didn't want it to end.

Early the next morning, I descended the mountain at my own pace, like a bouncing rubber ball. An armed escort struggled to keep up with me as I leaped from one landing to the next, skied over mudslides, and skidded down scree. Slaloming down the steep slopes of Mt. T. with total abandon, I had almost reached the ranger post at Burusi when suddenly I heard gunfire ahead of me.

I stopped in my tracks. My escort grabbed my arm and pulled me into a ditch beside the trail. His labored breathing as he crouched beside me, tightly gripping his AK-47 in his sweaty hands, finger on the trigger, suggested he was far more frightened than I was. I'd been near firefights before and something about this pattern of gunfire—unrelenting shooting until at least forty rounds had been expended—suggested something more haphazard. When the gunfire ceased, my armed escort and I slowly, carefully, and quietly proceeded down the trail. When we reached the post, we found two rangers holding a poacher with a broken leg and his dog. Despite the fact that the guards were firing at the poacher as he ran, he was not apprehended until after he tripped over a stump and broke his leg. Not a single bullet found him or his mutt. And yet as easily as their forty rounds of erratic gunfire had missed the intended target, they could have hit an unintended target like me.

We are going to take care of all who come. We're going to do what's right and worry about how we pay for it later on.
—Georgia governor Sonny Perdue

Metro Atlanta had a touch more New Orleans about it. In the wake of Hurricane Katrina, the city had opened its doors to evacuees. "Many folks got blown to Atlanta by the storm," said our cab driver, an African American woman, as she drove Jillian, David, and me from the airport to our hotel. "They got it bad over in Nawlins," she added sorrowfully. "Real bad. And who's gonna help them? Not FEMA. Lie don't care who tell it. Not George W. Bush. That fool needs a checkup from the neck up. Hell, it's down to *us*. I'm putting up my cousin Lisa and her five kids."

On the two previous occasions that I had visited Atlanta, I'd been part of a delegation of stupid gorilla folk that were wined and dined and shown around all the beauty spots in a chauffeur-driven limo, places like Zoo Atlanta and Atlanta Zoo (which is what it was called before Terry Maple turned it around), our progress slowed only by our host's need to stuff his face with grits. Not this time.

After checking into our hotel, an unremarkable downtown sky-scraper squeezed in between the global corporate headquarters of household brands, we decamped to a nearby sports bar, where we met Jason Drangel, our lawyer from New York. It was a far cry from Fat Boyz, but I still found resonance in that bar.

"We've got a case, right?" I asked Jason as I nursed my beer, a Sol stuffed with a wedge of lime. "I mean, we both began using the name 'Dian Fossey Gorilla Fund' at the same time, in the summer of 1992."

"They're claiming prior use," said Jason.

"But they can't. I was there. We changed the name at the same goddamn time."

"Well, then, you've got a case. But at what cost? They'll fight you tooth and nail, and their lawyers have agreed to take this on pro bono. You'll end up spending donors' money."

"Thankfully, our accountant Lian had the good sense to put those legal fees aside for a rainy day," said Jillian. "So we've at least got enough to pay for this rainy bloody day."

"The first thing I will ask them tomorrow," said David, with a reasoned tone, "is why couldn't you have picked up the phone and called us, instead of serving us with legal papers?"

———————————

The hearts and homes of Georgians were opened as never before. And while the rest of the townsfolk were busy trying hard to be charita-ble, two gorilla charities were duking it out in legal arbitration on the umpteenth floor of a legal office in downtown Hotlanta. A nondisclosure agreement (NDA)—that pixilation of events—prevents me from disclosing what went on up there. But suffice to say, it was shameful. Lie took the elevator. Truth took the stairs but got there in the end. At one point I considered opening up a window and jumping to my death.

We gave up the name and the web address too. Even now, to add insult to injury, if I log on to the wayback machine and look up a PR triumph on a blue-chip company's website that Jillian and I had pulled off in our heyday, the link takes you to DFGF International. Fuck them!

We became the Gorilla Organization. And to build our brand we had to start again from scratch, which cost us money we didn't have. Mercifully, around this same time, in a final act before cancer claimed his life, Robert Lewis sent us a donation made up of the remainder of Dian Fossey's estate. They may have had her name, but we had $120,000 of her money, which we turned into an endowment, the interest from which pays for an annual grant awarded to the best indigenous gorilla conservationist.

Atlanta and the NDAs broke me. The trajectory of my career had already degraded to a dangerously low orbit by then, so it didn't take much for me crash and burn. But boy was I angry. No way was I resigning now, if only to stick it to those bastards in the United States.

The Gorilla Organization hit the ground running with a fresh brand-building venture that no doubt would keep me busy for many more years to come. It had all the potential to renew my purpose. But I needed a break from gorillas. I asked my trustees to grant me a six-month paid leave from my job as executive director and they agreed.

My sabbatical would begin in August 2006. I intended to spend it working on a debut novel, though I didn't yet know what it was about. Probably the Congo jungle. Jillian was none too happy about this arrangement, especially after I told her I planned to spend it in Kampala. "Sheet," said Darren. "We gonna get higher than a Georgia Pine!"

18

A BURNT-OUT CAREER

We went with this crazy hippie guy. . . . We were trying
to find this mine, and we needed him because apparently
there are soldiers. And . . . basically he's Dennis Hopper out
of *Apocalypse Now*. And I thought, *Oh, what are we doing?*
Eventually, yes, we ran out of water.
—Steve McQueen, CBE, discussing the filming of
Gravesend and a Dian Fossey Gorilla Fund
guide who aided the crew for a time

I COULD NOT sleep. The nocturnal sounds of the jungle were completely drowned out by the din of transistor radios playing rumbas all
around me, the chatter of young men bragging and old men haranguing, and the shrill laughter of prostitutes that echoed off the high
canopy. My sleeping arrangement was a Yucatán hammock suspended
in a thatch-roofed hut, the walls of which had yet to be sealed with
mud. Smoke pervaded from the stoves of some three hundred artisanal
miners who lived in this camp in the middle of the jungle. Many
were still awake, and as they moved about to socialize, the beams
of their torches swung through the latticed walls of my hut, casting
strange shadows.

I was a bit anxious in this dissonant corner of the Congo River
basin. It was not my usual habitat. But circumstances demanded that

we spend the night in this remote mining camp, a hamlet of ragtag thatch huts and lean-tos spread out across a two-acre forest clearing, about forty kilometers southeast of Walikale, in Congo's South Kivu Province. In every direction beyond our camp, there were no other people for miles. People we knew about, that is. It was easy to imagine unseen forces moving through the tangle and taking their positions. Nearby, there could easily have been a company of rebels, remnants of the Interahamwe perhaps, or Congolese Mai-Mai. I knew they were out there somewhere.

Before setting out on our expedition, we visited a UN peacekeeping base on a hillside near Walikale and met the base commander, a Brahman wearing tennis whites. "Things are really going well here now," he told us. "We patrol the Kisangani highway on a daily basis." The paved bit, that is—a mere thirty-five-kilometer stretch in a jungle as vast as Afghanistan.

In *Apocalypse Now*, Francis Ford Coppola's movie about the Vietnam War based on Joseph Conrad's *Heart of Darkness*, a brooding Captain Willard, having just accepted his mission to assassinate Colonel Kurtz, rasps, "Shit . . . charging a man with murder in this place was like handing out speeding tickets in the Indy 500." The same could be said of the arrest warrants issued by the International Criminal Court to Congolese warlords. Hard to find a military officer from any ranks of this conflict who hasn't, at some point, recruited child soldiers, intimidated or killed villagers, and been involved in dodgy mineral dealings. Like Kurtz, the warlords' methods may be unsound, but their modus operandi is hardly original.

Much had gone into preparing for this trip. It began in January 2006, when *Apes in Danger* aired on the BBC to critical acclaim. The gorilla episode featuring yours truly leaping up mountains in deepest darkest got the highest ratings. "This is the Wild West," I say, sitting in the back of a pickup truck speeding through the Congo jungle. "Everything here is minerals. Minerals, minerals, minerals. Nobody's producing food, no one's doing anything other than mining. There's no health, no education. Gorillas are natural resources that are hugely valuable to this country. But valuable if they're left alive in that forest."

When I look at the footage now, I see a burnt-out look in my eyes. I had clearly reached the end of my tether. But I wanted to be the poster boy for the coltan crisis. *Apes in Danger* caught the eye of the public, including Turner Prize–winning British video artist Steve McQueen, who asked his assistant Pinky Ghundale to arrange a meeting with me to discuss a filming expedition to the Congo. On a cold winter morning, at the American Hotel near his home in Amsterdam, I sat down to breakfast with the filmmaker.

Steve was a large, buttoned-down man in his late thirties, with boyish charm and a preference for a Brideshead style, in contrast to his West Indian heritage. "With this film," he said, "I want to show the striking parallels between the twenty-first-century 'coltan rush,' fueled by demand for consumer electronics, and the nineteenth-century rubber boom. This is the kind of stuff that inspired Joseph Conrad to write *Heart of Darkness*."

"So you want me to arrange for you to visit a coltan mine?"

"Yes," he said between sips of tea. "We'll be four people: camera operator, camera assistant, sound person. Could you look into whether we can film a rebel group?"

"That would be risky," I said. "We may encounter Mai-Mai rebels whether we like it or not. A Channel 4 crew were recently held hostage by an errant general in South Kivu for three days. I think it would be better if we plan on the hop, rather than alert anyone to our imminent arrival. I will check with Henry Cirhuza, our man in the Congo, to see what the latest security concerns are and arrange for whatever filming permits you may need."

Seven months later, Steve and I reunited in Goma. Accompanying him was director of photography Sean Bobbitt and camera assistant Gordon Segrove. Having a resource center there enabled me to start in poll position. You can never know enough about your next destination. In the jungle there are no vistas; it's impossible to gain perspective—everything you see is within a few meters of where you stand or else you cannot see it.

Henry Cirhuza was my fixer and would keep the rest of the expedition on point. His first job when we arrived in Walikale was to organize letters of permission from the local administrator, and recruit armed guards, porters, a cook, and a priest. We needed the priest to negotiate a spot where we could pitch our tents for the night, and acquire provisions of poultry, meat, and vegetables. Our last night of civilization was spent in the Walikale Guest House, an unfinished, raw-cement, six-roomed house, with a bent nail in the doorframe of every room for security. Funny how the standard of accommodation, which declines the farther into the bush you go, seems so much more luxurious on the way back. From where I was lying, in my unfinished thatch hut, that guesthouse is the goddamn Hilton.

No one knew quite what to expect the next morning when, after a hearty breakfast of Spanish omelets and boiled potatoes, we piled into the back of a pickup truck and drove out of town. After just a few kilometers the road disintegrated, forcing us to abandon our vehicle. A human caravan of twenty-one souls then continued on foot.

The path ahead looked unpromising, little more than a mud track. The route had once been a major highway, and the Germans who built it had cleared enough jungle that there was scant shelter from the oppressive, midmorning sun. In the confines of the equatorial forest the temperature was a sultry thirty degrees Celsius (eighty-six degrees Fahrenheit), and it was windless. But, as the jungle beyond it was impenetrable, we had little choice but to stick to this "road," maneuvering through swaths of thick mud and deep ruts.

The porters ran shifts carrying the two 35mm cameras and kept their spirits up with a medley of marching songs that they sang throughout the day. Everyone we met along the way was courteous and good-natured. Children cried, "Monique! Monique!" because the only other outsiders they had ever encountered were UN peacekeepers, known locally by their mission acronym, MONUC. In every village we were greeted like liberators.

The priest did his thing, and the cook, his. Each day ended with a generous meal of goat or chicken stew, potatoes, and the chef's special salad: tuna fish mixed with mayonnaise and tinned spaghetti. The following morning, outside our tents, dozens of children had gathered to await their chance to catch a first glimpse of a *mzungu*.

Walking an average of ten kilometers a day, it took us three days to reach the mining village. We didn't arrive in very good shape. Sean Bobbitt had horrifying blisters on his feet, the result of trudging through swamps in boots that were not waterproof. And we had only a third of our water supply remaining. Henry and I thought the three cubic meters of water we shipped in from Goma would be sufficient for this expedition. We hadn't banked on the film crew bathing themselves in the stuff for the first couple of days.

———————

Steve, Sean, and Gordon were fast asleep now, each in his own pup tent, having been zipped up since dusk. Not me. I was wide awake in the midnight hour, eyes darting in every direction, bereft of chums to share my bottle of Johnnie Walker Green Label with. The night before Steve had joined me for a dram. I suspect he thought I was out of my depth.

I was. This was way outside my comfort zone. Still, he came to me, not the other way around, and I did everything I could to prepare. Now that I found myself in these strange, unnerving surroundings, however, I was having doubts. And as the restless miners moved around their camp, casting phantasmagoric shadows about my wooden cage with their torchlights, I began to wonder if I might be going crazy.

I saw Henry approaching. "*Vipi* (Swahili for "What's up?")?" I asked.

"Isn't this a bizarre place?" he said in French. He was surprisingly quiet and unassuming for a Congolese, and a stalwart in the campaign to save gorillas. And he had always been a reliable barometer for the security of any given destination in the Congo. A Bashi, born and raised on the shores of Lake Kivu, he knew the territory well. Every expedition should have a Henry. Still, I suspected, like me he felt a little out of his depth as well.

"We should do this kind of safari more often," I told him.

Henry smiled. "You think you can convince others to come here?"

"Probably only adventuresome types. You need to be strong to stay the course. Sure, you'll have to endure wading through swamps, trudging through mud, plenty of bushwhacking, and swarms of insects. Portable mosquito nets and waterproof footwear are a must. There'll be nowhere to plug in your gadgets. Everything will be basic, just as it is now. On this circuit there'll be no safari chic, only the thrill of knowing you're one of the first outsiders to tread here."

"It sounds like a *safi* idea, boss," said Henry, using the Swahili word for "proper," while nodding his head in approval. "The Kivus could certainly use some tourist dollars. Do you think insecurity will allow? Things are calm now. But you know the situation in the Kivus."

"Security always screws up my plans," I gasped, kissing my teeth. I looked east to try and coax the first rays of sunlight through the trees. And then one struck me between the eyes. "People think I have a jones for war zones, but it's these apes. They tend to live in scary places."

In the end, Steve McQueen and his crew shot only twenty minutes of footage at the coltan mine. Plans to go elsewhere were scrapped. Sean Bobbitt's blisters were becoming worse and worse, opening up like rift valleys in his heel and between his toes. He needed immediate medical attention, so we returned to Walikale. Once there, we took him to the local hospital run by Médecins Sans Frontières (MSF), a charity that penetrated deeper into war zones than most others. The doctor told Sean he needed to be airlifted out straightaway. At the same time, I learned the Antonov I'd chartered had been held up in Bukavu with a broken wheel.

The Walikale airport was the only place with a telephone network. When I say airport, I mean a short stretch of the Kisangani highway that gets cordoned off to allow the planes to land. We decamped there to see if we could hitch a ride on one of the few daily flights flying supplies in and flew minerals out. Sean could no longer walk, so we sat in the departures lounge, a poky wooden gazebo on the soft shoulder of the highway, and waited.

The first plane to land was an Antonov twelve-seater. Its wings nearly struck our lounge as it raced down the runway. It came to a standstill only a few meters from where the barrier had been lowered to keep travelers off the road. Using a tiller that they fastened to the plane's front tire, the ground crew then rotated the aircraft one hundred and eighty degrees. It was quickly unloaded and loaded again. We explained our predicament to the Russian pilot, who just shrugged and said, "I've maxed my load already with minerals."

"We'll pay you $2,000 to take the four of us and our equipment to Goma," I pleaded.

"I couldn't even take one of you," he replied, adding with a chuckle, "You'll never get those cameras out of here." As he started up his engines, my heart sank. I began to wonder if we would ever escape the jungle.

An hour later a white 4x4, festooned with MSF logos and flags and towing an empty trailer, pulled up to the airport. It had obviously come to pick up a load of medical supplies from an incoming flight. I figured it was unlikely Doctors Without Borders would be flying minerals out. As the plane approached the runway another MSF 4x4 pulled up, and a White woman got out. I went up to her in the hope I might appeal to her better nature.

"My client is in a bad way and needs immediate medical attention," I said. "May we please hitch a ride on your plane?"

"I don't know who you are," she snapped. "You could be anyone. There are all kinds of negative forces operating in this area."

"I'm a Canadian gorilla conservationist," I said, calmly handing her my card.

She told me her name was Dr. Leslie Shanks, and that she was also Canadian. "I am currently acting head of MSF in the Congo," she added. "And our policy is to never give lifts to strangers. Why don't you let me have a look at your client's wounds?"

"We've already seen a doctor this morning, in your hospital," I said with exasperation, "and he told us to airlift him the hell out of here as soon as we could."

As she deliberated, the MSF plane pulled up behind her, and the ground crew began unloading boxes of medical supplies. It was then I noticed the copilot was someone I knew, another fellow Canadian. We had met some months earlier in Butembo. He greeted me warmly and promised to have a word with the Belgian pilot. But after he returned to the cockpit, the propellers began to whine. This was not a good sign.

"I suppose I could call head office," said Leslie, looking at her mobile phone. "Let me see if I can reach . . ." But her words were drowned out by the sound of the MSF plane taking off, empty. She looked up in astonishment. Realizing she had been trumped by her own pilot, she then simply turned on her heels and began to walk away.

Steve McQueen rose to his feet and followed her. "Shame!" he cried. The sight of him striding loftily down the road/runway after her, while thrusting an indignant hand in the air, is one I shall never forget. "Shame, madam! Shame on you!" Spoken like a true gentleman. She hurried to her car and then quickly drove away. Shameful, indeed, for a person in her position.

We eventually got Sean out. As a result of our trip, Steve made the film *Gravesend*.

———————

The sound of grinding generators was everywhere. Power cuts were endless. There really wasn't much going on in Kampala anyway, but the mood was benign, and it gave me time to reflect. An afternoon spent under the dapple of the big tree down at the Blue Mango was just the tonic, though they might have played the music loud enough to hear over the goddamn generator.

"If you drink at midday, you are bang to rights to be doing blow by sundown," said whoever I was with. I don't remember who. It might have been Darren. Or it might have been a Ugandan rasta complimenting me on my flow. "*Malaika, mulaya, muyaye, muyeyo*," they said, meaning "Angel, whore, gangster, cokehead." They called me "my nigger" too. Being the Blackest *mzungu* in KLA was not something I was particularly proud of, because I felt like I was losing my true identity. A lifelong love affair with the Bright Continent had lured me in farther and deeper than I should have gone. I was lost.

This was no dignified way for a forty-four-year-old director of an international NGO to behave. My midlife crisis was spiraling out of control. I wore black leather pants to the clubs. (In the tropics?) The girls seemed to like them. I was a debauched, coked-up narcissist roaming the clubs, dazed and confused, grooving to predictable bass lines and sniffing strangers' cheap perfumes. I never followed the wrong scent. I simply lost the scent and forgot what I was hunting for. Cocaine was my emotional placeholder. I used the charity's credit card, with its photo of a cute little gorilla, not only to draw the cash I needed to buy the stuff but also to carve it up. The credit card no longer worked, it was so caked in coke. Blow lit up my days and nights.

My heart belonged to the African savannas, jungles, and coasts. That's where I first encountered most things good and bad in my life. It was my proving ground as a child and once again as a professional adult. But that was out there, beyond the traffic jams and lingering smell of sewage. I was stuck in KLA, hip-hop heaven, on a downward spiral of indiscriminate women and fast 4x4s, riding in the Blackback with Patrice in the after hours, cruising up and down neon streets with a thumping soundtrack. The week before, while I was distracted, a tag team of two Burundian pros stole $2,000 from my safe and my silver Adam Ant gorilla ring. No matter. Without asking how the money got stolen, the charity reimbursed me and later claimed it on its insurance.

I took stock of my career. There wasn't much left of it now. This was my last act, the antihero's unheroic end, the beginning of the end for me. I'd had too many failures, was an also-ran man, a close-but-no-cigar lummox in the right place at the wrong time. People who once thought I was a class act turned away. I'd let everyone down and thrown away whatever integrity I had for a good time. I wasn't as clever as I thought. I filled the gaps with bullshit. As a vetreran fundraiser, I knew how to arrange bullshit so that it looked and smelled like roses.

I was now totally immersed in my own marketing mendacity. I went places I never went and met people I never met. I had this twisted notion that I had to have a good time all the time.

───────────

As another night unfolded like indigo fabric, Jillian sat opposite me on the veranda at the Golf Course Apartments, smiling at me with that big sweet grin of hers, scratching her mosquito bites and looking a little worse for wear for the bottle of Amarula she'd just single-handedly downed. She had come to stay with me in Kampala for a week. I tried to hide my philandering from her, but she eventually began asking me about the women whose phone numbers were in my phone. I told her they had put them there after snatching my phone from me in a bar and that it was entirely out of my control. Somehow she believed me.

Whenever she left the veranda, even for an instant, I'd take another sniff from my coke shaker, a handy little half-gram dispenser I kept hidden. I was impressed by my wife's staying power. She'd drunk seven Tusker beers and now a whole bottle of elephant candy. I really should have been doffing my hat to her. But I had nothing more to offer our marriage. Pumping slowly, blood scarcely spilling, the lifeblood had been irretrievably drained from it, and I knew it would end soon.

She left and I was alone. The rain had stopped, the clouds were lifting, and a breeze blew across the golf course, rustling the leaves in the wide, spreading trees. A feeling of emptiness came over me. What was it about the African night that was so gloomy? And the sultry night tore down into a thousand strips. A constrictor had wrapped itself around me and was tightening its coil, slowly draining me of lifeblood. No amount of bourbon or coke, it seemed, could dissuade this slimy reptile from its predatory designs on me. It had me in a grip that grew ever tighter. I could no longer breathe because of it. Then the constrictor relaxed its grip and let me slip in under my sheets and dream. I was drowning in python skin, and I could feel myself being sucked into the jungle foliage, disintegrating into the rotting roots and stinking leaves that festered all around me in febrile decay.

But then I awoke suddenly and sat upright, drenched in sweat. My bed was hot, and the sheets twisted like a snapshot of a hurricane. The fan had stopped when the power was cut after I'd gone to bed. It was completely dark. I was alone. Soon I was back on the veranda.

Darkness prevailed and sounds took over, beyond the trippy dub loops oozing from my iPod speakers, the steady pleading of bullfrogs and crickets in the dark. Everything was in flux, as my thoughts flipped back and forth in time; one minute I was in the Congo jungle and the next in KLA. After midnight the night transformed. The creatures fell silent. Nothing stirred. There was no sound. Nothing to be heard. Interminable peace. Not even the constrictor was awake at that paralyzed hour before the dogs, cockerels, and muezzins sounded daybreak. Africa was a blank sheet without history or future—just the black, black, black of now.

This was when Africa remembered the time before time, when there was no color, no light, and no sound. The senses had not yet been born. In the jungle, from a seething miasma came a heartbeat. A slow, creeping light spread slowly across the golf course—gray and colorless adumbrated shapes and forms, light without emotion. And then, in a moment of natural brouhaha, dawn exploded with brilliant color, dazzling rays, and the big band brash horns of a thousand screeching birds.

Should I stay or should I go? I craved the jungle. It was a metaphor for my life: impressive to behold from afar, rich in texture up close, but destructive as it rambled in every direction, and dark and dangerous at its core. If only I could manage to climb above the canopy, I might still get some perspective, maybe find some direction. In the jungle, the beast was absent. He had no place in that overgrown paradise, that Eden that never asked us to leave. We came from there, and yet we barely understood the jungle. It appeared evil; witness a swarm of ants taking down a tree frog. But that was simply unenlightened self-interest. There were times in the jungle when it was so hot and humid and windless I wished I could just crawl out of my skin. I aimed to return. I wanted to be back there pacing my own perimeter, sniffing out the unknown, dragging out carcasses. The women I slept with in KLA didn't give a damn about my adventures in the jungle, but without those adventures I'd have been swallowed whole.

In a clearing in the jungle a table is set, laid out with meticulous attention to detail, with silver service and white-gloved butlers. It's a banquet in my honor. Douglas is there along with a few other patrons, supporters, and colleagues. Koko, Ziz, and Effie are there too, trying to blend in. Fat chance, you big apes. I loves ya. A few things are noticeable by their absence, such as reality. Still, every creature present is slow clapping me and cheering me up to the table, inviting me into their circle. It seems they really want me to be there with them at their exclusive banqueting table. "For he's a jolly good failure . . ." I sing with a wink and a grin as I confidently step forward to take my place at the feast. The guests tilt their heads, smile knowingly, and then shrug. They're with me all the way, baby, they totally have my back because that's how I want them to be, that's how I've arranged this.

I'm trying to let my conscience off the hook. What do I care? I'm no longer a part of their expedition. In the end, no matter how enamored with the continent, the protagonist always finds a way out of Africa, to leave the Bright Continent behind for safer, cooler realms.

Not me. Africa consumes me.

19

LEGACY

When the silverback's got more silver than back, it's time to
move on, before he gets moved on.

—Guy Ritchie, *The Gentlemen*

"Bartender, a beer, please," I say, leaning into the bar.

"Cold or warm, sir?" he asks.

"After the journey I just made, it'll have to be cold."

The bartender smiles, reaches into a glass-fronted fridge, and
retrieves a frosted bottle of Virunga Mist, Rwanda's new craft beer.
I examine its label. Virunga is written in bold green Gothic letters,
and beneath it is a woodcut illustration of the rain forest transected
by a path leading to three distant volcanoes. On the back of the bottle
there's a map of the mountain gorilla habitat under which is written
Your Virunga Adventure Starts Here.

I take a swig. It's smooth and rich but a little too sugary for my
taste.

These days everyone is cashing in on gorillas. Gorilla tourism is
Rwanda's biggest foreign-currency earner. Visitors on their way to
Volcanoes National Park run a gauntlet of signs and billboards adver-
tising gorilla-themed businesses like Beyond the Gorillas Experience,
Five Volcanoes Boutique Hotel, La Paillotte Gorilla Place, and Villa

Gorilla. Rwandans are no longer as ambivalent about their mountain gorillas as they used to be when the only place they were talked about was in the pages of *National Geographic*. I take some credit for that.

Virunga Mist in my hand, I wander across the hotel grounds and admire the actual Virunga massif. Six volcanoes are lit up like a son et lumière by the last rays of the day. The smell of burning eucalyptus triggers an avalanche of memories, of the many times I scaled those slippery slopes, took the great and the good—polymath, celebs, titans of industry—to meet their hairy mountain cousins in the wild. "There be gorillas," I sigh, then shudder as I recall some of my experiences. "And demons too."

My current coterie of clients is gathered on the lawn to watch a traditional dance show that's being staged to welcome them. We've just driven in from Kigali. I'm loath to join them and force a smile for what is clearly an unpolished performance staged for tourists. Besides, safari guides are expected to be surly misanthropes who drink too much and say very little. They'll understand me better after they hear my gorilla talk tonight: "Gorilla Tactics: How to Save a Species." It's the same talk I gave a week ago, nine thousand miles away, to a sold-out Robert Bateman Centre in the old Steamship Terminal in Victoria, British Columbia's inner harbor.

I'd moved to Victoria from Kenya a year earlier and, following a decade-long hiatus, had revived my fundraising career. Turns out South Vancouver Island has a thriving volunteer sector and experienced charity fundraisers are in high demand. I had to be selective in what career highlights I chose to share with potential employers, and I left out the grittier chapters and my tragic fall from grace. After dusting off my glad-handing hat, I was back in the money-raising game. There were some new developments—like e-appeals and social media fundraising—but the mechanics were still the same. In five years, I raised a million dollars for mental health and environmental causes. Eventually, I started my own fundraising consultancy, Blue Gorilla

Giving, providing "guidance in cause related goals for both donors and beneficiaries."

I recently consulted for Emmanuel Bugingo, who used to run DFGF Europe's resource center in Ruhengeri and now runs Partners for Conservation, a nongovernmental organization in Rwanda. His work is a logical extension of the community-based program that Luiz Fabbri set up and Jillian developed. Basically, Emmanuel takes Western tourists who have visited or are about to visit the gorillas and shows them how community conservation works, and demonstrates that it is the most effective way to ensure the survival of an endangered species when its habitat is surrounded by densely populated, poor communities. Women's empowerment and finding markets for co-ops are among the aims of Partners for Conservation. It gives them access to a flow of international clientele, which can potentially connect them to overseas markets. If handled properly, Partners for Conservation has great potential for growth.

Emmanuel and I go way back. I cannot forget the time he came through for me when I really needed him to. It was early February 2006, and I was having lunch with travel guru Richard Bangs in a seafood restaurant in Santa Monica. I was on the last legs of a fundraising tour of California, but I'd run out of prospects and was tired of asking the same people for the same old donations. Fundraiser fatigue had set in, and I wasn't having much success. Then I met Richard. "To mark World Water Day," he said, "which the UN has designated as March 22, I was planning a trip to Nepal. But after hearing about your water cisterns, I think we'd get more bang for our buck coming to Rwanda and making the connection between water and gorilla conservation. If we pay for it, could you build a new water cistern in six weeks? Is that possible?"

"Hang on, I'll check." I stepped out of the restaurant and called Emmanuel on my cell phone. He said he'd speak to the contractors in Ruhengeri and let me know. Ten minutes later he called back and said it was touch and go but could be done.

"You're on," I then told Richard.

Back in Africa, I began making arrangements for the trip. Yahoo.com was paying on the understanding that Richard and his crew would post daily multimedia reports on its website. Didrik Johnck would get footage, and John Canning would take stills. Patrice and I would drive down from Kampala in the Blackback, pick up the crew at the Kigali airport, and take them to the Virungas. The cement in the water cistern was still drying. Would it be ready in time for World Water Day in a week?

My phone rang; it was Richard Bangs in L.A. "I was at a cocktail party last night," he said, "and I ran into Daryl Hannah. I told her of our project to help finance a cistern at the edge of the gorilla habitat, working with you and the Gorilla Organization, and she volunteered to help, saying, 'I've always wanted to see the gorillas!'"

"So she's coming!?"

"Yup."

I was beside myself. I knew how these things worked. To be seen on the arm of a hot Hollywood movie star would go a long way toward restoring my tarnished, wild-eyed image, and really stick it to my detractors. "*Boo yakka!*" I cried. "I'm back in the game."

Daryl Hannah was a class act. She was low maintenance and had more humility than all the other celebrities I'd ever wrangled put together. From the moment Patrice picked her up from Kigali airport (he found her sitting on her rollaboard outside in the rain), she made life easy for all those around her. And during her four-day stay, she contributed much more to the tasks at hand than she was asked to do, staying up late to help the crew with film edits before the clips got sent back to Yahoo.com via a high-speed link, and then getting up early the next morning to track mountain gorillas again and again.

Daryl was sensational. At the edge of the park, with a hiking stick that a ranger had given her, she reenacted her fight scene with Uma Thurman in *Kill Bill: Volume 1,* and she then did a standing back flip that made my heart skip a beat. When I told her *Blade Runner* was one of my favorite films, she said, "Mine too. It was the first movie I made. I thought they'd all be like that." She was tall and gorgeous and sexy, and she kept herself in great shape. Hiking in Virunga with her was such a pleasure.

No, I didn't try it on with her, as so many have assumed. I still had a few shreds of dignity left in me. Besides, Jillian was there as well, though she didn't join us on any of the treks. I don't remember her being there, however. I suppose I was too preoccupied with my exquisite client. "I'm just gonna stay here now," she sighed after her wild encounter, "Say hi to my family. I'm gonna go live with the gorillas."

In *Adventures with Purpose: Dispatches from the Front Lines of Earth,* a book that Richard Bangs later published in 2007, he describes the purpose of our trip. "The money for gorilla salvation goes to many good works, such as training trackers, clothing and arming antipoaching squads, removing snares, researching behavior, even giving inoculations. But the Gorilla Organization, which Greg heads, is devoted to what he calls 'a holistic solution,' one that invests in community development surrounding the park. His theory is that if the lives of the two and a half million people who live in the shadow of the Virungas are improved because of the presence of the great apes, they will come to say to the more shortsighted, 'Hell, no. You're not coming into the gorilla habitat. The gorillas are our bread and butter here.' And the gorillas' presence is the reason for a local supply of clean water, as we are to witness."

As planned, Daryl opened the water cistern on World Water Day. Emmanuel, working alongside the Rwandan parks authority, organized a fitting celebration. Dignitaries gave speeches, dancers performed, and there was a big fete afterward. It demonstrated once and for all that Rwanda had become an all-singing, all-dancing, gorilla-loving nation. We all had a good time, and the gorillas got some swell PR from it. But the coolest thing Daryl did for us was when we met President Kagame in Kigali. I wore a tie with more gorillas on it than survive in Virunga; Daryl wore sneakers without shoelaces. Kagame told us that he had lived in Virunga for several years when he led the RPF and made forays back and forth from Uganda, but he never saw a mountain gorilla during that time. It was only after he became president that he went on a gorilla trek. "A four-hour slog in the rain," he said.

Daryl had asked Jillian and me beforehand if there was any issue we wanted her to press with the head of state, and there was. When the time was right, Jillian gave her the signal, and the actor let rip her concerns about a new sanctuary the wildlife authority wanted to build near the park for orphaned gorillas, which we believed might quickly turn into a zoo. It worked. Kagame put the kibosh on it, much to the annoyance of Rwanda's head of wildlife.

On the way to the airport to catch her flight home, Daryl kept asking Patrice to stop so she could get out of the car, grab a garment from her rollaboard, and gift it to a woman she'd seen walking along the side of the road. She did this again and again until she had no more need for her rollaboard, and boarded her departing flight bareback.

Daryl and I remained friends. I met her a couple of times for coffee in L.A. when I passed through. And in 2021, after I asked her to lend her name to a campaign to save a fifty-acre wood north of Victoria, she and her husband, Neil Young, donated $25,000 and wrote the following: "Anyone interested in addressing Climate Change in earnest understands that true solutions to the crisis we face lie in embracing interconnectedness, generational thinking, and planning for resilience. In order to truly do these things, it becomes clear that it is essential to prioritize conservation and protection of intact ecosystems on land and water bodies. Resilience best takes the form of decentralization. . . .

It is precisely saving these intact ecosystems, particularly old-growth forests, whether small or large, as they perform so many functions (sequestrating carbon, providing habitats, filtering water, creating oxygen, rebuilding soil and of course bringing peace, joy and relief to those who get to spend time amidst these natural gems), as a crucial first step in effectively responding to the climate crisis."

———————————

I've been running gorilla safaris ever since. It's an obvious vocation for me. As a veteran, I've been handpicked to be the chief guide on a safari to mark World Gorilla Day 2018. My job is to prepare the clients for what they are about to experience and to be there with them when they experience it. I prefer that to being in charge. I'm a storyteller, not a tour guide. And I've supervised enough fuckups in my career to know that high-end clients are better off in the hands of professional outfitters, even if it means I have to settle for a finder's fee.

Back at the lodge bar I check on the progress of a two-gigabyte presentation file I'd stored in iCloud. Only 120 megabytes have downloaded. Why didn't I take care of this before leaving civilization? "Bartender, another Virunga beer!"

To participate in this five-day safari, my clients have each paid upward of $12,000 and traveled from South Africa, China, Malaysia, Israel, India, Mexico, Canada, Australia, and the United States to be here. For many, this is their first time in Africa, yet no one seems troubled by the standard of lodgings. The "lodge" we're staying at shall remain nameless. Each of its cabins has both a number and the name of a common bird: Canary, Crow, Pigeon. They are made of cement and inappropriately huge. Each cement block is connected by a convoluted maze of cement pathways that lead guests to a cluster of unsightly brick edifices: lounge, reception, restaurant, and bar. I was warned against staying here by a friend.

"But we're bringing our own chef from Kigali," I told her.

"For sure you will need more than a chef," she said.

Granted, I'm accustomed to a higher standard on the East African safari circuit, places that abide by a certain wilderness aesthetic. However, this lodge was the only place that could accommodate a gorilla safari of this size: nine foreign staff, two local tour operators, six local drivers, seventeen clients, and me. Besides, by staying there, we were putting more cash into the local economy.

Wealthy foreigners have appropriated wildlife and wild places from Africans. The *Out of Africa* idyll only ever allowed walk-on parts for Africans: the trusty bush sidekick, the witty old man, the smiling roly-poly mama, the wide-eyed *toto*. So much of the branding associated with safaris and game parks nostalgically harks back to colonial times when the White man was in control of it all and would never have allowed the destruction of Africa's wild places. East African game parks, like ski slopes and country clubs, are the orbit of the rich and famous—wealthy, self-made high achievers who crave distinction in an overpopulated world. The economic gap that exists between visitor and the visited is incongruous. But few come here to soak up local atmosphere; they're here for the natural beauty, to mingle with wild things.

Wild animals are nonjudgmental, don't ask for money, and look great in selfies. Nevertheless, being so loved by the well-off has been no guarantee of wildlife's survival. Africa's protected areas are shrinking. There are a few notable exceptions: Paul Allen, for instance, after foregoing lunch with the Beatles, went on to fund a raft of wildlife conservation endeavors in East Africa before he died. The Gates Foundation's record on wildlife conservation remains nonexistent. And yet everywhere I turn, I hear, "Bill stayed here." On the wall behind the bar at the lodge there's a photograph of the owner standing next to Bill Gates, who doesn't look like he's enjoying his stay. He's famous for leaving porters $400 tips.

I take comfort in knowing the program that Jillian and I had designed and implemented with our colleagues to save mountain gorillas in the wild was effective, and that it encouraged poor people living next to their habitats to become conservationists themselves and establish a front line of protection. Our MO was prohuman, which was uncommon in wildlife conservation back then and still is. What benefit do Africans get from protecting their wildlife? Not much. Despite the billions of dollars invested in wildlife protection, hardly any of it has gone toward changing the mindset of the average African and his or her attitude toward wildlife and nature. As a dedicated Afrophile, I made sure my efforts went some way to correcting that imbalance.

I put heart and soul into rescuing these great apes, but in the end, I destroyed my marriage, resigned my career, and abandoned England for Africa, where I lost myself. It wasn't all for nothing. In my twenty years at the head of a variously named organization, I played a key role in growing the wild mountain gorilla population, from 650 to 1,000—a 50 percent increase.

But it goes deeper than that. Since our first encounter the gorillas have shown me only guileless acceptance. Great apes are us. Our common ancestor lived around seven million years ago. If that's how far I must go back to find parity with my peers, so be it. I'm a gorilla man.

At 5:30 AM on World Gorilla Day 2018, I arise, step into my trekking gear, and wolf back a buffet breakfast before joining a fleet of stretch 4x4s taking us to Volcanoes Park HQ: the starting point for gorilla treks. Rwanda recently doubled the price of a gorilla trekking permit, from $750 to $1,500, so I expect to find the place deserted. Never has it been so busy. You cannot put a price on awesome. That's what the Rwanda Investment Board is banking on, but it doesn't have the benefit of economy of scale. Eight is the maximum number of people permitted to visit a gorilla group in a day, for no longer than one hour. Only ten gorilla groups in the park are open to visitors, hence full capacity is eighty visitors a day, which adds up to nearly $44 million a year in gorilla permits. Even at one-third capacity, that's a major earner for a small African nation.

Of all my encounters with gorillas, this one's the most memorable, for many reasons. It's World Gorilla Day, the temperature is around twenty-four degrees Celsius (seventy-five degrees Fahrenheit), with a few high stratus clouds to take the edge off the equatorial sun, and we are tracking Sabyinyo group. I'd met them a dozen times before, but not in the last five years. I'm excited about seeing Guhonda, whom I first met in 1996 when he was a stroppy young silverback who needed little provocation to charge. We find the group about three kilometers from the Congo border. Guhonda sits like Buddha in the shadow of the canopy, not as haggard as I expected the oldest silverback in Virunga to be. His deep cognizant gaze meets mine and holds it for longer than I am prepared for. That's not to say he recognizes me, though he seems to be prying into my psyche with his gaze. He outgazes me.

Drunk with awe and disbelief, my clients and I hang out for a spell with Sabyinyo's boisterous infants, females, blackbacks, and chilled-out old silverback. The experience never gets old. Suddenly, I'm shoved aside by a one-armed female (the victim of a wire snare) who then clambers over my legs like they're bamboo stalks while clutching her two-week-old baby—the youngest gorilla I've ever seen. She passes within inches of me, showing me her baby. She wants me to see her baby. I can smell it.

A fountainhead of emotion bursts from my heart. If not for me, and countless others who slogged tirelessly to save them, that baby may have never been born.